COLLAPSE OF THE CONSERVATIVES

VOLATILE VOTERS, BROKEN BRITAIN AND A PUNISHMENT ELECTION

STEVE RAYSON

BAVANT
PRESS

CONTENTS

"The most important thing a party must do in a campaign is listen to what the voters are saying."

Philip Gould

INTRODUCTION

We are talking about the collapse, no other word is sufficient, we are talking about the collapse of support for the Conservative Party.[1]

— PROFESSOR JOHN CURTICE

After his election victory in December 2019, Boris Johnson took a trip to Mustique to celebrate the New Year. He was basking in the warm glow of a remarkable political honeymoon. By March 2020, support for his Conservative government was running at 54%, a full 26 points ahead of the Labour Party.[2] It was the highest Conservative poll share ever in government and the party's biggest lead over Labour since Thatcher won the Falklands War in 1982.

Johnson's popularity increased further in the first half of 2020 with the outbreak of the COVID-19 pandemic, as the public put aside political differences to support the government during an extraordinary time of crisis. By March 2020, 72% of the public expressed satisfaction with the government's initial handling of the pandemic.[3] As the months wore on, the grim reality of lockdowns, economic turmoil, and mounting death tolls steadily eroded support for the government. But in early 2021, Johnson's popularity surged again following the successful nationwide rollout of the COVID-19 vaccination programme.

By May 2021, public satisfaction with the government's management of the crisis had climbed back up to 62%.[4] Seventeen months after their election victory, the Conservative Party had an 11-point poll lead over Labour and a commanding 23-point lead on who would be best at handling the economy (39% to 16%).[5]

On 6 May 2021, the Conservatives capitalised on their 'vaccine bounce' by making significant gains in the local elections. They secured an additional 235 seats on a swing of 8% and won control of 13 more councils. On the same day, they also won the constituency of Hartlepool in a by-election, taking it from the Labour Party with a remarkable 23% swing, the biggest for an incumbent governing party in a by-election in the post-war period. The scale of Labour's defeat was such that their new leader, Keir Starmer, reportedly considered resigning.[6]

Two days after the local elections, the front page of *The Times* was dominated by a large photograph of a triumphant Boris Johnson standing in front of a 30-foot inflatable of himself with his thumbs up. The headline read, 'Boris Johnson eyes decade in power'. The paper's political editor, Steven Swinford, claimed Johnson was "preparing for a decade-long premiership after a series of historic victories".[7]

Johnson's buoyant optimism appeared well founded. Despite the challenges of Brexit and the COVID-19 pandemic, his Conservative government had strengthened their grip on power. By late May 2021, the party had increased its lead in the polls to 18 points over Labour, 46% to 28%.[8] Political commentators claimed it was evidence, yet again, of the party's ability to shift and capture the mood of the public. An ability that had made it the world's most successful political party, according to *The Economist*.[9] Cabinet ministers, encouraged by their recent successes, suggested that Johnson would be prime minister for longer than Margaret Thatcher, who had held office in Downing Street for 11 years.[10]

Just three years later, on 4 July 2024, voters delivered arguably the most brutal result in British political history. Almost half of the Conservative Party's 2019 voters deserted them. The party's vote share slumped to just 23.7%, the lowest in their 190-year history. The party lost 251 seats, more than any party had ever lost at a general election.

In the traditionally Conservative home counties, the party was devastated. For the first time since 1906, Tories didn't win a majority of southern seats. In Berkshire, Bedfordshire, Buckinghamshire, Hertfordshire, and Oxfordshire, the party lost 26 seats, including previously safe seats, such as Henley, which they had held for over a hundred years.

It was a catastrophe for the party and its senior MPs. As the results were announced, cabinet minister after cabinet minister lost their seat, including Grant Shapps, Penny Mordaunt, Gillian Keegan, Steve Baker, Jacob Rees-Mogg, Johnny Mercer, Victoria Prentis, Mark Harper, and Michelle Donelan.

One of the last seats to declare was South West Norfolk, one of the safest Conservative seats in the country where Liz Truss held a 24,000 majority. Her majority was wiped out by the largest ever Conservative to Labour swing in a general election of 26.2%. Truss became the first former British prime minister to lose their seat in an election for almost 90 years.

Labour won a landslide 174-seat majority following a

professional, disciplined, and heavily targeted campaign, but it was a 'loveless landslide'. The party received just 33.7% of the vote. No majority government had ever received such a low share of the vote. Starmer's rebuilding of the Labour brand and the efficiency of the party's vote was critical to their victory, but the real story of 2024 was the collapse of the Conservatives rather than enthusiasm for Labour.

The extent of the Conservative collapse in just three years was truly remarkable. The question was, why?

~

There will be no shortage of books about the 2019–2024 parliament and the failures of Boris Johnson, Liz Truss, and Rishi Sunak. Some have already been written, and some are still being tapped into computers. There will be numerous insider accounts about the machinations inside the Tory Party and the party's four leadership elections. There will be descriptions of dinners at the Carlton Club and the tactical manoeuvrings of senior Conservative MPs as alliances were formed and reformed in the struggle for power. This is not one of those books.

This is a book that seeks to understand how and why public opinion moved so powerfully in just three short years. Commentators have variously sought to explain the collapse of the Conservative Party by referencing Partygate or the catastrophic Liz Truss mini-budget or the rise in immigration or soaring NHS waiting lists or the crumbling of public services. These events all mattered, but what was key was how they collectively shifted the public narrative, the stories people tell and share in their communities.

The public narrative is the core mechanism that helps people structure an understanding of events. It is not simply a script or story that is retold, it is a process of telling, listening, reflecting, and, importantly, incorporating the stories of others before being retold. It is this co-creation process that confirms the validity of the core story. Typically, these public narratives are stories of the past, the present, and a desired future.

This book draws heavily on evidence from elections, polling surveys, and focus groups to track the shifts in public opinion. More surveys, polls, and focus groups were conducted during the 2019–2024 parliament than ever before. Regular surveys tracked the public's views, including their satisfaction with political leaders, their views on economic competency, trustworthiness, and much more. Polls had also become increasingly sophisticated with the rise of multilevel regression and post-stratification (MRP) polls that allowed pollsters to estimate the state of the parties in specific constituencies and which were used to inform tactical voting choices. Companies also conducted and publicly shared feedback from hundreds of focus groups across the country, many of which were recorded or available to watch live.[11]

Part 1 of this book, *Volatile Voters*, seeks to provide the context within which public narratives were developed during the 2019–2024 Conservative government. It summarises the unprecedented series of political shocks and upheavals in the United Kingdom over the ten years from 2014 to 2024 and tracks how these events increased voter volatility and distrust of politicians.

Increased voter volatility was visible in the levels of vote switching across elections and in the rise of transactional and tactical voting. It was amplified by the growing voter distrust of the government and politicians more generally. By 2024, the level of trust in politicians had fallen to its lowest level in 40 years.[12] Higher levels of distrust can make the public more cynical and receptive to populist ideas. They also increase the likelihood of political disengagement and unpredictable protest votes.

Part 2 of the book, *Broken Britain*, explores how three different narrative strands emerged during the 2019–2024 parliament and coalesced into a single, coherent, and dominant public narrative. This narrative became the accepted explanation for the series of chaotic events that took place during the parliament and led to the collapse of the Conservative Party in the 2024 election.

The first narrative was 'nothing works anymore'. It resonated strongly with the public, 84% of whom felt public services had deteriorated under the Conservatives.[13] The broad nature of the narrative allowed the public to continually add their own examples, whether it was having to wait for an NHS operation, hitting a pothole, not being able to get a GP appointment, police not investigating crimes, trains being late, or sewage being pumped into their local river. The more the public shared and added their stories, the more powerful and compelling the story became.

It was also a narrative reinforced by the media, by pundits, pollsters, and opposition politicians. In their election videos Angela Rayner, Rachel Reeves, and Nigel Farage all claimed that 'nothing works anymore'. The same phrase was repeated continuously in focus groups, newspaper headlines, TV reports, and survey findings. By 2024, nearly two-thirds of people believed that nothing in Britain worked anymore.[14]

The second narrative to emerge was 'the Conservatives are incompetent'. The party's constant regicide resulted in a succession of leaders who each appeared unsuited to the role of prime minister and created a sense of disarray and incompetence. This view was reinforced by a series of failed promises, particularly on immigration, which really mattered to 2019 Conservative voters. Despite promising to reduce net migration, the numbers tripled, soaring to 745,000 in 2022.

The party's historical electoral strength, its perceived competence in managing the economy, was seriously undermined by the economic shocks of Brexit, COVID-19, the Ukraine war, and a global inflation surge. It was then completely demolished in September 2022 by Liz Truss's mini-budget, which firmly pinned a Tory rosette on the economic crisis and ensured the party took the blame for the rising cost of living, higher mortgage rates, and the ensuing recession.

By 2024, pollsters reported that two-thirds of voters thought the Conservative Party was incompetent[15] and 81% were dissatisfied with how it was running the country.[16] Robert Shrimsley, the *Financial Times* chief UK political commentator, argued that after 14 years of Conservative government, voters had concluded the country was "led by serial incompetents and in a worse state than it was a decade ago".[17]

The third narrative was 'the Conservatives should be punished'. It was the result of growing public anger at the collapse of public services, rising levels of poverty, and the behaviour of the Conservative government, which had been marked by allegations of impropriety, misconduct, corruption, fraud, and lying. Professor John Curtice observed that by June 2024, the overwhelming public feeling was not only that the Conservatives had failed and had to go, but they had to be punished for the damage they had caused. He noted that "a significant section of the electorate was willing to take whatever stick they found available and congenial to beat the Conservatives".[18]

The Economist felt the public was so aggrieved and so determined to hand out a punishment beating to the Tories that the election was going to be "an episode of mob justice".[19] Sam Coates, the deputy political editor of *Sky News*, said it would be "a revenge election"[20] where the driving force would be the public's determination to punish the Conservatives. The UK's first-past-the-post electoral system was ideally designed for the public to take their revenge, and voters took full advantage as heavy tactical voting removed the Conservatives from even their safest seats.

The popular television presenter and author Richard Osman offered no comfort to the Conservative MPs who lost their seats. He said they couldn't even look forward to appearing on the popular *Strictly Come Dancing* TV programme, as previous MPs such as Ed Balls had done, because "there is such a visceral dislike for what the Conservative Party have done over the last few years".[21]

These three strands – nothing works anymore, the Conservatives are incompetent, and the Conservatives should be punished – fused together and became a single powerful public narrative:

> *Nothing works anymore because the Conservatives are incompetent, and they should be punished.*

It was a story that was co-created, shaped, and validated by the public themselves, as they continually added and shared their own stories. It was also a story that provided a common sense explanation for recent events. Arguably, the narrative had become so powerful by the summer of 2024 that nothing could have saved the Conservatives in the general election.

Part 3 of the book, *A Punishment Election*, provides a detailed review of the 2024 election campaign and reveals how the collapse of the Conservative Party was exacerbated by:

- Labour, Liberal Democrat, and Green Party campaigns that all leveraged the public narrative and the public's willingness to engage in intense tactical voting to eject the Conservatives. They focused ruthlessly on voter efficiency rather than trying to increase their vote share across all seats. They targeted resources on specific constituencies where they could establish themselves as the main challenger and persuade people to vote tactically to remove a Conservative candidate. The success of these strategies was exemplified in North Herefordshire, where the Green Party overturned a 24,000 Conservative majority.

- A poorly planned and managed Conservative election campaign, which failed to create a convincing counter-narrative. A campaign that was also torpedoed by Sunak's decision to leave the D-Day commemorations early and a betting scandal which reinforced the public's view of corrupt and dishonest politicians who had to be ejected from office.
- The decision of Nigel Farage to lead Reform's campaign and to stand over six hundred candidates. The party provided a home for disillusioned former Leave voters, concerned about the Conservative Party's failures on issues such as immigration. The split in the right-wing vote enabled Labour to win back nearly all of the Red Wall seats it had lost in 2019, even though it secured fewer votes in these constituencies in 2024.[22]
- A defensive Labour Party campaign which sought to reassure voters by stealing the Conservative Party's positions on the economy, tax, crime, defence, and patriotism.

Part 3 also contains a detailed analysis of the election results, including the flow of votes between parties from 2019, voter demographics, tactical voting, and the disproportionate translation of votes into seats.

The final part of the book, *The Future*, explores the new and increasingly volatile electoral landscape after the collapse of the Conservatives. It examines:

- James Kanagasooriam's view that we are now in a world of sandcastle politics where parties build large and broad electoral coalitions only to see them washed away in a matter of years.
- The potential implications of the high levels of distrust in politicians, including the public's openness to populist ideas, lower levels of political engagement, and unpredictable shifts in voting patterns.
- How the success of targeted campaigns in 2024, where one party established itself as the primary challenger and built a tactical voting alliance against the incumbent, may influence and shape future election campaign strategies.

The book finishes by examining the specific challenges facing Kemi Badenoch, the new leader of the Conservative Party. These include how to respond to the rise of Reform, rebuild a reputation for competence, address the party's demographic challenges, and develop a narrative about the party's vision that appeals to younger, more socially liberal voters while at the same time seeing off the challenge of Reform on its right.

The party needs to recognise why it lost the 2024 election. At the party's autumn conference in 2024, there was little discussion about the collapse in public services. To move forward, the party must craft a narrative that reconciles its desire for lower taxes and a smaller state with the electorate's desire to improve public services.

An angry, anti-politics mood combined with new social, economic, and cultural cleavages means that future elections are likely to be increasingly fragmented and unpredictable. The Conservatives cannot rely on disaffected Labour voters turning back to them as they did in the past. The future is not what it was.

While many commentators argue the Conservative Party's lust for power will ensure it will be back in government again, its position is precarious. Centre-right parties in Western countries have struggled in recent decades. Many have either been displaced by parties further to their right or captured by more extreme elements within their own ranks. The Conservative Party has to recognise the potential gravity of its current situation. If it fails to adapt and address the challenges it faces, the 2024 election could mark an irreversible turning point in its electoral fortunes.

PART I

VOLATILE VOTERS

1

FRAGILE COALITIONS AND VOLATILE VOTERS

Political coalitions these days are more like sandcastles – impressive but liable to be swept away.[1]

— JAMES KANAGASOORIAM

The Conservative Party is often lauded as an election-winning machine, and its 14 years in power from 2010 might superficially suggest it had a solid and enduring mandate. However, the party's election results from 2010 were far from convincing and masked a remarkable degree of voter volatility. The party's grip on power was far more tenuous than it appeared.

In two of the three general elections of 2010, 2015, and 2017, the Conservatives failed to secure a majority of seats. In 2010 and 2015, the party's share of the vote was just 36% and 36.9%, respectively. In the 2014 European Parliament election, the Conservatives came third behind UKIP and Labour with just 23% of the vote. In the 2019 European Parliament elections, the

Conservative Party came fifth, with just 8.8% of the vote. It was the worst result in the party's history as its supporters switched to the Brexit Party, which came top with 30.5% of the vote.

In the general election of December 2019, Boris Johnson sought to win back Brexit Party voters on a platform of getting Brexit done, levelling up left-behind areas, controlling the country's borders, promising "colossal new investments" in public infrastructure[2] and pledging to increase public spending in key areas like health, education, and the police. Johnson was helped considerably by the Brexit Party's decision not to stand candidates in 317 seats. Nigel Farage said it was a decision to put the country first, partly out of fear of splitting the Conservative vote and letting Labour in, who, according to Farage, had broken their pledge to respect the result of the 2016 referendum.

Johnson and the Conservatives won 43.6% of the vote in the election and an 80-seat majority. After the election, the Conservative Party's support surged to over 50% in the polls, a full 26 points ahead of the Labour Party.[3] Adam Boulton, writing for *Sky News*, argued that British politics had "taken a decisive turn after a period of remarkable instability".[4]

Johnson's political sandcastle?

Johnson's election victory, with the largest Conservative majority since 1987, may have looked like a return to political stability – but beneath the surface, it rested on a fragile coalition. Many former Leave voters backed the Conservatives solely due to the absence of Brexit Party candidates, while many Remain voters supported them reluctantly out of a deep-seated fear of Jeremy Corbyn.

In the so-called Red Wall, Johnson successfully won over left-behind voters with his own brand of charismatic leadership and his pitch to 'get Brexit done', control the country's borders, and level up the country.[5] But there had been no Damascene conversion and no deep well of support. Voters in these areas were more frustrated with Labour and its Brexit stance than enthusiastic about the Tories.

Many Red Wall voters said they were lending the Conservatives their support to give them a chance to prove themselves. In essence, their support was conditional on the improvements that might flow from a Conservative government, which, if not forthcoming, would lead them to switch back to Labour or another party. For others, it was a purely transactional vote to 'get Brexit done' rather than overwhelming enthusiasm for the Conservative Party.

Many former Labour voters said they were switching to the Conservatives 'with a heavy heart'. This was something Johnson himself acknowledged. On 13 December 2019, standing behind a podium embellished with the words 'The People's Government', Johnson thanked first-time Conservative voters, saying, "You may have only lent us your vote, you may not see yourself as a natural Tory ... Your hand may have quivered over the ballot paper before you put your cross in the Conservative box ... I and we will never take your support for granted."[6]

The coalition of voters that Johnson assembled in 2019 was broad and inherently unstable, containing groups with conflicting views, from liberal Remain voters to socially conservative Leave voters. Professor Tim Bale, a historian of the Conservative Party, believed that this coalition would be "difficult to hold together" as there was no evidence of any deep ideological support for the party.[7] This was a view shared by Professor Paula Surridge, who held focus groups in the Red Wall areas. She said, "It is hard to find any sense that new bonds have been forged with the Conservative Party – our participants did not think that those who switched allegiance last time could now be counted on in the same way as Labour voters could in the past."[8]

When Jeremy Corbyn was replaced by Keir Starmer and the Brexit deal was finally signed, two of the core motivations for the 2019 first-time Conservative voters supporting the party were removed. The polling analyst James Kanagasooriam argued the Tories had built a giant political sandcastle that could easily be washed away with the tide by increasingly volatile and transactional voters.[9]

Volatile voters

In 2019, as the Conservative Party celebrated its sweeping 80-seat majority, many believed their grip on power was secure for at least two terms, but not everyone agreed. A month after the election, Professor Philip Cowley wrote an article for *The Times* headed: 'Events happen. Governments cock up. Labour doesn't have to lose.'[10] He argued that while few people would stake a large sum of money on a Labour government being formed after the next election, the electorate was becoming more volatile, with voters increasingly likely to switch parties between elections.

In 2015, an estimated 43% of people voted for a different party than they had voted for in 2010. There had been whiplash swings in the votes for political parties. For example, in 2015, Labour won only 30.4% of the vote. Just two years later, the party's vote jumped to 40%, and another two years later, it collapsed back to 32%, giving the party its lowest number of seats since 1935.

The 2019 vote did not signify a return to stable majority government or ideologically-based voting. It was, in reality, the result of transactional voting, which enabled a temporary coalition to be assembled to 'get Brexit done' and to stop Corbyn from becoming prime minister.

The increased volatility in voting prior to the 2024 general election was attributed to several factors, including:

- Falling party identification and party dealignment
- Greater frequency of elections
- Smaller party success and failure
- Major shocks that are salient and relevant to vote choice
- More cross-pressured voters leading to realignment
- More late deciders during campaigns
- More transactional and tactical voting

Party dealignment

In the 1960s, almost one in two voters said they had a 'very strong' identification with a political party. By 2005, that figure was just 10%, meaning voters were more likely to switch parties between elections. The 2019 election and the fall of the Red Wall continued to weaken the link between social class and party affiliation. For many years, Labour had been gaining support in managerial and professional occupations while the Conservatives had been gaining support in semi-routine and routine occupations. Professor John Curtice argued that by 2019, there was no longer much of a link between party support and social class.[11]

The changing nature of party support was documented by Jennings and Furling in their 2024 book, *The Changing Electoral Map of England and Wales.* They pointed out that in 1979, the higher the proportion of people in manual and semi-skilled jobs in a constituency, the bigger the Labour vote and the lower the Conservative vote.[12] This was still true by 1997, but the relationship had become much weaker. Labour's connection with blue-collar voters was breaking down, with many believing the party no longer represented people like them. By 2019, Jennings and Furling observed, "manufacturing had become positively associated with Conservative support – with the party tending to secure a higher vote in areas with larger workforces in blue-collar occupations".[13]

Elections and smaller parties

The growth in secondary elections has allowed smaller parties to increase their visibility, gain votes, and demonstrate they are a viable alternative to the established larger parties. Outside of general elections, voters can express their preferences in European elections, the Scottish Parliament, or the Welsh Assembly elections, local elections, and elections for city mayors and police and crime commissioners.

The success of smaller parties in secondary elections could be seen clearly in the 2019 European Parliament elections. The two parties with the largest vote share were the Brexit Party with 30.5% and the Liberal Democrats with 19.6%. While history shows that smaller parties can struggle to hold onto their voters in general elections, voters become more familiar with switching their votes between parties. They also develop a more favourable disposition to parties they vote for in secondary elections and are more open to being persuaded to switch votes in the future.

Political shocks

Fieldhouse et al. argue that party dealignment combined with electoral shocks has led to "substantial and dramatic increases in vote-switching".[14] They argue that shocks which are salient and relevant to party choice can cause people to re-examine their historic party loyalties and change the status quo in political systems. They provide five examples of such electoral shocks.

1. Immigration and the rise of UKIP. Following the Blair government's decision in 2004 to allow unrestricted immigration from the EU accession countries, immigration became a growing concern for the electorate, which resonated in elections, most notably in the rise of UKIP.
2. The 2008 financial crisis. The 2008 economic crisis led to a major policy shift focusing on austerity, which had long-lasting consequences. This shock also allowed the Conservatives to successfully question Labour's economic competence, coming as it did at the end of a period of Labour government.
3. The collapse of the Liberal Democrats after the coalition government. The Liberal Democrats' decision to join the Conservatives in government in 2010 angered their left-leaning voters, who deserted the party in 2015, causing the party to lose 49 of its previous 57 seats.
4. The Scottish referendum. The 2014 referendum caused a major political realignment in Scotland, resulting in a surge in support for the SNP and a collapse in the Labour vote.
5. Brexit and the 2017 election. The result of the EU referendum was the biggest shock to British politics in decades. It polarised voters, with 82% voting for the two main parties in 2017. Brexit appeared to create a realignment of voters, with a record number of people switching between Labour and the Conservatives.

When people are less attached to political parties, they are increasingly likely to vote on a transactional rather than an ideological basis. This means they may vote to achieve a specific objective rather than to support the principles or values of a particular political party. In 2019, many people may have voted Conservative to stop Jeremy Corbyn from getting elected rather than because of a deeper-rooted ideological affinity with the party. In 2024, people may have voted for the Green Party in seats like North Herefordshire to unseat the Conservative candidate rather than because of their support for the party's policies, such as unilateral nuclear disarmament.

James Kanagasooriam viewed much of the vote for the Conservatives in Red Wall areas in 2019 as a transactional vote. This view is supported by Professor Tim Bale, who wrote in 2021 that Boris Johnson should be concerned that "his relationship with many of the voters who switched to the Tories in 2019 is, at root, transactional rather than romantic".[15] This was backed up by anecdotal evidence. For example, one voter, Michael Hallihane, explicitly said, "I never voted Conservative in my life until after the referendum. And I saw it as a transactional vote."[16]

The growth in voter volatility and transactional voting makes broad and shallow political coalitions very fragile. In a coalition with conflicting values such as Johnson's, parties can find that policies that are popular with some supporters may alienate other parts of their coalition. For example, when COVID-19 restricted the Conservative Party's levelling-up investment ambitions, the party sought to appeal to Red Wall voters by focusing on cultural issues. They adopted a form of culture war rhetoric which alienated their younger and more liberal 2019 Conservative supporters.

Distrust

Political trust is generally high when people have confidence in their government and political leaders, and view them as trustworthy, fair, credible, and competent.[17] In Western democracies, politicians have tended to be more distrusted than trusted. This has been generally viewed as beneficial to democracy, as it ensures an ongoing evaluation of the performance of political leaders. Some have even referred to this liberal distrust as the 'guardian of democracy'. However, the political scientist Eri Bertsou argues it is important not to conflate this liberal distrust with political distrust, which, far from being beneficial, is a potentially damaging and destabilising force.[18]

It is critical to understand that political distrust is not merely a lack of trust where there is doubt and scepticism about the government's intentions but a strong and settled belief in the untrustworthiness of political leaders. Once the public becomes distrustful of a government or politicians more generally, it is hard to reverse this view.

Bertsou argues that there are three aspects to political distrust. The first is based on evaluating the competence of political leaders and government. The second is based on unethical and untrustworthy conduct, which the public sees as wrong or unfair. Public perceptions of untrustworthiness, corruption, bribery, and cronyism are all strongly associated with political distrust. The third is based on partisanship, where people are more likely to distrust politicians they disagree with.

Political trust has been declining for several decades. This has been attributed to political scandals, such as the MPs' expenses scandal in 2009, and the increasing prominence of cynical views about politicians. In 1986, 40% of people trusted the government to place the nation's needs above the interests of their party; by 2010, this had halved to 20%.[19]

The Brexit referendum also had a damaging impact on the public's trust in politicians. A group of academics studying trust in government observed that the failure to 'get Brexit done' had "resulted in a loss of political trust" and warned that there could be "a further downward spiral of distrust and disaffection".[20]

Higher levels of voter distrust can lead to more unstable electoral environments. Research by Voogd et al., published in 2019, found evidence that low levels of trust undermine the formation of stable party preferences and stimulate volatility.[21] They found that declining trust drives voters, particularly supporters of parties in government, to change their party preference. High levels of distrust also create opportunities for populist parties, which appeal to voters with simple solutions on the basis that the political and establishment elites cannot be trusted.

High levels of distrust can also lead to unpredictable behaviour where voters seek to punish existing political leaders by acting or voting in a contrary manner to register a protest against the existing government. Research by Okolikj et al. found that voters with high levels of distrust were more likely to vote for protest parties, even if such parties were far removed from their own ideological position, to express their distrust of political parties.[22]

Distrust can also lead to people opting out of the political system, which can be reflected in low levels of voting and political engagement. The 2020 British Attitudes survey found that turnout in the 2019 election was lower among people who said they almost never trusted the government.[23] The same survey also found that 62% of these people wanted a change in the current voting system and were "markedly more likely to have a populist outlook".[24]

In 2021, the Institute for Public Policy Research (IPPR) warned that growing distrust could "lead to a downward spiral of democratic decline, with voters disengaging, becoming polarised, or turning to populist leaders and causes".[25]

In summary, the growing levels of political distrust in the UK increased the potential for electoral volatility, including greater polarisation, support for populism, and a decline in political participation.

The Blue Wall and tactical voting

Steve Akehurst, director of the research group Persuasion UK, has argued that "younger voters are far more transactional and less attached to political parties than older generations".[26] In his view, this has significantly increased the potential scale of tactical voting, where people seek to make their vote count in a first-past-the-post system by trying to stop a candidate they dislike being elected.

Chris Hopkins, political research director at Savanta, has argued that tactical voting is also on the rise because voters have become "increasingly sophisticated in understanding how in a first-past-the-post system, their vote can be as effective as possible".[27]

Analysis by Professor Stephen Fisher before the 2024 election suggested that Labour and Liberal Democrat supporters were more willing to vote tactically for each other in 2024 than they were in 2019. This was primarily because Liberal Democrat voters were not worried about Keir Starmer to the degree they were with Jeremy Corbyn. Steve Akehurst's research suggested that Labour supporters in traditionally Conservative seats were very transactional and particularly open to voting for the Liberal Democrats or the Green Party to unseat a Conservative MP.[28] The increased willingness of voters to vote tactically potentially put the Conservatives at risk in a large swathe of seats, which became known as the Blue Wall.

This vulnerability became apparent just a month after the Conservatives won the Hartlepool by-election in 2021. On 17 June 2021, the party lost a by-election in Chesham and Amersham, a constituency which had been Conservative since its creation. It was won by the Liberal Democrats on a huge swing of 25 points. The Conservative share of the vote fell from 55.4% to 35.5%. The result was initially put down to local concerns regarding HS2 and the relaxation of planning controls. However, John Curtice argued that many of the Conservative Party's traditional voters were no longer sure about the party's direction.

There was also evidence in the by-election of significant tactical voting as Labour voters turned to the Liberal Democrats to remove the Tories. The degree of tactical voting was reflected in the Labour vote, which fell to 1.2%, its lowest-ever share of the vote in a Westminster election. It was a stark warning that the Tories were vulnerable to tactical voting in constituencies in Southern England.

Many of these constituencies had voted against Brexit and were becoming more liberal as younger, more liberal graduates moved out of London in search of cheaper housing. For example, Mike Martin, the Liberal Democrat MP for Tunbridge Wells, estimated that around 3,000 people had moved into his constituency every year since 2019. Tony Travers, the director of LSE London, a research centre at the London School of Economics, argued the Chesham and Amersham by-election result was the result of this gradual "erosion of the Tory party's traditional rock-solid voter base in the south-east of England".[29]

Travers believed that demographic changes were significant, noting that in a typical year, more than 200,000 people move out of London to the south-east and east. Travers argued that Labour votes were effectively being exported to the wider region. As evidence, he pointed to the 2019 local elections, where the Conservatives faced sudden and vast losses of councillors in places such as Chelmsford, Chichester, East Cambridgeshire, Guildford, South Oxfordshire, Vale of White Horse, Winchester, Woking, Surrey Heath, and Spelthorne.

The day after the by-election, Ed Davey, the leader of the

Liberal Democrats, took an orange mallet to a wall of blue bricks to symbolise his party's victory.[30] *The Guardian* used the photo in an article published on 19 June 2021, headed 'The Blue Wall: what next for the Tories after a shock byelection defeat?'[31] The article identified 29 Blue Wall seats where the Tory majority was below 30%, the Liberal Democrats came second, and the Leave vote was below 53%. These were:

Brecon & Radnorshire
Cambridgeshire South
Cambridgeshire South East
Chelsea & Fulham
Cheltenham
Chippenham
Cities of London & Westminster
Esher & Walton
Finchley & Golders Green
Guildford
Henley
Hitchin & Harpenden
Lewes
Mid Sussex
Mole Valley
Newbury
Romsey & Southampton North
Somerton & Frome
South West Surrey
Sutton & Cheam
Taunton Deane
Thornbury & Yate
Tunbridge Wells
Wantage
West Dorset
Wimbledon

Winchester
Witney
Wokingham

Steve Akehurst identified a similar group of Blue Wall seats, which were historically Conservative but could be lost as a result of tactical voting. Akehurst specifically identified seats where:

- Labour or the Liberal Democrats had overperformed their national swing versus the Conservatives in both 2017 and 2019.
- The Conservative majority was under 10,000 votes.
- A disproportionately large number of residents were graduates.[32]

These seats were mostly in suburban areas in England, often on the outskirts of cities or large urban conurbations. Akehurst argued that voters in these seats were more likely to focus on issues like housing and the environment rather than immigration. They were also more pro-EU and liberal than the new Conservative voters in the Red Wall and felt increasingly distant from the Tory Party.

The increasing willingness of people to vote tactically, combined with the changing demographic nature of Blue Wall seats, made the Conservative Party particularly vulnerable in these constituencies.

2

A DECADE OF POLITICAL SHOCKS

The days of predictable voting patterns are gone.[1]

— ANAND MENON

An unprecedented series of political shocks and upheavals in the United Kingdom marked the decade from 2014 to 2024. These seismic events included the closely contested Scottish independence referendum, the divisive Brexit vote, the global COVID-19 pandemic, the Partygate scandal, a severe cost-of-living crisis, record-breaking levels of immigration, an economic recession, the rapid turnover of Conservative prime ministers, and the disastrous Liz Truss mini-budget that sent markets into turmoil.

As we noted in the previous section, political shocks can act as catalysts, altering public perceptions of political parties and accelerating shifts in political allegiances. This is particularly the case when voters have fewer ties to existing parties and an increasingly wider choice of viable parties to vote for. In these circumstances, a series of political shocks can reconfigure the electoral landscape.

Shocks create significant and specific risks for governing parties as they are typically held accountable for events. This particularly applies to economic shocks, which can damage a governing party's reputation for competence, even if the crisis is global. The global financial crash damaged the Labour Party's public reputation for economic competence even though global leaders considered Gordon Brown to have played a stabilising role.[2]

Political shocks have the potential to increase voter volatility by reshaping public opinion at two levels. Firstly, shocks can potentially detach voters from their previous party affiliations. This can destabilise voter coalitions and drive significant shifts in voting patterns, leading to greater transactional, tactical, and protest voting. Secondly, shocks can shape the level of political trust, namely the confidence people have in the government and the extent to which they see their political leaders as trustworthy, credible, fair, and competent.[3] Shocks have huge potential to create and reinforce voter distrust in politicians.

It should be noted that a severe shock or period of crisis is not always bad for the government of the day. One observed phenomenon in a crisis is an initial 'rallying-round-the-flag' effect – first proposed by the American political scientist John Mueller.[4] This rally effect can be reflected in the sudden and substantial increase in public approval of a political leader.[5] Professor Will Jennings has suggested that the bounce in Boris Johnson's satisfaction ratings in early 2020 was an example of a 'rally-round-the-flag'.[6]

These rally effects, however, may not endure for long as the public begins to scrutinise the efficacy of the political leadership and the actions it has taken to resolve the crisis.

Mueller noted that a rally that sends approval ratings soaring could be reversed in a matter of months, particularly if the press and the opposition step back from supporting a national unity response to a crisis and instead begin to criticise the government.

In this chapter we review the rolling series of political shocks that occurred from 2014 onwards and track how they:

- damaged the public's confidence in the leadership of the Conservative Party, including their competence, credibility and trustworthiness
- increased the level of distrust in politicians more generally
- fragmented the 2019 Conservative voter coalition
- increased voter volatility and increased the likelihood of transactional and tactical voting
- made the public more open to populist appeals.

The analysis draws on a wide variety of data sources, including:

- a multitude of polling surveys that look at voter intention, favourability ratings, confidence in the government, and a variety of other issues
- discussions that took place in focus groups during and after each event
- election results, including secondary elections such as local elections, by-elections, and European elections
- long-term research studies on political trust undertaken by the British Social Attitudes survey, the National Centre for Social Research survey, and the Ipsos annual Veracity Index survey, amongst others.

2010–2019

In the 2010 general election, the Conservative Party, led by David Cameron, secured 36.1% of the popular vote but fell short of achieving a parliamentary majority. This outcome necessitated the formation of a coalition government, with Cameron partnering with the Liberal Democrats – a relatively rare occurrence in British politics. While coalition governments are often characterised by instability, the Conservative-Liberal Democrat alliance that governed from 2010 to 2015 proved to be remarkably cohesive. In retrospect, this five-year period stands out as one of the more stable chapters of the Conservatives' period in power.

Despite this relative stability, support for the Conservatives in opinion polls ranged from 41% in December 2011 to just 27% in March 2013.[7] This low point followed the February 2013 by-election in Eastleigh, triggered by the resignation of Liberal Democrat MP Chris Huhne. While the Liberal Democrats managed to retain the seat, albeit with a reduced majority, the most significant aspect of the by-election was what happened to the Conservatives. The Party's support fell 14 points as they were pushed into third place by the UK Independence Party (UKIP).

UKIP's leader, Nigel Farage, claimed it was not a "freak result" but represented growing support for his party.[8] Cameron, by contrast, brushed off the result, saying, "This is a by-election. It's mid-term. It's a protest. That's what happens in by-elections."[9] The result, however, foreshadowed the potential for large numbers of voters to switch from the Conservative Party to a more populist right-wing party.

During his period as prime minister, Cameron was responsible for two major political shocks. These were the result of two extraordinarily risky bets on binary referendums. The first was the Scottish independence referendum in 2014, which he survived narrowly, with 55% voting that Scotland should not be an independent country. However, the consequences of the referendum had a significant impact on Scottish politics as the campaign led to a voter realignment which reverberated for many years.

Around 90% of those who voted for independence in the referendum switched their allegiance to the SNP in the subsequent general election. To some commentators, it was seen as an increase in transactional voting, with voters primarily focused on achieving Scottish independence and setting aside other ideological considerations. The referendum had the effect of turbocharging the SNP, who went on to win a landslide 56 seats in the 2015 election, an increase of 50 seats on 2010.

The second high-risk bet that Cameron placed was designed to head off the rise of UKIP and, in his words, to stop Conservative Party members "banging on about Europe".[10] Cameron promised to hold an in/out referendum on membership of the European Union if the party won the 2015 general election. In the subsequent election, the Conservatives won a majority of ten seats on a vote share similar to that they had won in 2010 (36.9%).

In large part, the Conservative Party's victory was due to a collapse in the Liberal Democrat vote, which fell from 23% to 7.9%, causing them to lose 49 of their 57 seats. The Liberal Democrats were widely seen as being punished by voters for propping up Cameron's government and backtracking on key promises such as scrapping university tuition fees.[11] The Conservative Party also ran an effective campaign targeting and winning Liberal Democrat seats.

The huge swings in support for the Liberal Democrats and the SNP at the 2015 general election highlighted the growing volatility of the electorate.

The Conservatives' majority in 2015, and the party's ability to govern on its own rather than in a coalition, might have been expected to herald a period of greater stability. However, Cameron's promise to hold a Brexit referendum plunged the country into a period of immense political chaos. The referendum took place on 23 June 2016, and the UK voted to leave the European Union by 52% to 48%. Cameron's bet failed spectacularly. He resigned the morning after the vote and was replaced by Theresa May, who became the UK's second female prime minister after Margaret Thatcher, in July 2016.

The referendum result was the single biggest shock to British politics in decades. The binary nature of the vote had the effect of polarising voters, as it had in Scotland, and detaching many from their historic political affiliations. In the following general election in 2017, a record number of people switched directly between the two main parties. It appeared that how people had voted in the referendum became an important part of their political identity.[12] A joint British Election Study report in 2019 argued that "for the first time in modern history, non-economic attitudes including immigration and Europe were equally as important as left-right in sorting Conservative from Labour voters".[13]

The Brexit referendum also damaged voters' trust in politicians on both sides of the debate. Each side believed the other side had acted unethically and lied during the campaign. Many Remain voters believed the Leave campaign had been dishonest about the consequences of Brexit and lied about the £350m on the side of the Brexit bus that they said would go to the NHS and about mass migration from Turkey.

Leave voters, on the other side, pointed to the scaremongering about the consequences of Brexit. For example, just before the referendum, a poll in *The Guardian* put Leave ahead on 53%, creating a sense of panic inside the government. It led to a joint press conference where George Osborne and the Labour shadow chancellor, Alistair Darling, announced that it would be catastrophic if the UK voted to Leave. They claimed it would require an immediate emergency budget with spending cuts and tax rises of tens of billions of pounds,[14] including a 2% rise in the basic rate of income tax, a 3% rise in the higher rate of income tax, a £2.5bn cut in NHS spending, a £2bn cut in spending on pensions, and over a billion pounds of cuts in defence and education. Osborne also said that 820,000 jobs would be lost within two years, that house prices would fall 18%, and there would be a 12% fall in sterling. Despite these dire predictions, after the vote there was no emergency budget or increases in taxes, although there was an initial 20% fall in sterling.

After the referendum, the percentage of the public that trusted politicians to tell the truth in a tight corner fell from a low of 11% to just 6%.[15] Fieldwork carried out in October and November 2016 for the Ipsos Veracity Index revealed that trust in politicians had "dropped notably".[16] In 2015, 21% of people said they would generally trust politicians to tell the truth. A year later, this had dropped to 15%.

Theresa May had the unenviable task of negotiating and getting agreement to a Brexit deal with the European Union. Her small parliamentary majority meant that she was continually vulnerable to rebellions from Conservative MPs who stymied her attempts to gain an agreement on a deal. May's Brexit proposals were rejected three times in parliament, as an unlikely alliance formed between Eurosceptic Conservative MPs and pro-Remain Labour MPs, effectively blocking her plans and deepening the political impasse. In an attempt to break the deadlock, May decided to go to the country in 2017 to seek a working majority.

After a poor campaign, May failed to win an overall majority of seats in the 2017 election, but the polarising effect of Brexit was visible in the result, with 42.3% of the vote going to the Conservatives and 40% going to Labour. Over the next two years Brexit dominated UK politics and support for the Conservatives fell steadily as May tried and failed to get agreement to a Brexit deal.

In April 2019, Nigel Farage launched the Brexit Party to fight the upcoming European Parliament elections.[17] Almost immediately, the opinion polls shifted as Conservative voters defected to the new populist party. In the European Parliament election on 23 May 2019, the Brexit Party came top with 30.5% of the vote as large numbers of Conservative supporters deserted the party over its failure on Brexit.

The Conservatives were trounced, coming fifth with just 8.8% of the vote, their worst share of the vote ever. The Labour vote also declined by 10% to just 13.6% as they were pushed into third by the Liberal Democrats, whose vote trebled from 6.6% to 19.6%. It was the first time ever that two political parties had finished ahead of Labour and the Conservatives, as over three-quarters of people voted for alternative parties. It was a further indication of growing electoral instability, with voters increasingly willing to switch their votes between parties, albeit in a secondary election.

The 8.8% Conservative vote in the European elections was a blow from which Theresa May could not recover. A month later, she resigned and was replaced by Boris Johnson, who became the third Conservative prime minister in just three years.

3

BORIS JOHNSON

We are going to restore trust in our democracy.[1]

— BORIS JOHNSON, 24 JULY 2019

In an attempt to break the ongoing Brexit deadlock in parliament Johnson sought to call an early election for October 2019. Under the Fixed Term Parliaments Act, this decision required two-thirds of all MPs to vote in favour. Johnson failed three times in parliament to secure enough votes. Finally, he supported a Liberal Democrat plan to change the law and returned to parliament with a bill requiring a simple majority rather than a two-thirds majority. Labour, conscious of being seen as blocking an election, finally supported the proposal, and it was agreed that an election would be held on 12 December 2019.

Boris Johnson and the Conservative Party won the election with an 80-seat majority, promising to 'get Brexit done'. Johnson also pledged to redress the country's economic imbalances and to create "superb public services and infrastructure".[2] He promised to invest £28bn in strategic and local roads, construct 40 new hospitals, and build 300,000 houses a year by the mid-2020s.[3] He also said he would expand public services, including 50 million more GP surgery appointments a year, and the recruitment of 50,000 more nurses and 20,000 more police officers.

Johnson's proposals resonated with the public after years of austerity, and in the months following the election, support for the Conservatives increased.

The COVID-19 pandemic

Johnson's ambitious investment agenda was brought to a shuddering halt almost immediately by the outbreak of the COVID-19 pandemic. Britain's first cases of the coronavirus were announced on 31 January 2020, the day the country finally left the European Union. On 23 March 2020, in response to the COVID-19 crisis, Johnson announced a country-wide lockdown, ordering people to stay at home and forcing a dramatic pivot in government priorities and spending.

As the pandemic took hold, Rishi Sunak, the new chancellor, announced a £5bn emergency response fund to support the NHS. This was followed by a much more expensive furlough scheme as economic activity collapsed. The scheme provided grants to employers to cover 80% of their staff's wage and employment costs, up to a total of £2,500 per person per month. The scheme was initially for three months but was extended in May until the end of October 2020. The Institute for Fiscal Studies (IFS) put the scheme's huge £80bn cost into context by pointing out that it was more than the government spent on the education system in a year.[4] The final cost of the furlough scheme was estimated at £96.9bn,[5] while the total cost of the government's COVID-19 measures was estimated at between £310bn and £410bn.[6] After the COVID-19 pandemic, there would be no money for 'colossal' investments in a levelling-up programme.

There was strong initial public support for the government's handling of the COVID-19 crisis. In March 2020, a YouGov survey found that 72% of people thought the government was handling COVID-19 'very' or 'somewhat' well. A Hanbury Strategy survey in the same month found that 67% were satisfied with the government's handling of COVID-19.[7]

By the end of March 2020, multiple polling surveys put support for the Conservative Party at over 50%, giving them a 20-point lead over Labour. As noted earlier, Professor Will Jennings suggested that the increase in Boris Johnson's satisfaction ratings at this time was an example of a 'rally-round-the-flag' in a period of crisis.[8]

In May 2020, Johnson's adviser, Dominic Cummings, was alleged to have made a trip with his family from London to County Durham in breach of government guidelines banning non-essential travel and instructing people to stay at home. There was an outpouring of public anger at Cummings' behaviour and claims that there was 'one rule for them' and another for ordinary people. Emily Maitlis, on *Newsnight*, said that the public felt "fury, contempt and anguish" and that Cummings had made the public "feel like fools".[9] There was also concern in the scientific community that the episode would make people less likely to follow government guidelines. In June 2020, following the Cummings incident, an Opinium poll found that public support for the government's handling of COVID-19 had fallen sharply, with only one in three people expressing support for the government's pandemic measures.[10]

The YouGov COVID-19 tracker, established to assess satisfaction with the government's handling of the crisis, showed a sharp fall after the Cummings scandal. The percentage of people who believed the government was handling the pandemic 'very' or 'somewhat' well fell from 59% in March 2020 to 45% in July 2020 and to just 35% in November 2020.[11] During this period, research by Ben Davies and his colleagues at the University of Kent also found a marked increase in general political distrust.[12]

In December 2020, Johnson introduced new lockdown measures and placed a third of the population under new restrictions to counter a new strain of the virus. People in the south-east and east of England, including London, were told they couldn't mix with other households over Christmas. They were instructed to stay at home, and indoor leisure and entertainment venues and all non-essential shops were forced to close. The decision to 'cancel' Christmas with four days' notice dominated the headlines of the Sunday papers on 20 December 2020. There was criticism of Johnson's "characteristic dithering", which meant people had already booked train tickets and purchased extra food for family gatherings.[13] *The Sun* commented that millions of people would be rightly furious and the Prime Minister would never be forgiven if the science used to support the new restrictions turned out to be 'dodgy'. The *Daily Star* said voters no longer had confidence in Johnson.[14]

By the end of December 2020, 56% of the public thought Johnson was doing badly as prime minister, compared to 37% who thought he was doing well.[15] The public's unhappiness with the government was also reflected in the polls. The 20-point poll lead that the Conservatives had held over Labour in April 2020 had disappeared in just nine months. The BBC poll tracker put support for the Conservatives down at 38% equal with Labour,[16] while Focaldata published a poll putting Labour two points ahead of the Conservatives. To lose a 20-point lead in such a short time was yet another indication of voter volatility and a warning about the public's growing distrust of the government.

The vaccine bounce

In January 2021, the government published its UK COVID-19 vaccine delivery plan, which aimed to give 15 million people in priority groups their first dose of the vaccine by the middle of February 2021. The programme was a great success, and by Valentine's Day 2021, the government had achieved its ambitious target. By 15 April, 17 million more doses of the vaccine had been administered, and by June 2021, all adults aged 18 or over could get their first dose of a vaccine.

The successful vaccine rollout turned around public perceptions of how the government was managing the pandemic. Satisfaction with the government's handling of COVID-19, which had been falling throughout the latter half of 2020, jumped to 62% in May 2021.[17] Grant Shapps argued that Johnson should be given the credit for constantly pushing hard to increase the speed of the vaccine rollout,[18] and the Prime Minister was duly rewarded in the opinion polls, as the Conservatives established a ten-point lead over Labour at 44% to 34%.[19]

In little more than a year, the Conservative poll lead had yo-yoed. In March 2020, the party had a 20-point lead. By December, this lead had completely disappeared, and Labour were ahead. Just five months later, in May 2021, the party was in the lead again with a ten-point advantage over Labour.

On 6 May 2021, there was a by-election to replace Mike Hill, the Labour Member of Parliament for Hartlepool, who had resigned over allegations of sexual harassment. Hartlepool had been a constituency held by the Labour Party since it was created in 1974. It was one of the Red Wall seats that didn't fall to the Conservatives in 2019. Paul Williams, an NHS doctor and former MP, was selected as the Labour candidate. He had formerly represented the nearby constituency of Stockton South but lost his seat at the 2019 election. The selection was accused of being a stitch-up by some local Labour Party members, concerned that Williams had strongly advocated for a second referendum, whereas the constituency had voted 69% to leave the EU in 2016.

The Conservatives won the by-election on a 16% swing, with their candidate, Jill Mortimer, winning 52% of the vote. It was the biggest swing towards an incumbent governing party in a by-election in the post-war era. It was also only the second time since 1982 that a governing party had won a by-election seat from an opposition party.

Starmer was heavily criticised after the loss. Corbyn ally Len McCluskey, the Unite general secretary, said, "People don't know what his vision is. People don't know what Labour stand for anymore."[20] A headline in *The Guardian* claimed, 'Starmer concedes Labour has lost the trust of working people.'[21] It was later reported that Starmer considered resigning after the by-election defeat.[22]

Hartlepool was portrayed as a major win for Johnson, but the reality was more complex. In 2019, Labour's vote in Hartlepool had dropped by 15%, and the Conservatives might have won the seat easily if it had not been for the Brexit Party splitting the right-wing vote. Their candidate Richard Tice had won a quarter of the vote and deprived the Tories of victory. The absence of Tice in the subsequent by-election enabled Mortimer to win comfortably.

On the same day as the by-election, there were local elections in over 145 councils, with around 5,000 council seats being contested. It was the first nationwide election fought collectively by the three new party leaders, namely Keir Starmer, Ed Davey, and Boris Johnson. As predicted by the polls, the Conservatives made significant gains on the back of their 'vaccine bounce'. The party gained 235 seats and won control of 13 more local authorities, while Labour lost 327 seats.

Boris Johnson was jubilant, claiming it was a "mandate for us to continue to deliver".[23]

On 8 May 2021, the newspaper front pages were adorned with images of a smiling Boris Johnson. *The Times* front page had a picture of Johnson alongside a giant inflatable of himself with his thumbs up. The headline was: 'PM eyes decade in power.'[24] Cabinet ministers suggested that Johnson could surpass Margaret Thatcher's 11-year tenure in Downing Street.

After the local elections, polling companies reported that the Conservatives had established a large lead over Labour. For example, a Redfield & Wilton Strategies poll gave them a nine-point lead over Labour, 42% to 33%, while Survation's first poll after the local elections gave the Conservatives a lead of 11 points, placing them at 44% and Labour at 33%. It appeared that the Conservative Party and Johnson had successfully navigated the rough waters of Brexit and COVID-19.

Cracks in the dam

Despite the Conservative Party's electoral success in May 2021, Johnson's personal reputation had been significantly damaged by a series of events. The first was Johnson's handling of media reports in early 2020 about a lavish refurbishing of his flat in Downing Street. There were claims that the refurbishment, including the luxury wallpaper, had exceeded the £30,000 a prime minister could spend on renovations, and a Tory donor, Lord Brownlow, had paid the additional costs. A payment which had not been properly declared.

When challenged on the matter, Johnson insisted he had personally met the costs. His denials prompted someone to leak an email from Lord Brownlow, in which he agreed to donate to cover the extra costs. Despite this clear evidence, Johnson doubled down, saying he had made all the payments himself. The subsequent investigation by the Electoral Commission confirmed that £112,549 of Johnson's flat refurbishment had, in fact, been paid by Huntswood Associates, whose director was Lord Brownlow. After the investigation report was published, surveys found that nearly a third of people believed Johnson was less honest than other politicians,[25] while a survey by YouGov found that 55% of the public thought Johnson was untrustworthy.[26]

In April 2021, Johnson was forced to deny allegations by Dominic Cummings that he had said he would rather "let the bodies pile high in their thousands" than impose a further lockdown.[27] On 26 May 2021, Dominic Cummings repeated the allegations before the Science, Technology and Health Select Committee, where he gave seven hours of testimony. He repeatedly said Johnson was unfit to be prime minister. Cummings' remarks were widely reported and made the evening news headlines. Cummings claimed the Prime Minister was like a shopping trolley – erratic, easily swayed, and lacking a clear direction – and that "tens of thousands of people died who didn't need to die".[28]

On Thursday, 17 June 2021, the Conservatives lost the Chesham and Amersham by-election to the Liberal Democrats. The scale of the defeat indicated the potential for a Blue Wall realignment, as discussed and detailed in Chapter 1. If only half the swing achieved by the Liberal Democrats in the by-election was applied across the region in a general election, the electoral map would change swiftly and perilously for the Conservatives in the south-east of England.

On Friday, 25 June, *The Sun* published pictures of the health secretary, Matt Hancock, kissing his aide Gina Coladangelo in his office at the Department of Health, in what was a clear breach of the COVID-19 rules he had helped design. Hancock resigned the next day. Tory MP Andrew Bridgen told *BBC News* it was not the affair that forced the resignation but "the hypocrisy of being someone who makes the rules and then broke the rules".[29]

The breach of the rules by Matt Hancock immediately cut through with the public, and confidence in the government plummeted. The percentage of people who felt the government were handling COVID-19 very or somewhat well fell by almost half from 62% in May 2021 to 34% in July 2021.[30]

The series of COVID-19 scandals had a marked impact on public trust. By the end of the summer, 60% of people believed Boris Johnson was untrustworthy and the same percentage said they had no confidence or very little confidence in the government's handling of the COVID-19 pandemic.[31]

The Paterson affair

While public anger was growing about Johnson's handling of COVID-19, his relations with his own Conservative MPs were severely damaged by his handling of what became known as the Paterson affair. The Conservative MP, Owen Paterson, had been investigated by the Parliamentary Commissioner for Standards after being accused of breaking lobbying rules for MPs. The Commissioner reported that Paterson had lobbied on behalf of specific companies for which he did paid consultancy work. The investigation revealed he had failed to declare his interests and used his parliamentary office and stationery for his consultancy. The Commissioner concluded there had been "serious" and "egregious" breaches of the parliamentary lobbying rules, which she claimed were the worst seen in many years.[32]

The Commons Standards Committee, after considering the findings, recommended that Paterson be suspended from parliament for 30 days. In line with the established process, on 3 November 2021 a motion was proposed in the Commons inviting MPs to approve the punishment, which would have triggered a recall petition in his constituency. Boris Johnson was determined to save Paterson from suspension and hatched a plan with his former boss, Charles Moore, over dinner at the Garrick Club. Johnson agreed to whip Conservative MPs to vote for a motion that would postpone consideration of Paterson's suspension and establish a new committee to investigate the disciplinary process for MPs. Johnson's use of the three-line whip to save Paterson was considered unethical by former Conservative ministers,[33] and 13 MPs broke the whip to vote against the motion. A further 60 abstained, including Theresa May. The motion passed by 250 votes to 232.

The outcome caused outrage among opposition MPs, the media, and the public. The *Daily Mail* ran a critical front page under the headline 'Shameless MPs sink back into sleaze' and noted Paterson had taken £500,000 from the firms he had lobbied for in "an outrageous breach of the rules".[34] It was no longer possible for Johnson to hold the line, and he did a sharp U-turn, saying that a vote would still take place on whether Paterson should be suspended after all. The decision upset Conservative MPs who had reluctantly voted to postpone the suspension under pressure from the whips and who had been subject to public anger for doing so. Paterson responded by announcing his intention to resign his seat which he did on 5 November 2021, causing a by-election.

The leader of the Scottish Conservatives, Douglas Ross, commented that Johnson's handling of the affair was "extremely poor". In *The Times* on 20 November 2021, a Johnson arch loyalist and cabinet minister was reported to have said, "I'm worried about him ... The mood on the back benches is really, really bad. There's nothing for them to unite behind, there's no economic vision, no plan."[35] Another was reported as saying the No 10 operation was a "shitshow" and "there's just no political judgment there".

In November 2021, COVID-19 was also back in the

headlines. Cases of the Omicron variant were rising, and the government moved to implement its Plan B, advising people to work from home, wear face coverings in indoor venues and introducing vaccine passports. The proposed restrictions were unpopular with Conservative MPs, 99 of whom voted against the vaccine passport measures, which only passed due to Labour support.

Support for the Conservatives continued to fall, and by the end of November 2021, their ten-point lead of the summer had evaporated. The BBC poll tracker put the Labour Party and the Conservatives level in the polls at 37%. Johnson responded by claiming these were normal mid-term blues that would be shrugged off in due course. In fact, they were about to get a lot worse.

Partygate

On 1 December 2021, the *Daily Mirror* published an exclusive story that would become known as Partygate. The front-page headline read: 'It's one rule for them: Boris Party Broke COVID-19 rules.'[36] The headline was accompanied by a photo of Johnson drinking a cocktail. In the article, Pippa Crerar wrote about Johnson having given a speech at a packed leaving party in November 2020 and also claimed there had been a Downing Street Christmas party with staff taking part in a festive quiz and exchanging Secret Santa presents.

Downing Street did not deny the claims of parties, but a spokesperson responding to the *Daily Mirror* claimed, somewhat implausibly, that COVID-19 rules had been followed at all times. When asked in the House of Commons about the parties, Johnson claimed that "all guidance was followed completely in Number Ten".[37] In the following week, further revelations were published in the press about parties and events in Downing Street. Most damaging was ITV's broadcast of a leaked video of Johnson's spokesperson Allegra Stratton. During a rehearsal for media briefings she was seen joking about holding a Christmas party in Number 10 Downing Street.[38]

The public again felt like they were being taken for fools, and the Partygate story immediately cut through to voters. The scale of the public anger and disgust was huge. Sajid Javid pulled out of broadcast interviews after asking for, and not receiving, reassurances that staff had followed the rules in Downing Street. A Savanta ComRes survey found that 72% of respondents, including 58% of Tory voters, felt there was one rule for the government and one for everyone else. On 9 December, the press criticism of the government was scathing, even from Tory-supporting papers such as the *Daily Mail*, which ran the front-page headline, 'One rule for them, new rules for the rest of us'.[39]

The public anger was driven by a deep sense of unfairness and hypocrisy. People had been legally obliged to stay away from friends and family even if they were dying in hospital while parties were being held in Downing Street. A stark contrast was drawn between the Queen sitting alone in St George's Chapel at Windsor on the eve of Prince Philip's funeral and a party held on the same evening in Downing Street involving a suitcase full of wine.

Johnson's personal poll ratings crashed after the Partygate revelations. By the end of December 2021, the percentage of people who felt he was untrustworthy had jumped from 60% in July to 69%,[40] while 75% of the public didn't think he was telling the truth about the parties and 71% of the public thought he was doing a bad job as prime minister.[41] It was little surprise that 72% thought he should resign.

The Partygate scandal also damaged trust in the Conservative Party. The percentage of people who believed the party was untrustworthy jumped from 56% in July to 64% in

December, with only 10% of people still thinking they were trustworthy.[42]

On 16 December 2021, the Conservatives lost the North Shropshire by-election that had been triggered by the resignation of Owen Paterson. The Liberal Democrats overturned the 23,000 Conservative majority with a huge swing, taking a seat the Tories had held for 115 years. The Conservative MP, Sir Roger Gale, said the by-election had been "a referendum on the prime minister's performance".[43] Paul Goodman, writing in Conservative Home, the party's unofficial news blog, said there was a growing view that No 10 "doesn't tell the truth", and a vote of no confidence in Johnson was becoming more likely than not.[44]

At the end of the year the BBC poll tracker put support for the Conservatives down at 32%, seven points behind Labour, while the *Sky News* poll tracker had the Conservatives six points behind. A YouGov poll put the Conservatives on just 30%, the lowest since Johnson took over as leader. According to the polls, over a hundred Conservative MPs were in danger of losing their seats, and the party would be wiped out in the Red Wall.

The start of 2022 brought further bad news for Johnson. First, Christian Wakeford, the Conservative MP for one of the Red Wall seats, Bury South, defected to Labour. Second, Sue Gray, who had been tasked with doing an internal investigation into the Downing Street parties, published an update on her inquiry and reported that there had been inappropriate gatherings, a drinking culture, and a failure of leadership. Third, the government's ethics adviser, Lord Geidt, publicly criticised the Prime Minister's conduct during the investigation into the refurbishment of the Downing Street flat. He accused Johnson of failing to provide him "with all the material" and described Johnson's failure to mention his communications with Lord Brownlow as "extraordinary".[45] Johnson said the omission was due to a mix-up when he had changed mobile phones and offered a humble apology.

On 17 January 2022, Dominic Cummings published a blog post accusing Johnson of lying to parliament about the parties in Downing Street and saying they had been warned that the parties broke the rules.[46] He referred to an email invite to one of the parties from Martin Reynolds, who ran Johnson's private office, which said, "Bring your own booze!" A few days later, the email invite was leaked to the press. The public's distrust of Johnson jumped still further after the revelations. According to a YouGov survey in February 2022, fully 75% of the public felt he was untrustworthy. Rumours began to emerge that Liz Truss and Rishi Sunak were readying themselves for a leadership contest.

In April 2022, the news continued to be unrelentingly grim for Johnson. The police, who had been urged to investigate the breaches of COVID-19 regulations in Downing Street, handed down 126 fixed penalty notices, including for Johnson and Sunak, the most senior politicians ever to be punished by the law. A group representing families bereaved by COVID-19 said there was "simply no way" either could continue in their jobs and that both were "truly shameless".[47] A YouGov Poll published on 12 April 2022 found that three-quarters of people thought Johnson had 'knowingly lied' about Partygate.

In a focus group held by More in Common, participants said Johnson had proved he couldn't be trusted.[48] One participant said they were sick of all politicians. In another Savanta focus group, a participant commented, "I am reluctant to change from a lifetime of voting Conservative and being a strident supporter of the Conservative Party. ... But I cannot condone the behaviour of this Prime Minister. I will not vote Conservative again if Boris is the Prime Minister."[49]

After the COVID-19 crisis, the government continued to be damaged by allegations of incompetence, corruption, and growing reports of fraud. The Bounce Back Loan Scheme (BBLS) had been introduced by the government in April 2020 to provide rapid access to finance for small businesses affected by the coronavirus pandemic. In June 2021, it was revealed that basic fraud checks had not been carried out when providing these loans. As a consequence, the scheme was open to fraud and defaults. It was estimated that £17bn would not be repaid.[50] Journalists started to document cases of fraudulent claims and published dozens of examples where loans had been misused, such as to buy cars and expensive watches.[51]

Trust in the government was also undermined by its use of 'VIP lanes' to award contracts for personal protective equipment (PPE) during the COVID-19 pandemic. In January 2022, the High Court ruled that the government's use of this fast-track process, which allowed MPs and members of the Lords to recommend firms that could assist with PPE, was unlawful. Campaigners had claimed it was open to abuse. One of the most high-profile cases involved a Tory peer, Michelle Mone, who had recommended a newly created company that went on to receive £200m of government contracts without mentioning that she and her husband would be beneficiaries. At first, the couple denied they were involved, but it was later discovered that Mone's husband had been paid at least £65m from the company's profits on the PPE contracts, and then transferred £29m to a trust which benefited Mone and her three children. The surgical gowns provided by the company, at a cost of £122m, were found to be unsuitable and never used by the NHS.

Mone became a symbol of Conservative Party dishonesty and corruption. In the summer of 2021, she had posted a photograph on Instagram of her and her husband on their new luxury yacht, the *Lady M*. It wasn't the first time Mone had taken to social media to flaunt her expensive life. In November 2020, her wedding had graced the pages of *Hello! Magazine*, including photos of Mone in her designer dress and Jimmy Choo shoes. In December 2020, while the UK was in tier 2 and tier 3 COVID-19 restrictions, she had posted photos of their honeymoon at a five-star hotel in the Maldives.

Mone was just one of many people who profited from their senior Tory Party connections via the 'VIP lane'. There were at least 24 PPE contracts worth £1.6bn awarded to those with known connections to the Conservative Party.[52] There was a growing sense among the public of inappropriate and potentially corrupt behaviour as the procurement process was investigated. The percentage of people who believed the Conservative Party to be untrustworthy increased further in June 2022 to 65%.

A global inflation shock

Inflation had been running at around 2% in the summer of 2021, but was beginning to rise across the world following the reopening of the global economy after the COVID-19 pandemic. There was an unprecedented surge in demand for shipping, causing container freight rates to skyrocket to levels ten times higher than those in 2021. Manufacturing sectors, still reeling from supply chain disruptions, struggled to match the escalating consumer demand, leading to widespread product shortages and consequent price hikes across various goods. The swift revival of industrial activity also sparked a dramatic upswing in energy consumption. This sudden increase in demand, coupled with geopolitical tensions and supply constraints, catapulted oil and gas prices to multi-year highs, further fuelling inflationary pressures and exacerbating a cost-of-living crisis.

By December 2021, inflation in the UK had more than doubled to 5.4%, the highest in three decades.[53] The *Daily Telegraph* said, "Britain faces worst cost of living crisis for a generation",[54] while the Resolution Foundation warned that "Spiralling energy prices will turn the UK's cost-of-living crisis into a catastrophe."[55]

Trust in the Conservative government's ability to manage the economy fell away as inflation increased. In January 2022, a Deltapoll survey for the *Daily Mirror* found the Labour Party had overtaken the Conservatives on economic competence, with 42% backing Keir Starmer and Rachel Reeves on the economy compared to 36% who backed Boris Johnson and Rishi Sunak.[56]

In the same month, Carnegie UK published a report on democratic wellbeing that examined trust in politicians after the COVID-19 pandemic. It found that less than half of the English public (45%) felt that democracy worked well in the UK, and the overwhelming majority did not trust MPs (76%) or the UK government (73%) to make decisions that would improve their lives.[57]

At the start of February 2022, the UK energy regulator Ofgem announced a 54% rise in the consumer energy price cap from 1 April 2022, which was forecast to increase average bills by £693 to £1,978. The scale of the increase forced the government to announce a support scheme to offset some of the rising energy costs. In late February, things got markedly worse when Russia invaded Ukraine, sending energy prices even higher. The BBC reported that UK energy bills could "top £3,000 a year".[58]

In the press, there was growing criticism that the government had not built the domestic sources of clean energy and grid connections the country required and had exposed Britain to international gas markets. Others noted that French billpayers were protected by the country's investment in nuclear reactors and their energy bills were around 50% cheaper than those in Britain.

By April 2022, inflation had risen to 9%. The IFS estimated

that the surging cost of food meant that inflation was more like 11% for the poorest households. Two-thirds of people believed the government was handling the economy poorly. As a result of the crisis, the Prime Minister's and the Chancellor's personal ratings plummeted to -45 and -44 respectively.

The Labour Party was now ahead of the Conservatives on the 'holy trinity' – public voting intention, best prime minister, and economic management.[59]

Rapidly rising inflation forced the government to provide more assistance to poorer families. In June 2022, it announced that over eight million households would receive a 'cost-of-living' payment of £650 to help ease the pressures they were under. Rishi Sunak said it was part of a package worth at least £1,200 for vulnerable families.

To help tame inflation, the Bank of England Monetary Policy Committee started increasing the bank's base rate. It was increased to 0.5% in February 2022, to 0.75% in March, and to 1% in May 2022.[60] Several former Bank of England officials felt the bank had been too slow to spot the signs of inflation in the post-pandemic period and that it had raised interest rates too slowly to control a surge in inflation. There was also particular criticism that the bank had continued an extensive bond-buying programme when there were signs the economy was rebounding.

At the start of May 2022, Johnson was pressed on the cost-of-living crisis on the TV show *Good Morning Britain*. The Prime Minister was told of 77-year-old pensioner Elsie, who could only afford to eat one meal a day and who used her free bus pass to ride the bus all day rather than use energy by being at home. Johnson responded by reminding viewers that the 24-hour Freedom bus pass was something that he had introduced.

Susanna Reid responded by saying, "Marvellous, so Elsie should be grateful to you for her bus pass!" Johnson's response was widely seen as crass and insensitive. Furious commentators on social media said the remark was "disgusting" and a demonstration of how "out of touch" the Prime Minister was with the realities of struggling people.[61]

The Conservative Party went into the 2022 local elections with falling support. Polls put the party at 33% nationally, six points behind Labour.[62] In the elections, the Conservatives lost 350 council seats and control of 13 councils, including the symbolic Westminster City Council.

The final Sue Gray report, issued on 25 May 2022, was damning for Johnson. Subsequent polls found that three-quarters of people believed he had misled the House, and two-thirds of people thought he should resign. After the report's publication, Labour established a double-digit lead in the polls. On 3 June 2022, Boris Johnson and his wife, Carrie, were booed as they made their way into St Paul's Cathedral for the Platinum Jubilee Service of Thanksgiving.

In June 2022, inflation rose further to 9.4%, and the BBC poll tracker gave the Labour Party a nine-point lead at 40% to 31% for the Conservatives. Tobias Ellwood was reported to have asked his fellow Conservative MPs if they could continue to govern given "the erosion of the trust with the British people".[63]

On 23 June 2022, the Conservative Party lost by-elections in Wakefield, and in Tiverton and Honiton. The by-elections were called after two disgraced Tory MPs resigned. Parish, the Conservative MP for Tiverton and Honiton, had resigned after admitting to watching pornography on his phone in the House of Commons, while Ahmad Khan, the Conservative MP for Wakefield, had resigned after being convicted of child sexual assault. In the subsequent by-elections, Labour won Wakefield with an 8.6% swing, while in Tiverton and Honiton, the Liberal Democrats won with a 29.9% swing.

The scale of anti-Conservative tactical voting in Tiverton and Honiton confirmed the willingness of people to vote tactically to remove the Tories. The Liberal Democrats had overturned the Conservative Party's 2019 majority of 24,239. At the time, it was the largest vote majority to be overturned in modern political history and the sixth-largest swing against a governing party since 1945. Peter Kellner, the political commentator and former head of the YouGov polling firm, observed there had been "ferocious tactical voting" in the by-election and sounded a warning for the party that "strategic anti-Conservative tactical voting could decide the next election".[64]

Tory MPs started suggesting that Johnson's time was up. At the start of June 2022, Graham Brady, as Chair of the 1922 Committee, received enough letters from Conservative MPs to trigger a vote of no confidence. Conservative Home said 55% of its readers wanted Johnson to go, but in the subsequent vote of confidence, Johnson survived with 59% of the votes of MPs. The *Daily Telegraph* headline summed up the reality: 'Hollow victory tears Tories apart – Johnson's authority crushed'.[65]

The Pincher affair

The final and ultimately fatal shock of Johnson's tenure came at the end of June 2022. Chris Pincher, who had been made the party's deputy chief whip by Johnson, resigned the whip after allegedly groping and sexually assaulting two men at the Carlton Club. Pincher had previously been accused of sexual assault in 2017, and MPs felt that further action had to be taken. However, Johnson disagreed and when challenged he claimed publicly that he wasn't aware of previous allegations and complaints against Pincher.

The Prime Minister's claim was demonstrably untrue. While Johnson was at the Foreign Office, there had been an official complaint and an investigation into Pincher. Sir Simon McDonald, the former permanent under-secretary of state for foreign affairs, had briefed Johnson personally on the matter.

In the light of Johnson's public denial on 5 July 2022, McDonald wrote to the Parliamentary Commissioner for Standards, Kathryn Stone, about Johnson's and Downing Street's statements on Pincher. He said he had to write as "No 10 keep changing their story and are still not telling the truth."[66]

The letter was described by *The Guardian* in an editorial as an "extraordinary, devastating intervention".[67] It claimed this further example of flagrant lying was the end game for Boris Johnson.

Further damaging revelations followed. It was said that Johnson, far from not knowing about the Pincher allegations, had referred to him as "handsy" and Dominic Cummings claimed Johnson had joked about Pincher back in 2020 as being "Pincher by name, pincher by nature".[68]

Johnson's constant lying and poor judgement were the last straw for Rishi Sunak and Sajid Javid who both announced they were resigning on 5 July 2022. In the next 24 hours, 36 more ministers resigned. William Hague encouraged Johnson to step down rather than lose a vote of confidence. When Michael Gove went to see Johnson to also advise him to step down, he was sacked. Johnson replaced Sunak as chancellor with Nadhim Zahawi, who, just two days after his appointment, also called on Johnson to step down, saying publicly, "You must do the right thing and go now."

Johnson resigned at lunchtime on 8 July 2022.

Sebastian Payne, in his book *The Fall of Boris Johnson,*[69] argues that Johnson was ultimately bought down by the three Ps, Partygate, Paterson, and Pincher. While it was the 57 ministerial resignations[70] after the Pincher affair that forced Johnson to resign, it is also arguable that the very high level of public distrust in the Prime Minister and his honesty made his position untenable.

Looking back at Johnson's period in government, Anthony Seldon and Raymond Newell, in their book *Johnson at 10: The Inside Story*, concluded that not since 1916 had a prime minister been so poor at appointments, so incompetent at running cabinet government, or so incapable of finding a stable team to run Number 10.

When Johnson resigned, 71% of the public thought he was doing a bad job,[71] and the Labour Party held an 11-point lead over the Conservatives, whose support had fallen to 30%.[72] The party had also lost their lead over Labour on the economy, immigration and crime. Only 60% of those who had voted Conservative in 2019 were planning to do so again.[73] Johnson's coalition of voters had fully fractured in a few short years.

Despite his failings 55% of the party membership – around 170,000 mainly white, male pensioners – still supported Johnson and thought MPs had been wrong to force him to resign.[74]

Johnson's impact on public trust

The impact of the Johnson premiership on public trust is difficult to overstate. He had doubled down on blatant untruths, such as the payments for the refurbishment of his flat, the gatherings at Downing Street, and his denials that he had knowledge of Chris Pincher's behaviour. Three-quarters of the public felt he was untrustworthy and so did a great many Conservatives. When asked in the subsequent Tory leadership debate if Johnson was honest, Tom Tugendhat swiftly replied, "No."[75]

By the summer of 2022, public confidence in the government and the broader political establishment had plummeted to alarming levels. An Ipsos survey published in

July 2022 found that just 21% of people thought the Conservative Party was fit to govern,[76] the lowest number for either main party since Ipsos had started tracking the metric in 2011. The survey also found that only 12% thought the Conservative Party kept its promises.

The erosion of political trust more generally was starkly illustrated in a survey published by the Office for National Statistics (ONS) in July 2022,[77] which was conducted just before Boris Johnson's resignation. The findings painted a bleak picture of the political landscape. Only one in five respondents (20%) expressed trust in political parties, while an overwhelming 62% explicitly stated their distrust of all political parties, indicating a pervasive crisis of confidence and trust that transcended party lines.

4

LIZ TRUSS

I have a bold plan to grow the economy through tax cuts and reform.[1]

— LIZ TRUSS, 6 SEPTEMBER 2022

The Conservative Party ran a leadership election in the summer of 2022 to replace Johnson, with candidates needing to secure support from 20 colleagues to stand. Eight secured the necessary support and five made it through to the leadership TV debates. During these debates Liz Truss heavily criticised Sunak for presiding over "the highest tax burden for 70 years".[2] Sunak's riposte was to strongly criticise Liz Truss's economic plans, arguing they would increase inflation and "tip millions into misery".

Insiders report there was dislike bordering on contempt between Truss and Sunak.[3] Truss dubbed Sunak the 'socialist' chancellor and promised to reverse the tax rises he had announced as chancellor. Sunak in turn eviscerated her proposals to fund tax cuts through borrowing, which he said were morally irresponsible as they would pile debt onto future generations, as well as economically irresponsible given the growth in inflation. He warned that cutting tax would encourage spending as prices were rising, which would force up interest rates and increase the costs of the borrowing.

During the contest, voting intention figures from Savanta ComRes revealed that the Labour Party had opened up a 15-point lead over the Conservatives. The *Daily Express* said the Tories were "reeling" after the "brutal" polling figures gave Labour its largest lead since 2013.[4]

The leadership candidates were whittled down by a series of ballots, leaving just Liz Truss and Rishi Sunak. The choice between the two candidates would be made by the Tory Party membership. The Conservative Party historian Tim Bale noted the party membership represented just 0.4% of the electorate and their views on all subjects were far to the right of the public. On 5 September 2022, the leadership results were announced. Truss won comfortably, securing 57.4% of the vote compared to Sunak's 42.6%. The party's members had chosen the libertarian, tax-cutting ideology of Liz Truss. She offered no consoling words to Rishi Sunak when the result was announced to the membership. Instead, she ignored him and triumphantly marched to the stage.

The election of Liz Truss was widely celebrated by the right-wing press. "Cometh the hour, cometh the woman," said the *Daily Mail*, while the *Daily Telegraph* said Truss deserved "a chance to show what she and the government are capable of delivering before judgement is passed".[5]

The public was less convinced about Liz Truss. Only 12% of people thought she would be a good or great prime minister, while 52% thought she would be poor or terrible, and 65% believed she was out of touch with ordinary people.[6] Two days after her election, on 7 September 2022, the BBC poll tracker gave Labour an 11-point lead over the Conservatives, at 42% to 31%.[7]

Writing in *The Times*, William Hague, the former Conservative leader, said the party could not change its leader again before an election without being "the laughing stock of the country and the world".[8]

The mini-budget crisis

Liz Truss came into Downing Street with a mission to "get shit done".[9] She cleared out and replaced staff that had served under Boris Johnson and appointed a new cabinet comprised entirely of her loyalists. She also immediately sacked Tom Scholar, the permanent secretary to the Treasury, as part of her mission to tear up what she called Treasury orthodoxy. Nicholas Macpherson, the former permanent secretary who had served three chancellors during his 11 years in the job, was aghast and commented, "Tom Scholar is the best civil servant of his generation. Sacking him makes no sense. His experience would have been invaluable in the coming months as government policy places massive upward pressure on the cost of funding."[10]

Truss was immediately faced with a series of challenges. On her third day as prime minister, Thursday, 8 September 2022, Queen Elizabeth II died at 3.10 pm. On the same day, Truss was grappling with a further crisis over energy costs. Following continued rises in global energy prices Ofgem announced that the cap would be increased again, adding a further £700 a year to average household bills.

Inflation was already over 10%, and the public was hurting. The reaction of one participant in a focus group in Bassetlaw was typical of many. "Somebody's going to have to do something to step in ... or something's gotta break I think. Something's got to give somewhere to help us out."[11]

Truss had to act on her leadership promise to limit the impact on consumers. Her new chancellor, Kwasi Kwarteng, announced the introduction of a new but less generous price cap of £2,500, which would remain in place for two years. Truss and Kwarteng were opposed to a levy on energy company profits to pay for the policy and instead said the costs would be met by over £100bn of additional government borrowing.[12]

Truss and Kwarteng believed that cutting taxes was the primary means of achieving economic growth. They were impatient to change the government's policies and to implement their plan of driving growth through deficit-funded tax cuts alongside deregulation and privatisation. On Friday, 23 September 2022, just four days after the funeral of Queen Elizabeth, the new chancellor delivered a ministerial statement to parliament entitled 'The Growth Plan', which set out a series of economic policies and tax cuts. It was referred to in the media as a mini-budget.

The mini-budget reversed Sunak's proposed increases in National Insurance and the proposed increase in corporation tax from 19% to 25%. Instead of increasing taxes to help fund the deficit, Kwarteng aimed to cut taxes by £45bn a year by 2026 and to increase government borrowing by billions of pounds in future years.[13] His proposals included a 1% cut in income tax, a reduction in stamp duty and the abolition of the 45% top rate of tax for people earning over £150,000 per annum.

The right-wing press was jubilant. The *Daily Mail* applauded the budget with the headline: 'At Last! A True Tory Budget.'[14]

The Institute for Fiscal Studies estimated that after the mini-budget, government borrowing in 2022/23 would climb to £190bn and remain at well over £100bn, even once the energy support package was withdrawn.[15] The government refused to have an independent assessment of the budget by the Office for Budget Responsibility (OBR) until November 2022. Paul

Johnson, the director of the IFS, said, "Today, the chancellor announced the biggest package of tax cuts in 50 years without even a semblance of an effort to make the public finance numbers add up. Instead, the plan seems to be to borrow large sums at increasingly expensive rates and put government debt on an unsustainable rising path."[16]

Government debt had already increased by hundreds of millions of pounds to support the country through the COVID-19 pandemic and was approaching 100% of GDP. The mini-budget proposed substantially increasing this debt to fund the government's tax cuts and the new energy package. Investors started to question how the debt was going to be repaid. It was unclear how the government could finance the extra debt without considerable cuts in services or significant tax increases.

Liz Truss's claim that the policies would drive up growth, which would pay for the debt, was given short shrift by economists and the market. Investor confidence in government debt fell, which forced up the yields or interest on government debt as investors demanded a higher risk premium.

On Sunday, 25 September 2022, Kwasi Kwarteng appeared on the BBC's *Morning Politics* show. He said his budget was just the beginning, and there was more to come. The implication was the government was going to increase government debt still further. Investors and economists were incredulous.

It was Liz Truss's heroine Margaret Thatcher who had said, "You can't buck the market." She made the comment in 1988, when Nigel Lawson had sought to keep the pound down by cutting interest rates and intervening in foreign exchange markets. On Monday, 26 September 2022, Liz Truss was to discover the brutal truth of Thatcher's warning about the power of the markets. When the Asian markets opened, investors dumped the pound, and its value fell to $1.035, its lowest value against the dollar in history. When the London market opened, the FTSE 100 Index fell by 2.3%. In an unusually blunt intervention, the International Monetary Fund asked the Prime Minister to think again about her "large and untargeted fiscal packages".[17]

The jump in the risk premia the markets applied to UK gilts (government bonds) pushed up gilt rates, the interest rate on government debt, by over a percentage point within a week. This was a greater change than gilt markets typically saw over the course of a year. The rise in gilt rates forced down the price of government bonds, creating a major crisis for pension funds which had used bonds as collateral for liability-driven investments (LDIs).

The government appeared unaware that the falling price of government bonds was creating a major problem for pension funds. Within days, several pension funds were close to being insolvent. The Bank of England was forced to intervene and promised to buy long-term government bonds "on whatever scale" was necessary to ensure financial stability.[18]

Prior to the mini-budget in August 2022, the Bank of England Monetary Policy Committee (MPC) had increased the main interest rate to 1.75%, which was 1.5% above where it had been at the start of the year. However, there was a view that the MPC had been too slow to increase rates to curb inflation, which was running at 9.9% in August 2022, and that rates had to increase further and faster. On 22 September 2022, the day before the mini-budget, the MPC increased the base rate by a further 0.5% to 2.25%. The market believed that interest rates would need to go higher. This caused mortgage providers to withdraw lending offers, even before the mini-budget, in anticipation of much higher rates.

The perceived need for higher interest rates to control

inflation, which was running at over 11%, was validated by the subsequent decisions of the MPC, which increased the base rate to 3% in November 2022, to 4% in March 2023 and to 5% in July 2023. Mortgage rates followed the same upward trajectory, which was a disaster for those about to buy a property or come off a fixed-rate mortgage deal.

The simple story was that the sharp increases in interest and mortgage rates in late 2022 and early 2023 were solely due to the catastrophic mini-budget. However, rising interest rates were a global phenomenon. In the US, the Federal Reserve had already raised its rate to 3.25% in September 2022 to curb inflation and raised it further to 4% in November 2022.

Catherine Mann, on the rate-setting committee, said the Bank of England had been too slow to act to curb inflation. It is arguable that the sharp increase in interest rates and mortgage rates in the months after the mini-budget was partly because the Bank of England and the MPC were having to play catch-up in the fight against inflation.[19] However, the mini-budget allowed the opposition and the press to pin all of the blame on Liz Truss.

The mini-budget quickly became known as the KamiKwasi budget and Truss's approval ratings crashed. When the Conservative Party conference opened on Sunday 2 October 2022, Truss's popularity had fallen to -59, a figure lower than Jeremy Corbyn or Boris Johnson at their lowest points.

In the face of mounting public criticism, Conservative MPs began withdrawing their support for Truss's budget proposals. On the BBC Michael Gove said he didn't believe the 45p tax cut was right and was "profoundly concerned".[20] Truss was informed by Graham Brady that Tory MPs would veto the 45%

tax cut if it came before the House, which forced Truss to summon Kwarteng to reverse the policy.

On Friday, 7 October 2022, the Office for Budget Responsibility wrote to the Treasury, warning the Chancellor that the mini-budget had created a £72bn black hole in the nation's finances. The papers were briefing that the cabinet secretary and head of the Treasury were insisting the cuts in corporation tax had to be reversed. Kwarteng's position was becoming untenable, and Graham Brady informed Truss that he had to be sacrificed. The following Friday, Kwarteng found out he had been sacked on Twitter. By this point, Truss had lost all credibility. Worse, she was becoming a laughing stock.

On the same day, the historian Dominic Sandbrook published an article asking the question, 'Is Truss the worst PM in history?'[21] He concluded that not only was she the least impressive person to have become prime minister since the advent of universal suffrage, but when you compared her to previous prime ministers such as Thatcher, Callaghan, and Blair, it was hard not to weep.

The Economist ran a column with the headline, 'Liz Truss has made Britain a riskier bet for bond investors.' It argued that after deducting the 10-day mourning period following the death of Queen Elizabeth, Truss had caused huge economic and political turmoil after just seven days in power, comparing that duration to the "shelf-life of a lettuce".[22] The *Daily Star* picked up and ran with the comparison. Their video team began broadcasting a livestream of an iceberg lettuce next to a framed photograph of Truss, asking the audience whether she could outlast the lettuce. Within the first five hours of the stream, it had received more than 50,000 likes.

On Friday 14 October 2022, Liz Truss held a press conference following the sacking of her chancellor, Kwasi Kwarteng.[23] She looked around the room like a surprised owl. The more she spoke, the more she appeared hapless, helpless, and completely out of her depth. She chose a *Daily Telegraph* journalist to ask the first question. If she was expecting a softball question from the paper traditionally loyal to the Conservatives, she didn't get it. They asked, "Can you explain to the public why you think you should remain as PM?"

In the face of all the facts, Truss said, "I acted decisively to ensure we had economic stability."[24] She took a few more questions and then fled the conference after just eight minutes.

Jeremy Hunt was appointed as the new chancellor, and set about reversing almost all of her mini-budget decisions.

The Conservatives under Truss were haemorrhaging public support. Opinium published the results of their latest MRP poll based on a survey of 10,495 respondents which forecast, presciently, that Labour would win 411 seats in a general election.[25] It estimated that the Conservatives would be reduced to 138 seats, a loss of 227. The MRP poll published the predicted result for every seat in the country, allowing worried Conservative MPs to check how bad things looked in their own constituencies.

The public's confidence in the Conservative Party's management of the economy had collapsed. Rory Stewart claimed Liz Truss had "totally destroyed" the Conservatives' economic credibility.[26] When asked by YouGov which political party would be the best at handling the economy, twice as many people said Labour (32%) as the Conservatives (15%).[27] The party's reputation for economic management was no more. They had lost their lead over Labour and would never regain it prior to the 2024 election. Lee Cain, the former director of communications at 10 Downing Street, commented that Truss had successfully pinned a Tory rosette to the economic crisis.[28]

Truss's position was becoming untenable. There was growing talk in Conservative circles of changing their leadership rules so that Truss could be removed and replaced with a new leader. On the morning of Monday 17 October 2022, the story became front-page news.

'Plot to Topple Truss this week' – *Daily Mail*

'Tories hold secret talks on crowning new leader' – *The Times*

'Truss faces challenge within days' – *The Independent*

'Tory MPs: Quit Now' – *Daily Mirror*

Later in the day there were shouts of "Where is she?" in the House of Commons after Truss failed to appear for an urgent question about the appointment of the new chancellor. Penny Mordaunt, to much hilarity, informed MPs that Truss was not hiding under a desk afraid to come out. It was apparent to everyone that Truss had lost the confidence of Tory MPs.

On Wednesday, 19 October 2022, any lingering support for Truss amongst Conservative MPs evaporated. During the day Suella Braverman was fired by Truss for sending an official document from her personal email and responded by calling on the Prime Minister to resign. That evening, Truss's fate was sealed by a contentious vote on fracking. The Labour Party had put forward a motion to ban fracking and shale gas extraction, which gave the Conservative MPs a dilemma. The 2019 manifesto had clearly promised a moratorium on fracking but Liz Truss had pledged to overturn the ban.

Conservative MPs were told by the whips' office that the motion was effectively a confidence motion in the government, and they were on a three-line whip to vote against. Up to 60 MPs threatened to rebel, and in the face of the size of the rebellion, the government appeared to change its mind and said the vote was not a confidence vote. It left Conservative MPs confused about whether they could rebel or not.

The government won the vote, but there were reports of MPs being bullied and manhandled through the lobbies. The resulting chaos caused huge anger amongst Tory MPs. There were rumours the chief whip, Wendy Morton, had resigned and had been seen running through the lobby in tears. The Tory whip Craig Whittaker was reported as saying "I am f***ing furious and I don't give a f*** anymore."[29]

The next morning, Graham Brady visited No 10 and informed Truss that she no longer had the support of the party's MPs. She had to resign, or she would be forced out in a vote of confidence. She resigned at 1.30 pm outside 10 Downing Street, becoming, after only 45 days, the shortest-serving prime minister in British history. Her resignation speech lasted just 90 seconds.

When she became prime minister Truss had a net favourability rating of +41 among Conservative 2019 voters. When she left office this rating had fallen to -49.

Public support for the Conservatives had completely collapsed, falling much further than it had under Johnson's darkest days. A poll from Redfield & Wilton put support for the Conservatives on just 20%. Labour were polling at 56%, giving them a 36% lead.[30] It was the largest lead recorded by any polling company for any party since October 1997. At the end of October 2022, the BBC poll tracker also gave Labour a 30-point lead in the polls.[31]

The impact on public trust

A YouGov survey in October 2022 found that trust in the Conservative Party had fallen to a record low.[32] Over two-thirds (68%) of people felt the party was untrustworthy, while just 8% of the public thought it was trustworthy.

When the IPPR published its latest research on political trust in late November 2022, it said it was shocked by the extent to which the recent political chaos had "undermined trust in politics".[33] The percentage of people believing that politicians were only out for themselves had increased from 57% in May 2021 to 66%.[34] The IPPR argued that the speed of the nine-point change was particularly concerning. The previous nine-point increase had taken place over seven years, and the one before that had taken 42 years. The Institute concluded, "Put simply: trust in British politics is in freefall."[35]

The high levels of public distrust in politicians were similar across the political spectrum. For example:

- Leave voters (68%)
- Remain voters (67%)
- Conservative supporters (64%)
- Labour supporters (69%)
- Middle-class voters (65%)
- Working-class voters (66%)

It became clear that the collapse in political trust was not confined to the Conservative Party. The percentage of people who trusted political parties of any colour fell from 20% in 2022 to only 12% in 2023.[36]

5

RISHI SUNAK

I will unite our country, not with words, but with action.[1]

— RISHI SUNAK, 25 OCTOBER 2022

In her resignation address, Truss said that she and Graham Brady had agreed there would be a leadership election "to be completed in the next week". It was agreed that candidates would require a hundred nominations from Conservative MPs to expedite the process. Boris Johnson expressed interest in standing and quickly returned from his holiday in the Caribbean with 58 of his colleagues declaring their support for him. Penny Mordaunt also sought support for a leadership bid, but withdrew prior to the close of nominations after failing to secure the 100 nominations.

Rishi Sunak announced his candidature and, potentially worried that MPs on the right would support Johnson, did a deal with Suella Braverman where she would back him in the leadership race and, in exchange, be reappointed home secretary. This was seen as a sign of Sunak's weakness in the party. In the following days, he secured the support of 193 of his fellow MPs, over half of the parliamentary party.

Reports suggest that Johnson, to many people's surprise, did secure the 100 nominations but withdrew after concluding he couldn't win.

On 25 October 2022, Rishi Sunak, at the age of 42, became the youngest prime minister since 1812 and having served as an MP for just seven years. He also became the UK's fifth prime minister in six years.

~

The public and investors were no longer sure what the party stood for. The previous Conservative leaders had radically different ideologies, leadership styles, and policy approaches. Cameron had blended modern Conservatism with austerity, a tight fiscal policy to reduce the government deficit, and opposition to Brexit. Johnson, by contrast, embraced Brexit and promised to reverse austerity with huge increases in government spending and 'colossal' investment programmes to level up the country. Following the COVID-19 crisis, Johnson also embraced tax increases and froze personal income tax allowances, which the Cameron government had so proudly increased. Truss, with the support of the party membership, had reversed Johnson's approach and sought to cut taxes. The public was entitled to be confused according to Ben Riley-Smith, in his book *Blue Murder* about the Conservative government.[2]

The party's approach to fracking summed up the lack of direction. Its 2017 manifesto had promised to legislate so that licences could be issued to undertake fracking for shale gas, while their 2019 manifesto reversed this policy, saying there would be a moratorium on fracking. In 2022, Liz Truss announced an end to the moratorium, only for Sunak to reimpose the ban a month later. Following the dramatic shifts in leadership one of Sunak's key challenges was to establish a clear sense of direction.

Sunak also had to ensure there was a clean break from Liz Truss, who the public blamed for the country's economic crisis, and to restore the public trust which had been so comprehensively damaged by the time he became prime minister.

When he became leader of the Labour Party, Keir Starmer put clear water between him and what went before. He made wholesale changes to the Shadow Cabinet, appointing 18 new members in the process. His clean break from what went before was symbolised by the suspension of Jeremy Corbyn, the previous leader, from the Labour Party. It may not have been possible for Sunak to suspend or expel Truss from the party, but he could have clearly distanced himself from her and her former colleagues. Instead, in his first speech Sunak said, "I want to pay tribute to my predecessor Liz Truss, she was not wrong to want to improve growth in this country, it is a noble aim. And I admired her restlessness to create change. But some mistakes were made."[3]

Sunak did not create a new cabinet in his image. He appointed only four new members to the cabinet, while bringing back previous members who had served under Johnson, such as Michael Gove and Dominic Raab, and allowing the majority of those that had served under Truss to continue.[4] He also brought back Suella Braverman as home secretary, just six days after she had been sacked for leaking restricted material. It was a decision criticised by Conservative MP William Wragg, as chair of the Public Administration and

Constitutional Affairs Committee. Sunak appeared to be pandering to the right with his support of Braverman, who had declared war on woke culture and who said that her dream would be to see asylum seekers sent to Rwanda. George Eaton, the senior political editor at the *New Statesman*, argued Sunak had prioritised party unity over political coherence but it was a sign of weakness, and it was unclear what he stood for.

According to Tim Shipman, chief political commentator of the *Sunday Times*, senior Tories were disappointed by Sunak's failure to set a clear sense of direction or political strategy. One senior Tory told Shipman that the party needed a vision and a narrative for the public, but none was forthcoming.[5] No one questioned Sunak's unrelenting work ethic or his sense of responsibility but people were unclear about his political ideology and vision. Tony Blair observed that the Conservatives appeared "divided between the traditional business-orientated Conservative Party and the Brexit-ideology party".[6]

Sunak took over in October 2022, at a point of economic crisis. Almost immediately the Office for Budget Responsibility (OBR) announced that GDP had fallen for two quarters in a row and the country was again in recession. The OBR's report predicted the UK's economy would shrink further during 2023, and there would be a reduction in households' disposable income.

Sunak and Hunt sought to re-establish the government's economic credibility by setting out a five-year programme of tax rises and public spending cuts worth £55bn to restore stability "in the face of unprecedented global headwinds".[7] The five-year programme allowed Hunt to push back some of the more painful cuts in public services to beyond the next election. He increased taxes by freezing allowances and thresholds for income tax, National Insurance, and inheritance tax for a further two years to April 2028. He also reduced the threshold for the top rate of tax and lowered the tax-free allowances for dividends and capital gains tax.

The Labour Party claimed his plans were austerity 2.0. Rachel Reeves argued the freezing of allowances was a major stealth tax but it was one she did not promise to change or reverse. The IFS argued that the government was postponing the most difficult decisions until after 2024, and claimed the UK was entering a "new era" of high taxation.[8]

The Tory campaign director Isaac Levido argued that Sunak should focus on the public's top concerns, which resulted in the Prime Minister outlining five pledges in a New Year's address on 4 January 2023. His pledges were:

- Halving inflation
- Growing the economy and creating better paid jobs
- Making sure the national debt was falling
- Reducing NHS waiting lists so people got the care they needed more quickly
- Stopping small boats

In announcing the pledges Sunak added, "I fully expect you to hold my government and I to account on delivering those goals."

Grant Shapps, the defence minister, felt the pledge on small boats was unrealistic. He commented that pledging to stop the boats was like pledging to stop crime.[9]

Sunak appeared to drop the commitments that Johnson had made in the 2019 election campaign; there was virtually nothing about levelling up, and nothing on controlling or reducing legal migration which had exploded under the Conservatives. Sunak's favourability rating, which started at -20 when he became prime minister, fell further to -29 in January.[10] By the end of the month, 56% of the public felt he was doing a bad job as prime minister[11] and while support for the Conservatives had improved slightly at 26%, the party was still a full 22 points behind Labour.[12]

In the spring of 2023, there was finally some better news for Sunak. The OBR forecast that the UK would probably avoid a further recession in 2023 despite the economy contracting by 0.2%. Inflation was also forecast to fall from 10.7% in the last three months of 2022 to 2.9% by the end of 2023, which was in line with Sunak's pledge to halve inflation. The spring budget kept the energy price guarantee package in place and provided a little more money for defence and childcare commitments. However, there were even tighter plans for public spending beyond April 2025.

The cost-of-living crisis had increased the pressure on public sector unions to seek higher pay increases as two in five people felt they were worse off than six months earlier and there was further talk of strike action. From the summer of 2022 onwards there had been strikes across a range of industries including the rail and bus networks, postal workers, teaching staff, civil servants, and NHS staff. In June 2022, 93,000 days were lost due to strike action, which had increased to 843,000 in December 2022.

Junior doctors took strike action in March 2023 in support of a 35% pay claim. Failure to reach an agreement with the government led to further strikes in April, with more planned for the summer. Tim Bale commented that the various strikes were bad for Sunak, who couldn't afford to allow the idea that nothing works anymore "to take hold and to become common wisdom".[13] Polls consistently showed that people thought the government was handling negotiations with the unions poorly. It was going to be impossible for Sunak to deliver his pledge to reduce NHS waiting lists in the face of a widespread junior doctors' strike. In September 2023, the number of people waiting for hospital treatment rose to a record 7.8m.[14]

By April 2023, support for the Conservatives and Sunak had improved; however, the BBC average poll tracker still gave Labour a 16-point lead over the Conservatives on 44% to 28%. More worryingly for Sunak, an Ipsos survey found that only one in four of the public thought the Conservatives were fit to govern.[15] The relative unpopularity of the party was confirmed in the May 2023 local elections. The party lost over a thousand seats (1,063), while Labour gained 537 seats and 22 councils. The Liberal Democrats gained 407 seats and 12 councils. The Greens also gained 241 seats, taking majority control of Mid Suffolk District and becoming the largest party on seven other councils. The Conservative Party lost votes both in Red Wall areas and the traditional Tory shires. After the elections, Labour became the largest party in local government, overtaking the Tories for the first time since 2002.

The Liberal Democrats did better than at any time since 2010. In the *Financial Times*, Robert Shrimsley argued that this was a particular cause of concern for the Conservatives as the elections saw a sharp increase in anti-Tory tactical voting, which enabled them to eat into Tory majorities in more affluent southern seats.[16]

The Conservative Party's national share of the vote in the local elections was estimated at 26%, confirming the party's poor poll ratings. The election losses undermined any narrative that the Conservatives were recovering under Sunak.

There were immediate recriminations and public infighting in the Tory Party. Conservative MPs opposed to Sunak said he was to blame as, ultimately, it was the country's woeful economic performance that caused the losses, and he had been chancellor or prime minister for the last three years. Other Conservative MPs sought to blame Truss, while others suggested that the Partygate scandal under Johnson was one of the main reasons for the scale of the defeat. This latter claim brought a strong response from Johnson's supporters, who argued Sunak had been the one who 'knifed' the most successful election winner in 50 years.[17] Former Tory MEP David Campbell Bannerman, who chaired the Conservative Democratic Organisation, blamed Sunak for a lack of leadership and higher taxes. "We are putting up taxes – the highest taxes for 70 years, and there's a price to be paid for that. We want to get back to more traditional, Conservative policies."[18]

Whatever the rights and wrongs of the various arguments, the very public infighting created an impression of a party that was tearing itself apart and not focusing on the problems facing the country. While prices were not increasing as fast as they had been at the end of 2022, people remained concerned about the cost of living. The economy and rising prices were at the top of the public's concerns, according to Ipsos, followed by the NHS and immigration.[19]

By-election shocks

The dire polls suggested the Tories could be removed from even their safest seats, and a series of by-elections confirmed their worst fears. On 20 July 2023, the Conservatives lost a by-election in the constituency of Selby and Ainsty to Labour. There was a swing against the party of over 20%, which overturned the previous 20,000 majority. On 19 October 2023, two further by-elections took place. In Mid Bedfordshire, where Nadine Dorries had stepped down, there was a swing of over 20% against the Tories, which enabled the Labour Party to overturn a 26,000 majority. In Tamworth, the former seat of Chris Pincher, there was an even greater swing of 23.9% against the Conservatives. At the time, it was the second biggest swing from the Conservatives to Labour since 1945. John Curtice called it "one of worst nights any government has endured".[20]

The by-election results were another clear indication that

large numbers of voters were prepared to vote tactically to remove incumbent Conservative MPs.

A YouGov survey in September 2023 found that trust in the Conservative Party had fallen back to an all-time low.[21] Just 8% of the public thought the party was trustworthy compared to 68% who felt it was untrustworthy. These were exactly the same figures as in the previous October, immediately after the Liz Truss mini-budget.

An immigration shock

> *We will take steps to take net migration back to the levels of the 1990s – tens of thousands a year, not hundreds of thousands.*[22]
>
> — CONSERVATIVE PARTY MANIFESTO 2010

> *There will be fewer lower-skilled migrants and overall numbers will come down.*[23]
>
> — CONSERVATIVE PARTY MANIFESTO 2019

When Cameron came to power, net migration was running at 250,000 people a year which he promised to reduce to the tens of thousands. Despite his promises, net migration rose steadily, peaking at over 300,000 in 2016. Tim Shipman has argued that the day net migration hit 330,000 in May 2016 was the day that the Leave campaign gained the upper hand in the Brexit referendum.[24] Immigration had become a salient public issue, with two-thirds of people in 2016 feeling that immigration was too high.

In 2019 one of Boris Johnson's major pledges was to take

back control over the country's borders, and while he would not be drawn on numbers he promised to reduce the overall level of net migration. Initially under his tenure the numbers fell but this was due to the COVID-19 pandemic rather than any changes in government policy.

Johnson decided to liberalise the UK's visa regime against the advice of immigration specialists. He reintroduced the two-year post-study visa that also allowed students to bring family members with them. This not only allowed international students to work while they were studying but also to work after their study had finished at any salary threshold or skill level and without any sponsor employer. In effect, this circumvented all the salary and other requirements of normal work visas, which were there to make migration more selective and beneficial to the economy.

Johnson's new liberalised immigration scheme resulted in considerable increases in net migration from outside the EU. On Thursday, 25 November 2023, official figures from the ONS revealed that net migration to the UK in the year to December 2022 had soared to 745,000, up from 184,000 in 2019. The population of the UK had grown by 1% in a single year, the fastest rate since the baby boom of the 1960s. The figure of 745,000 was half the size again of cities such as Leeds or Liverpool. Michael Gove admitted the record-breaking numbers were putting unsustainable pressure on Britain's broken housing market.[25] Sir Simon Clarke, a former cabinet minister, echoed the views of many when he claimed the level of legal immigration was unsustainable "both economically and socially", adding there was "no public mandate" for it and it was overwhelming the UK's public services.[26]

The former prime minister, Tony Blair, was critical of the policy changes after Brexit, saying, "We've now got higher levels of immigration than ever before, and we've swapped out usually single people coming from Europe for families from Asia and Africa."[27]

Net migration fell back a little in 2023 to 685,000 but it was still more than double what it had been before. The huge rise was driven by an increase in sponsored students and their family members, plus Ukrainians, Hong Kongers, and Afghans moving to Britain on humanitarian visa programmes.

The cumulative number of people that migrated to the UK in the three years between 2021 and June 2024 by country was as follows:

- 670,000 from India
- 310,000 from Nigeria
- 274,000 from China
- 166,000 from Pakistan
- 131,000 from Hong Kong
- 108,000 from Ukraine

Ed Conway, the economics editor at *Sky News*, commented that the numbers represented an enormous shift in migration to levels never seen before in the UK.[28] Louie French, the Conservative MP for Old Bexley and Sidcup, said the "unsustainable levels of migration" were having a "significant impact" on housing.[29] Martin Vickers, the Conservative MP for Cleethorpes, said voters' "anger and frustration will grow when they consider these legal migration figures".[30]

At the same time that legal migration was rising rapidly, there was also a steady increase in a backlog of asylum claims, which peaked in 2022 and 2023 at over 120,000 cases. In 2024, there were still over 80,000 cases waiting to be processed.

The public's attitude to migration was nuanced. Evidence from focus groups suggested that the public was more concerned about asylum seekers than legal migration. There was also evidence that attitudes to migration had become more positive since Brexit. Professor Rob Ford argued there had been "a big positive shift in views about the economic and cultural impacts of immigration between 2015 and 2021".[31] This view was supported by both Ipsos and Kantar, who found that the percentage of people saying immigration should be reduced had fallen from 65% in 2015 to 42% in 2022. The public was also supportive of migrant employment in the NHS and social care, in areas where there were labour shortages such as hospitality and agriculture, and of migration from Ukraine and Hong Kong.

The salience of immigration started to rise again in 2023, prompted by the soaring numbers and by increasing media attention on illegal small boat crossings, albeit these represented a very small percentage of all migrants. In September 2023, Ipsos reported that public concern about immigration was at its highest for six years and that it was "the most cited issue for over 65s and Conservative party supporters".[32]

In March 2024, a report from the National Centre for Social Research found that while just under half of UK adults felt the impact of immigration on society was positive, 42% believed the number of immigrants to the UK should be reduced, compared to 29% who felt it should be increased.[33] When the ONS asked people in June 2024 what they thought were the important issues facing the UK, over half (52%) said immigration. This was much lower than other issues, such as the NHS and the cost of living, but it was the number one issue for many 2019 Conservative supporters.[34]

As Ipsos had previously found, the concerns about immigration were directly correlated with age, with 65% of those aged 50 to 69, and 75% of those aged 70 and over, believing immigration was one of the most important issues facing the country. To many 2019 Conservative voters, it appeared the government had completely lost control of the country's borders.

Forced to act on the record levels of legal immigration, Sunak reversed Johnson's more liberal migration policies at the start of 2024. He introduced a ban on most international students' family members, a ban on care workers' family members, a higher income threshold for British citizens' families and higher salary thresholds for workers outside of health and care. There was general agreement that these policies would result in net migration falling quite significantly later in 2024.

The government was also conscious that two-thirds of people, and an even greater number of Conservative supporters, felt it should be doing more to stop illegal immigrants. Small boat crossings in the Channel had risen from the low hundreds in 2019 to around 45,000 in 2022.[35] The growing numbers and associated public concerns had prompted Sunak's pledge to stop the boats and the government's plan to deter migrants crossing the Channel by saying that any asylum seeker entering the UK illegally from a safe country, such as France, could be sent to Rwanda and have their claims processed there.

Sunak failed to stop the boats, despite negotiating a successful returns agreement with the Albanian government resulting in a marked decrease in Albanians crossing the Channel. In the first quarter of 2024, there were 12,600 crossings, a 16% rise on the same period in the previous year.[36] To the public Sunak had clearly failed to fulfil his pledge to stop the boats.

The government's handling of immigration was eroding public trust, particularly with its own supporters. It had promised to 'take back control' of the country's borders – a key pillar of the Brexit campaign – and to reduce overall numbers of migrants. Conservative voters in 2019 had trusted the government to follow through on its promises. Instead, the government did the opposite and liberalised migration policies, leading to a huge increase in legal migration. Many 2019 Conservative voters viewed the latest numbers as a direct betrayal of their trust.

The disconnect between pre-election promises and post-election actions served to exacerbate the already growing sense of disillusionment among 2019 Conservative voters. For many, the perceived dishonesty on immigration epitomised a broader pattern of dishonesty in politics, further deepening the chasm of distrust between the public and their elected representatives. The government's failure to align its immigration policies with its previous rhetoric not only intensified scepticism about its integrity but also fuelled broader questions about the authenticity of political commitments in general.

Another recession shock

In October 2023, at the Conservative Party conference, Sunak promised to be 'bold' and 'radical'. However, what he offered was a mishmash of policies, including the dismantling of HS2, increasing the legal age to buy tobacco, and reform of A-levels. There was no bold vision, and despite missing half of their own levelling-up targets, there was no focus on levelling up. Sunak appeared oblivious to the political embarrassment of announcing the cancellation of the HS2 leg to Manchester in Manchester.

In the last quarter of 2023, GDP fell by 0.3%, a larger fall than economists were expecting. This followed a decrease of 0.1% in GDP in the previous quarter. This meant the UK was in a technical recession but it was the word 'recession' that hit the headlines on 15 February 2024.

> 'UK economy fell into recession after people cut spending' – BBC

> 'UK tips into recession in blow to Rishi Sunak' – *The Guardian*

> 'UK economy officially enters recession as GDP falls again' – *The Sun*

> 'UK economy falls into recession in major blow for Rishi Sunak' – *Daily Mirror*

> 'Britain falls into recession, with worst GDP performance in 2023 in years' – CNN

The news of the recession a year after the mini-budget simply reinforced voters' belief that things were falling apart and the Conservatives were not competent to manage the economy. According to a YouGov survey published on 23 October 2023, three-quarters of the public thought the government was handling the economy badly.[37]

In a desperate attempt to change the public mood, Sunak's government made two successive cuts in National Insurance. On 22 November 2023, the chancellor Jeremy Hunt cut the main rate of National Insurance from 12% to 10% from 6 January 2024. He also abolished Class 2 National Insurance paid by self-employed people earning more than £12,750 and cut the Class 4 National Insurance for the self-employed from 9% to 8%. The cuts failed to move the polls. In December 2023, the Labour Party still held a 19-point lead over the Conservatives according to the BBC poll tracker.[38]

On 6 March 2024, Jeremy Hunt tried again with another cut of 2% in the main rate of National Insurance, which was to be funded by £10bn of unspecified cuts in public services. The

Labour Party supported the reductions, with Keir Starmer claiming the proposals would still leave working people paying more tax because of freezes in tax thresholds and that taxes were already at a 70-year high.[39]

The decision to cut National Insurance and fund the reduction through unspecified spending cuts appeared to fly in the face of public concerns about crumbling public services and infrastructure. According to surveys, 57% of the population believed the government should prioritise funding public services compared to just 27% who favoured giving people a tax cut.[40] *The Spectator* reflected the views of many when it claimed "cutting National Insurance won't save the Tories".[41] The public was concerned about the NHS, public services, immigration and the continued high cost of living, including food prices, rents, and mortgage rates, not cutting National Insurance.

The Chancellor claimed the two National Insurance reductions would save the average worker £900 a year. The reality, as pointed out by Keir Starmer, was that stealth taxes such as the freezing of tax allowances meant that a typical worker on £35,000 a year would still be worse off even after the National Insurance cuts. More people would also be dragged into tax or higher tax brackets as their earnings rose. According to the OBR there would be over three million more taxpayers, two million more higher-rate taxpayers and half a million more additional rate taxpayers by 2028. The IFS pointed out that the National Insurance cuts would also not be enough to prevent taxes as a share of GDP rising to record levels within five years.

The cuts in National Insurance again failed to move the polls. On 3 April 2024, the *Financial Times* revealed that the Conservative Party's popularity under Sunak had fallen as low as it had under Truss. The paper's Poll Tracker put the Conservatives on just 23%, over 20 points behind Labour.[42]

In April 2024, the Conservative Party brand image hit a new low, according to an Ipsos survey, which claimed, "The

Conservative party's ratings across several metrics are the worst since they came to power in 2010."[43]

When he first became prime minister, Sunak's personal ratings were stronger than those of his party.[44] However, the more the public got to know Sunak, the less favourable his ratings became. By the end of his first year as prime minister his ratings had tumbled to -28 with 73% of people describing him as weak. By the time the election was called in 2024, Sunak's personal ratings were worse than those of Michael Foot in 1983 and Jeremy Corbyn in 2019.

6

A VOLATILE AND DISTRUSTFUL ELECTORATE

The rolling series of economic and political shocks in the decade from 2014, as documented in the previous chapters, was unprecedented. Many of these shocks had been self-inflicted such as Brexit, Partygate, the dramatic rise in legal migration and the Truss mini-budget. The Conservative Party's response to the shocks, including the rapid regicide that resulted in five different prime ministers from 2016 to 2022, made them look chaotic and incompetent.

The political shocks, and the government's response to them, had the effect of detaching voters from the party. By the start of 2024, almost half of 2019 Conservative voters said they would not be voting for the party in the next general election.

The 20-point lead that the Tories held over Labour in the polls in March 2020 was completely reversed four years later, with Labour holding a polling lead of over 20 points.

In 2019 the Conservatives had a 47-point lead amongst the over-65s but by April 2024 it had fallen to just three points. Every other age group favoured Labour by at least 13%. The Conservatives also trailed Labour in every region and were polling behind Labour on every issue except defence and security.

A series of by-elections during the parliament revealed that voters were prepared to switch their support between parties and engage in large-scale tactical voting. Elections had become more volatile with huge swings in support for challenger parties such as the Liberal Democrats, the Brexit Party, and the Greens. By 2024, seats with 20,000 majorities were no longer safe.

The actions of the Conservative Party and its leaders also led to a huge increase in voter distrust. In April 2020, 32% of people felt the Conservative Party was untrustworthy. By June 2024, this had more than doubled to 68%.[1] Writing in the *Financial Times,* John Burn-Murdoch observed that, "Many voters came to see the Tories as synonymous with dishonesty and unfitness for government."[2]

According to the British Social Attitudes survey the political and economic turmoil had resulted in "significant changes in the public mood". The survey's 2023 report concluded, "All in all, it appears that people's trust in governments and politicians, and confidence in their systems of government, is as low now as it has ever been over the last 50 years, if not lower."[3]

The behaviour of Johnson and others, such as Hancock and Cummings, who contravened COVID-19 rules during the pandemic had a "corrosive effect" on public trust, according to the survey. From 2021 to 2023, the percentage of people that trusted the government to place the needs of the nation above their party most of the time fell from 24% to 14%. More dramatically, the percentage of the public that trusted politicians to tell the truth in a tight corner fell from a low of 12% to just 5%.[4]

In June 2023, the House of Commons Privileges Committee published its report on Johnson's Partygate denials and concluded that the former prime minister had deliberately misled parliament.[5] An Ipsos survey later in the year revealed that the level of trust in politicians had fallen to its lowest level in 40 years. Just 9% of people said they trusted politicians to tell the truth, making them the least trusted profession in Britain.[6] According to Ipsos almost all of the decline in trust in Britain's politicians over recent decades had come about during the Conservative parliament of 2019 to 2024.[7]

A YouGov poll for *Sky News* also found that levels of public distrust had increased substantially during the 2019–2024 parliament. High-profile incidents such as the infected blood scandal, the Post Office Horizon scandal, the Grenfell Tower fire and political scandals such as Partygate all eroded public trust. By 2024 the number of people saying they 'almost never' trusted the government to place the country's needs above the interests of their own party had almost doubled from 26% in 2019 to 49% in 2024.[8]

In 2020, Remain supporters were more likely than Leave supporters to say they 'almost never' trusted governments or politicians. By 2023, the position had reversed, with Leave voters being more distrustful. By 2024, a significant proportion of the electorate distrusted all political parties and there was increasing anger about perceived political dishonesty and corruption.

In 2024, Ipsos conducted a study called 'The People Behind the Polls' where they followed a group of people during the 2024 election campaign and got their reactions to events such as the TV debates. This qualitative research survey found the public had a "complete distrust of politics and politicians".[9]

An analysis of the British Election Study panel in 2024 found that over 70% of those aged 18–60 agreed that 'politicians don't care what people like me think'.[10] The figure was 76% for respondents aged 30–44.

The 41st British Social Attitudes report published on 12 June 2024 confirmed that public trust in government had fallen to a new record low.[11] Almost half of people said they would 'almost never' trust British governments of any party to place the needs of the country above the interests of their own political party, more than ever before.

These higher levels of public distrust have the potential to destabilise the electoral landscape by:

- undermining attachments to political parties and the Conservative Party in particular, thereby undermining settled party preferences and increasing instability
- causing greater suspicion and cynicism about the actions of all governments
- increasing the use of transactional and tactical voting to punish an incumbent government's perceived dishonesty or incompetence
- creating opportunities for populist parties to appeal to voters on the basis that the political and establishment elites cannot be trusted
- creating unpredictable behaviour as voters seek to express their frustration by engaging in a protest vote or other actions
- lowering levels of engagement and voting

PART II

BROKEN BRITAIN

7

PUBLIC NARRATIVES

To secure an electoral victory, a political party must convince the public of its competence to govern. This requires politicians to become adept storytellers, and craft a compelling narrative that sets out a desirable vision of the future and establishes the party's competence to govern.

Elections are fundamentally about competing narratives as parties seek to ensure their story, their view of the world, is the one that is accepted by the public. Successful political campaigns select events that are considered important and build a narrative architecture with a single overriding story. These narratives seek to help the public make sense of complex issues and sub-stories by incorporating them into a coherent story which aligns with a particular political perspective.

David Gergen, a former US presidential communications adviser, argues political parties need a short, concise narrative that is easy to understand and can be repeated constantly in the hope that it will cut through.[1] There is a psychological benefit to repetition, as the more people are exposed to something, the more they are likely to see it as true. According to academic research, people assess whether a plausible statement is likely to be true by the number of times they see it repeated.[2] Shorter stories are easier to comprehend and share, which is why political campaigns strive to create slogans that summarise their narrative, such as 'Take Back Control' or 'Make America Great Again'. Each of these slogans is also an effective narrative that tells a story of the past, the present, and the future.

Facts on their own are not enough to win a political argument. What matters is the interpretation of the facts. You cannot assume that people will reason to the same conclusion given a set of facts. Political narratives provide the interpretation; they turn a series of facts into a coherent explanation for a sequence of events.

The public narrative

The public narrative is a story that resonates with people, is widely shared and becomes the accepted explanation for what has happened or is happening in their society. The most powerful public narratives become what the Italian philosopher Antonio Gramsci described as 'common sense' or common knowledge, something that is accepted by the community or audience as self-evident. Like the slogans above, they typically tell a story of the past, the present, and of a desirable future. An election campaign is fundamentally a competition to shape the public narrative.

There will always be a great many stories on the TV, on the radio, in newspapers, and on social media. These will include many competing political narratives, but very few will become the public narrative or the accepted explanation for events. A successful narrative is one that particularly resonates with people, one that enables them to make sense of things in the context of their own experience and one that aligns with other narratives they are familiar with. In simple terms, a story that fits with their perception of reality, even if it is not necessarily true.

The most powerful narratives are those co-created by the public. These tend to be broad stories that resonate with the audience and provide space for them to add their own examples. For example, if the core narrative is 'system X is broken', people can confirm the validity of the story by adding examples from their own lives or those of their friends and family. It is this co-creation by the audience that makes a public narrative so compelling. The addition of personal examples validates the core premise of the story and becomes a testament to its perceived truthfulness. By contrast, if the story doesn't resonate with people's own experiences or those of their friends and family, the overall narrative will not gain traction and risks being rejected by the audience.

To become a public narrative a story needs to be widely shared. This requires a shorthand, simple version that enables it to be shared and retold across a community using everyday language. The slogan 'Make America Great Again' was originally used by Ronald Reagan as a concise way of telling a story of the past, the present, and the future. Obama's 'Yes, we can', Thatcher's 'Labour isn't working', and Johnson's 'Get Brexit done' were equally effective short narratives. The core story must resonate with people even if it does not reflect the complex truth of a situation such as 'Take back control'.

A concise narrative enables the core essence of a story to be readily shared in a social setting, such as over a drink in a bar, at work, or even in a focus group or in response to a question from a journalist. The more a particular story is repeated, the more familiar it will become and the more likely it is to dominate and influence people's thinking. It is incredibly difficult for a political party to shift opinion in the face of a compelling public narrative that has taken hold.

The public narrative that emerged after the COVID-19

pandemic and which took hold in the run-up to the 2024 election was 'Nothing works anymore'. It was a phrase, along with 'Broken Britain', that was repeated endlessly both in the media and in conversations up and down the country. It was a broad narrative of decline but one which implied things needed to improve. This second part of the book explores how this narrative took hold.

8

NOTHING WORKS ANYMORE

We believe in superb public services and infrastructure.[1]

— CONSERVATIVE PARTY MANIFESTO 2019

In the run-up to the 2010 election, David Cameron promised to fix 'broken Britain'. It was a phrase he repeatedly used to describe what had happened to the country under the Labour Prime Minister Gordon Brown. 'Broken Britain' became a popular alliterative phrase and gained its own Wikipedia page which said it described "a perceived widespread state of social decay in the UK" from 2007 to 2010.[2]

By June 2024, the phrase had a new meaning. It was used to describe the country after 14 years of Conservative government and encapsulated the feeling that the party had broken the country so badly that nothing worked anymore. When interviewed by Laura Kuenssberg on the BBC, the television presenter and journalist Susanna Reid said that people feel “things are broken” and “there’s a sense that after fourteen years of the Conservatives in government, nothing works”.[3]

The idea that nothing worked anymore, and that Britain was broken, was reflected repeatedly in newspaper and magazine headlines.

> ‘Broken Britain? 76% say UK is becoming a worse place to live as taxes and NHS crisis take toll’ – *Evening Standard*[4]
>
> ‘From NHS to local councils, nothing in Britain works anymore’ – *The Sun*[5]
>
> ‘Broken Britain is back and victims let down, says commissioner’ – *The Times*[6]
>
> ‘In Broken Britain, even the statistics don’t work’ – *Financial Times*[7]
>
> ‘Britain is broken – and nobody can be bothered to do anything about it’– *Daily Telegraph*[8]
>
> ‘Why does nothing work in Britain today?’ – *The Independent*[9]
>
> ‘Broken Britain: what went wrong?’ – *The Spectator*[10]

The Spectator article quoted above talked of the country “falling apart”, of a “shambolic” NHS, “inadequate” sewage systems and airports in “chaos”. The *Daily Mirror* carried a front-page headline saying, ‘Schools in crisis ... hospitals in crisis ... armed forces in crisis ... councils in crisis ... police in crisis ... prisons in crisis ... courts in crisis ... Even hospices are in crisis', and claimed these crises were the price the country was paying for Tory tax cuts.[11]

In focus group after focus group, people highlighted their own experiences of 'broken Britain' and claimed that 'nothing worked anymore'. By June 2024, 62% of people felt that 'nothing in Britain works anymore'.[12]

To understand how the narrative 'nothing works anymore' became so powerful, we have to go back to the early years of the Conservative government. The 2010 to 2015 parliament was dominated by George Osborne's austerity policies. When the Conservatives took power they declared their aims were to reduce the government deficit and to grow the economy. Fundamentally, they believed that the country was spending too much on public services and sought to reduce the deficit primarily by shrinking the state rather than increasing taxation. The government promised to make over £6bn of cuts after just two weeks in office.

George Osborne successfully created a narrative that pinned the need for austerity on the previous Labour government, which he claimed was to blame for the country's fiscal plight.[13] It was a narrative that was given momentum by Labour's former chief secretary to the Treasury, Liam Byrne, when he left a note for his successor which said, "There's no money left."[14] Ministers leaving notes for their successors is a convention and Byrne intended his note to be a private joke, but David Laws made the note public in a press conference, saying it was an honest assessment of Labour's disastrous fiscal policies. Byrne was heavily criticised as the Conservatives made extensive use of the note throughout the austerity years. David Cameron regularly brandished a copy during campaign stops in the 2015 election. In the BBC *Question Time* debate in 2015, he said, "I became Prime Minister at a time when there was no money left" and held up a copy of the note. He continued, "That is the situation I inherited, and so we have had to make difficult decisions over these last five years."[15]

The scale of the public expenditure reductions the Conservative government proposed in its austerity programme was historically unprecedented. The Office of Budget Responsibility described the government's plan from 2010 onwards as "one of the biggest deficit reduction programmes seen in any advanced economy since World War II".[16] The government ring-fenced the NHS, schools, and foreign aid from the worst of the cuts, which meant that there were very significant cuts in spending on other public services. Funding to local authorities was cut in half, while spending by the Ministry of Justice was cut by 25%.

In 2015, the Conservatives unveiled proposals to make a further £37bn worth of cuts. Between 2010 and 2019, British public spending fell from 41% of GDP to 35%.

The Conservative government also dramatically scaled back public capital investment despite being able to borrow at historically low interest rates. There were large cuts in spending on the maintenance and construction of new schools, hospitals, and prisons. These short-term decisions all meant that future governments were likely to have to significantly increase capital spending in later years.

Substantially shrinking the state only made sense if the demands on the state were forecast to fall or there were massive efficiency gains to be had. Neither appeared to be true. The country's population was growing and demands on the state from an increasingly elderly population were likely to increase. In 2023, the then permanent secretary to the Treasury reflected on this period and said with hindsight the government should have taken advantage of the low interest rates to borrow and invested more.[17]

When Boris Johnson became prime minister in 2019, he sought to reverse austerity and adopted a radically different approach to fiscal policy. His chancellor Sajid Javid announced that for the first time since 2010 all government departments were to receive a budget increase. Johnson claimed to believe in excellent public services and said his government would create a colossal new levelling-up investment programme. However, this approach was almost immediately stymied by the COVID-19 pandemic.

The pandemic lockdown in 2020 resulted in the biggest contraction of the UK economy in three hundred years. The country's tax revenues fell dramatically during this period, requiring the government to increase borrowing massively to fund its COVID-19 interventions, which pushed the deficit up to almost 100% of GDP. To help control the deficit, the government also announced tax rises, most notably freezing tax thresholds and increasing the rate of corporation tax, but alongside these increases there were also further cuts in public service spending. Johnson's successors Liz Truss and Rishi Sunak both prioritised tax cuts over public services spending and departments were again squeezed by budget increases that were less than inflation, resulting in further real terms reductions in expenditure.

The next section highlights the impact that 14 years of budget reductions had on various public services.

Local government

> *We will give democratically accountable local government much greater power to improve their citizens' lives.*[18]
>
> — CONSERVATIVE PARTY MANIFESTO 2010

One of the areas hit hardest by the Conservatives' austerity programme was local government. In 2010/11 George Osborne reduced central government grants to local authorities by almost 10%. It was the start of a major squeeze on council spending. The central government grant to local government more than halved between 2010/11 and 2015/16.

By 2018, total local government spending power had dropped by 25% in real terms.[19] Spending on highways and transport fell by 23.6%, planning services by 35.7%, cultural and related services by 36.8%, and non-schools education by 31.6%. By 2024, council budgets were a third lower in real terms than they were in 2011. Remarkably, this reduction took place at a time when the country's population was increasing faster than at any point since the 1950s[20] and when the needs of the country's elderly population were also increasing rapidly.

The majority of council spending is statutory, with councils having to provide services such as education and social care. Adult and children's social care accounted for two-thirds of the budgets of upper-tier authorities by 2024, and the costs of care were increasing. Councils had a duty to provide support for children in care and were forced to use for-profit companies that, in 2024, provided three-quarters of care home places. The fees charged by the private sector homes rose by 72% in the five years from 2019 to 2024, with the average weekly bill per child in 2024 being £5,980 or £310,960 a year.[21]

Local council spending on social care for the over-65s fell by 35% between 2010 and 2018. A paper in the *British Medical*

Journal argued that cuts in social care may have accounted for 45,000 excess deaths between 2012 and 2014.

The statutory nature of much of council spending meant that spending on other non-statutory services had to be reduced dramatically. This resulted in the wide-scale closure of facilities,[22] including 1,376 libraries, 200 museums, more than a thousand publicly accessible swimming pools, 1,629 or 60% of public toilets, 1,243 council-run youth centres, 1,168 council-run children's centres and 40% of Sure Start Centres. The cuts also resulted in half a million council staff losing their jobs.

Many deprived areas also lost large-scale EU grants for disadvantaged communities following Brexit, which were inadequately made up for by the government's new UK Shared Prosperity Fund. A fund which Sunak later pledged to abolish during the 2024 election campaign to fund the proposed return of national service.

The cuts in local government spending were not evenly distributed, with deprived, traditionally Labour-voting communities suffering the largest cuts. In August 2022, Rishi Sunak boasted to a garden party in Tunbridge Wells that, as chancellor, he had redistributed money from deprived urban councils to wealthier rural communities.[23] David Gauke, a Treasury minister from 2010 to 2017, also admitted that the deprived parts of the country that had benefited most under Labour were forced by the Conservatives to make greater reductions in their budgets. "There was a rebalancing that went on," Gauke commented, adding, "Did it go too far? Maybe it did."[24]

In Liverpool, where the Conservatives had not won a parliamentary seat for 40 years, spending per head fell more than in any other city in the country. The consequences were devastating as Liverpool City Council's core spending power was cut by 35% in real terms between 2010 and 2023, a loss of nearly £330m per year when adjusted for inflation. The council was forced to cut 3,000 jobs. As of December 2023, the local authority's debt had grown to £580m. Two-thirds of the council's budget was spent on social care. Official data revealed that in Liverpool in 2024, 27,000 children, nearly one in three, were living in relative poverty, a record high.[25]

Severe cuts in highways and transport budgets meant that by 2024 local councils faced an estimated £14bn backlog in road maintenance, with up to 50% of roads judged to be at risk of complete deterioration within 15 years. According to the Ipsos Public Services Index, only 7% of voters were satisfied with road maintenance. After 14 years of Conservative rule, the *Financial Times* said the country's roads were in a dire state. The AA motoring organisation said it was called out to 631,852 'pothole-related incidents' in 2023, while the RAC reported that the number of callouts for pothole-related breakdowns had increased 40% on the previous year.

Potholes became the physical manifestation of the Conservative Party's austerity policies and symbolised Britain's crumbling infrastructure. Pollsters were surprised at how big an issue they were for people. "When you ask people 'What are the issues for your local area?', it's astounding how much potholes comes up. It really is one of the big motivators," commented Luke Tryl of the political consultancy More in Common.[26]

In November 2023, in recognition of the growing concerns about the state of the country's roads and the scale of the problem, Rishi Sunak reallocated money from the cancelled HS2 rail line to filling in potholes. Announcing the funding, Sunak said for too long politicians had shied away from tackling the scourge of potholes.[27] This was somewhat ironic given the constant cuts in highways budgets he had presided over. As with many other areas it appeared that the Conservatives were only just waking up to the damage done by years of austerity.

By January 2024, one in five local councils claimed they would be insolvent within a year, as their forecast income was insufficient to meet their forecast spending. Councils in this position are required to issue a section 114 notice and to take action to address the shortfall. In 2020, Croydon Council issued a section 114 notice, which was followed by two further notices as it struggled to balance the books. In 2023, the council was given permission by the government to raise its council tax by 15% as it sought to manage its £130m budget deficit. Other councils, such as Birmingham, Woking, and Nottingham, also issued section 114 notices.

Over a decade of cuts to local council budgets culminated in a loss of civic pride and the devastation of local services. An Ipsos survey found that satisfaction levels with local councils had almost halved in three years.[28] This was entirely predictable given the scale of the cuts to local government which forced them to increase council tax despite people receiving fewer services. However, 45% of people blamed the Conservatives rather than their local council for the crumbling of local services.

Health

> *We will back the NHS which matters more to families than anything.*[29]
>
> — CONSERVATIVE PARTY MANIFESTO 2010

When the Conservatives came into government in 2010, they inherited falling waiting lists from the previous government. About 2.5m people were waiting for non-urgent procedures and the number of people waiting more than three months had fallen from 700,000 to just 7,000. Satisfaction with the NHS was running at 74% according to the British Social Attitudes survey.

In 2010, David Cameron was conscious that many people were nervous about the Conservative Party's management of the health service, which Nigel Lawson had claimed was "the closest thing the English have to a national religion".[30] In his election campaign, Cameron said repeatedly that he would back the NHS and stressed his personal commitment to the health service because of the support it had provided to his severely disabled son, who sadly died at the age of six.

Andrew Cooper, one of Cameron's senior political advisers, said the NHS was "an issue of existential political importance for the government".[31] The level of public support for the health service meant the government had to demonstrate that the NHS was safe in its hands. In their 2010 manifesto, the Conservatives said their priorities could be spelled out in three letters – NHS.

The importance of the NHS to the public meant the service was ring-fenced from the worst of the Conservative spending cuts. The health service received more funding and hired more doctors under the Conservatives, but the budgets did not rise in line with the increasing demands of a growing and ageing population, the increased costs of medical treatment and a surge in mental health problems. NHS prescriptions for antidepressants in England almost doubled between 2011 and 2023.

In 2008, Michael Marmot, director of the UCL Institute of Health Equity, identified ways to reduce England's health inequalities, making suggestions in six policy areas, including better access to childcare, walking and cycling programmes, social-security reforms, and measures to improve people's sense of agency at work. The new Conservative government accepted his findings, but according to Marmot, they failed to implement them.[32] In 2018, he wrote, "For men and women everywhere the time spent in poor health is increasing."[33] He argued the UK's health performance since 2010, which included rising infant mortality, slowing growth in children, and the return of rickets, made it an outlier among comparable European nations. Marmot also believed that a decade of frozen healthcare spending had undermined the country's response to the pandemic. Marmot concluded, "The damage to the nation's health need not have happened. ... It was a political choice."[34]

The waiting lists which had been falling in 2010 increased steadily under the Conservatives. The number of people waiting for an NHS procedure increased from 2.5m in 2010 to over 4m by the start of 2020. That number shot up after the COVID-19 pandemic to 6.4m in March 2022. By July 2023, the number of people waiting to start routine hospital treatment had increased further to a record 7.47m.

As the waiting list increased, so did the median waiting time, which almost doubled from 7.5 weeks at the start of February 2020 to 14.8 weeks at the start of 2024. The number of people waiting over a year to start treatment soared to 385,000, and the proportion of cancer patients who started treatment within two months fell from almost 90% in 2010 to less than 60% by the end of 2023.

To improve the performance of the NHS and reduce waiting times the government needed the support of the NHS staff but rather than rewarding staff for their work during the pandemic the government imposed a below-inflation pay award. The proposal created an angry backlash, and staff raised the prospect of strike action. The government's treatment of health workers resulted in the Royal College of Nurses balloting their members for strike action and going on strike for the first time in their history in December 2022.

In 2022, the British Medical Association (BMA) sought a 35% pay rise for junior doctors to catch up on 15 years of below-inflation pay awards and balloted their members about strike action. More than 98% voted for strike action and the BMA announced a 72-hour strike starting on 13 March 2023. Junior doctors represented almost half the medical workforce, which meant the impact of any strike would be severe and include cancelling operations. NHS England said that by the end of January 2024, the strike had cost the health service £1.5bn.[35]

Resolving the dispute should have been a government priority, but negotiations failed, with the government refusing to offer more than 6% plus a lump sum of £1,250 for junior doctors. A series of further strikes by junior doctors took place, including strike action from 27 June 2024 to 2 July 2024, during the general election campaign.

The longer the dispute continued, the more the public blamed the government rather than the unions or the doctors. From April 2023 to June 2024, the number of people blaming the government rose by seven points from 41% to 48%.[36] The failure to resolve the doctor's strike meant that it was impossible to reduce waiting lists, which were so politically damaging to the Conservative Party. With over 7m people on waiting lists, almost everyone had a story of how a family member or friend was affected by the delays. One in eight people across the UK were waiting for an NHS operation at the time of the election in 2024. Frustration with the delays and backlogs in treatment led to a surge in people paying for their treatment in private hospitals. In 2023, there were a record 898,000 admissions to private hospitals.[37]

One of the major problems that hospitals faced was discharging people. In 2023, there were an estimated 13,000 people who, while fit to be discharged, had to stay in hospital due to a lack of social care.

By the time of the pandemic, adult social care and other forms of social care were largely delivered by private companies, many of which were owned by private equity firms, who saw major opportunities in the care sector. In 2023, the government was spending over £20bn a year on adult social care, which was expected to grow to over £30bn by 2030 due to the growing number of elderly people.[38]

The biggest cost for care homes was staff wages which typically make up 50 to 70% of costs. As a consequence, private care companies sought to recruit staff at low wages, lower than those in the public sector, which reduced the attractiveness of care roles and led to high levels of turnover. By 2023, there were 165,000 staff vacancies in social care.

After the COVID-19 pandemic, there were growing concerns about the financial viability of care homes which were having to manage with much higher heating bills, food costs, and wage bills. Back in 2011, one of the larger providers, Southern Cross, had gone into administration and in 2019, Four Seasons, the second-largest provider of care homes, had also gone into administration.

The failure to adequately fund social care at a time when demand was rapidly rising had a severe impact on the health service. In 2024, Jeremy Hunt admitted that cuts in social care under the Conservative Party's austerity programme went too far and had a major impact on the NHS. In an interview with Rachel Sylvester he said, "The squeeze on local government finances meant that access into the social care system was reduced, and that pressure transferred to the NHS and that showed itself in people not being able to get out of hospital."[39]

There were increasing reports of queues of ambulances outside hospitals that were unable to unload patients because of a lack of spare bed capacity. There were reports of 17 ambulances waiting outside the Great Western Hospital in Swindon[40] and a similar number of ambulances queuing outside the Aberdeen Royal Infirmary.[41] Local newspapers were reporting tens of thousands of hours of lost time because ambulance crews were unable to pass over patients due to the lack of available bed spaces in hospitals. The Association of Ambulance Chief Executives said that nationally in England around two million hours were lost. Ed Davey, the Liberal Democrat leader, said people were dying as every ambulance service in England was in crisis and claimed the Conservatives were "too busy fighting each other to help our country".[42]

The NHS waiting list figure had become totemic; it was the accepted public shorthand for how well the NHS was working. By 2024, as waiting lists surged to record levels almost everyone knew someone waiting for a procedure. To the public it was clear that under the Conservatives the NHS was not working anymore.

Despite the Conservative government's promise to recruit more GPs, the number of fully qualified, permanent full-time equivalent (FTE) GPs fell by 7% after 2015, even though patient demand was rising. The number of people reporting difficulties in booking appointments was growing. In 2019, before the COVID-19 pandemic, satisfaction with general practices fell to its lowest level ever.[43] By 2023 over a million people had been waiting over four weeks to see their GP.[44] In 2024, just 40% of patients reported that they were satisfied with their GP, compared with 90% back in 1998.[45]

Between 2010 and 2024 the UK's population increased by six million people, primarily as a result of immigration, and this inevitably increased the pressure on the health service. Many people in areas of mass migration who struggled to get a GP appointment blamed immigration and the rise in the population. A research paper by three academics has argued that the NHS crisis may have contributed to the rise of Reform in the general election, especially in areas undergoing rapid demographic change.[46]

In the five years after the 2019 election, the number of working-age people off work due to long-term sickness rose by 800,000 to a record 2.8m. This may, in part, have been due to the impact of COVID-19 on health, but longer waiting lists were also a factor. Spending on disability and incapacity benefits rose by £18bn while spending on mental health in England increased to 10% of the NHS budget.

Professor Chris Ham, co-chair of the NHS Assembly, argued there had been a steady decline in the performance of the NHS under the Conservatives because the funding had not kept pace with a growing and ageing population, there were limited funds for capital investment, and there had been a neglect of workforce planning.[47] It was only in 2023 that the government agreed a workforce plan that doubled the training of doctors and nurses.

Conservative leaders argued these criticisms were unfair as the pressures facing the NHS were typical of the pressures on health services in other Western countries, which also faced the challenge of increasingly elderly populations, rising medical costs, and shortages of healthcare professionals. They also pointed out that the government had had to manage the NHS through an unprecedented global pandemic. Despite this, they argued, the government had delivered on some of their key 2019 manifesto promises on health, such as recruiting fifty thousand extra nurses and ensuring there were fifty million extra GP appointments.

While accepting these points the Health Foundation argued that underinvestment by the Conservatives in the NHS had led to fewer doctors, nurses, beds, and scanners than other European countries which meant the UK was poorly prepared for a pandemic. The Foundation also noted that obesity rates were higher in the UK and the underlying health of the nation was poor.[48]

In 2021, it was reported that four in five people struggled to access an NHS dentist.[49] In 2023, the Nuffield Trust published a report which found that there were six million fewer courses of NHS dental treatment provided in 2022/23 than in 2019/20. It said NHS dentistry was at its "most perilous point in its 75-year history".[50]

Fewer and fewer dentist practices were taking on NHS patients, leaving people to pay for dentistry in the private sector. Age UK reported that older people faced high costs for dentures as they couldn't access an NHS dentist. One in five people said they were put off going to the dentist because of the high costs.[51] Nuffield reported that more than half of all adults hadn't seen a dentist within the previous 24 months and more than two in five children hadn't had an appointment in the previous 12 months.[52] In 2024, the top reason for children aged between six and ten being referred to the hospital was tooth decay.

As waiting lists increased and people struggled to get GP appointments, public satisfaction with health services collapsed. In 2022, the National Centre for Social Research (NatCen) published its latest British Social Attitudes survey titled 'Broken Britain?' They revealed that satisfaction with the health service had fallen to its lowest level in 25 years. An Ipsos poll found that just 32% of patients surveyed were satisfied with their local NHS hospital, compared with 80% in 1998.

A YouGov poll for *The Times* published at the start of 2023 found that 80% of people thought the health service had got worse under the Conservatives, and 39% were no longer confident it would be there for them in an emergency.[53]

Surveys found that four times as many voters believed the National Health Service would be better managed by Labour than the Conservatives.

Housing

> *We will make it easier for everyone to get onto the housing ladder.*[54]
>
> — CONSERVATIVE PARTY MANIFESTO 2010

After the Second World War, councils built millions of homes, and by 1980, more than five million households, almost a third of all households, lived in council housing.[55] When Thatcher came to power in 1979, one of her flagship policies was Right to Buy, which allowed council tenants to buy their homes at very large discounts. The policy was popular. Over a hundred thousand people bought their homes each year after the policy was introduced. It created a new cohort of homeowners and potential Conservative voters. However, it also resulted in a severe reduction in council housing, as local authorities were restricted from using the receipts of sales to build new homes. This led directly to large shortages of housing and to increased council house waiting lists.

To address the shortage in housing, the Labour government in 2007 set a target of building 240,000 new additional homes a year by 2016, including 70,000 affordable homes, of which 45,000 would be new social rented homes. After 2010, in the early years of the Conservative government, net housing completions were far below the target of 240,000 new homes a year. They were:

- 2011/12 – 140,000
- 2012/13 – 130,000

- 2013/14 –142,000

The failure to deliver on the number of new homes while the population was rising put increasing pressure on the country's limited supply of housing as the population and the number of households continued to grow.

In recognition of the pressure on the supply of housing, the 2019 Conservative Party manifesto promised to build 300,000 homes a year by the mid-2020s. The government failed to achieve this new higher target. Net additional new dwellings in the four years between 2019/20 and 2022/23 averaged around 235,000.[56]

By June 2024, Britain's housing crisis had become so acute that housing experts argued the country needed to build the equivalent of another city the size of London to make up for five decades of below-target construction.[57] Their analysis revealed that in some places in the ten years from 2011 to 2021, just one home had been built for every ten extra people in the population.

Leicester was an example where migration from overseas was high and where population growth significantly outpaced housing completions. The city's population increased 11.7% in the decade to 2021. In 2022, the council declared a crisis when the waiting list for public housing went above 6,000 families. Michael Gove, when he was housing secretary, admitted that housebuilding had failed to keep pace with the growth in population.[58]

In 2023, 1.2m households were on council house waiting lists across the country. In some parts of London it was calculated that those on waiting lists might have to wait 55 years for a council home.

Housing in the UK was also older and more expensive than other countries, according to research from the Resolution Foundation.[59] In the UK, 38% of housing was built before 1946, compared to an average of 22% across Europe. These older houses typically performed less well in terms of energy efficiency and required more maintenance. In 2024, people in the UK were spending more per head on housing than any other major European country for older, colder, and smaller homes.

During the 2019–2024 parliament the costs of housing in terms of rents and mortgages jumped considerably. In December 2019 a two-year fixed-rate mortgage was 1.42%[60] but by January 2024 the average two-year fix had tripled to 4.73%. The high cost of property in the UK combined with rising mortgage rates meant that it was increasingly difficult for younger people to get on the housing ladder and to own their own home.

Average house prices across the UK were almost 70% higher in 2024 than when the Conservatives took office in 2010. However, while the costs of housing were increasing salaries remained flat in real terms. By 2024, the average home cost more than eight times average earnings and was up to 13 times average earnings in some cities.[61]

In 1960, the average age of a first-time buyer was 23. In 2024, it was 34.[62] In 1991, 67% of 25 to 34-year-olds owned their own home. By 2015, it had fallen to just 33%. In an effort to reverse this trend, the government introduced policies such as reductions in stamp duty for some first-time buyers. These policies, combined with lower house prices outside the south-east of England, and improved disposable income among this age group, saw the homeownership rate amongst 25 to 34-year-olds increase to 39% in 2024. However, it remained substantially below where it had been in the 1990s and early 2000s.

The rise in mortgage rates was particularly devastating for many young families who had been hoping to buy their own homes. Only one in eight people renting could afford to buy in their area, according to research from the Skipton Group. Even relatively high earners were struggling to get on the housing ladder. The case of software engineer Emma Harris was highlighted by the BBC. She earned £50,000 a year but said the cost of renting and bills took up about two-thirds of her salary. "I am not likely to ever own a house and it's just depressing," she said. "I want to cry. I want to scream. I want to shout, and do various other things but none of them solve the issue – that I don't have the money to put away each month to scrape together the money for a deposit."[63] The Skipton Group estimated that even among renters who were in the top 25% of earners, with an income of more than £71,250 a year, only 44% could afford to buy a first home.[64]

Those who were forced to rent were also facing much higher rents both in the private rented sector and in social housing. Average rents had increased from £159 a week in 2019 to £190 in 2023. The Resolution Foundation published a report on housing in April 2024, 'Through the Roof', which examined the state of the housing market. It reported that private sector rents had climbed by 15% in the previous two years and were rising at the fastest rate on record.[65]

The cost of renting mattered because a growing proportion of people were living in the private rented sector. Nearly a third of below-average income families headed by someone aged 30–49 were renting, three times as many as in the 1990s. The Resolution Foundation commented, "With many more families in the UK now renting, and renting for longer, the rising cost of doing so poses a significant challenge to living standards."[66]

For those trying to save for deposits to buy a home the soaring rents made the task much harder. To many of those seeking to get on the housing ladder, it appeared that the housing sector was broken and simply didn't work anymore.

The housing crisis also had broader implications, including growing levels of homelessness. At the end of 2023, research by Shelter found that over 300,000 people were homeless, including 140,000 children, an increase of 14% on the previous year.[67]

The criminal justice system

> *We will rebuild confidence in the criminal justice system.* [68]
>
> — CONSERVATIVE PARTY MANIFESTO 2010

The United Kingdom witnessed a steady decline in crime rates from the mid-1990s, a trend that continued after the Conservatives came to power. Home Office statistics show that between 2010 and 2023, overall crime levels plummeted by 54%. By 2024, incidents of violence, burglary, and car theft had reached their lowest points in three decades.

Crime should have been one of the Conservative Party's success stories, but instead, the public's confidence in the functioning of the justice system was eroded by the government's austerity policies. The level of spending cuts forced on the justice system led to a growing perception that the system was ill-equipped to deal with the challenges it faced. By 2024 there was widespread discontent about the state of the justice system despite historically low crime levels.

The courts

The Conservative government's austerity programme had a major impact on courts and prisons. After 2010, 43% of the courts in England and Wales (around 240) were closed, leaving almost half of local authority areas without a local court. This led to large backlogs of cases waiting to go to court. In July 2024, crown courts had a backlog of 68,000 cases, while the magistrates' system had a backlog of 380,000 cases, according to the Law Society.

In 2024, there were a record 2,786 adult rape cases waiting to go to court in England and Wales, part of a record 10,141 sexual offences waiting to go to trial. In England and Wales in 2023, it took on average 777 days from a rape being reported to the police to the case being completed in court. In areas like West Mercia, it took 968 days.[69]

In some cases, the delays were well above the average. One rape case, which had been reported to the police on the day it happened in 2017, finally had a trial date set for May 2025, eight years later. One contributing factor was the collapse of a roof at Hereford Crown Court in 2020.[70] In 2023, 68,022 rapes were recorded by the police in England and Wales, but fewer than 3% resulted in someone being charged in the same year. To many people, it appeared as if the justice system was simply broken.

The prison service

The number of prisoners grew steadily after 2010. The Conservative government encouraged and pushed for longer sentences, resulting in the doubling of the number of adults sentenced to more than ten years in prison. Despite the growth in the number of prisoners, spending on prisons fell by 18% in real terms.[71] As a result, two-thirds of prisons became officially overcrowded.[72] In early 2024, in England and Wales, the number of prisoners reached a record high of 87,973, and this was projected to rise to 105,800 by March 2028. At the start of July 2024, prison governors warned that prisons were operating at almost full capacity.

As overcrowding increased, conditions in prisons deteriorated, and rates of suicide, self-harm, and violent assault increased significantly. An article in the *New Yorker* claimed the UK's prison system had "caved in, overrun by violence, self-harm, drug use, and staff shortages".[73]

The probation service

In 2013, the Conservative government made the decision to partially privatise the probation service, which had been operating relatively smoothly under the management of 35 regional probation trusts. These trusts, overseen by the National Offender Management Service (NOMS), which also managed prisons, were consistently rated as good or exceptional by the government.

Despite these strong ratings, the then justice secretary Chris Grayling moved forward with a plan to outsource parts of the service to the private sector in an effort to cut costs. His proposal shifted the supervision of low- and medium-risk offenders to privately run 'community rehabilitation centres'. This was done despite numerous warnings that the model would be ineffective.

The resulting calamity has been well documented by Sam Freedman in his book *Failed State.*[74]

With little preparation and no established market for probation services, the government handed contracts to companies with no real experience in this area. Of the 21 contracts awarded, 11 went to two major outsourcing firms: Sodexo, a French company known for providing catering services to schools and hospitals, and Interserve, a construction firm that later went into administration. Another major contractor, Working Links, collapsed in 2019 amidst allegations of fraud, with one of its probation centres rated as 'inadequate'.

The contract system included a 'payment by results' clause, designed to motivate companies to reduce reoffending rates. However, reoffending was influenced by factors like housing, benefits, and education – services outside the control of these companies. To minimise costs, some contractors met only the bare minimum requirements, opting to manage offenders through phone calls rather than meaningful, in-person engagement.

Eventually, the Ministry of Justice was forced to renationalise the service. By then, however, significant damage had been done. Valuable expertise had been lost, staff shortages were severe, and constant disruptions from reorganisations had shattered both the service and its morale. According to the National Audit Office, the cost of this failed privatisation experiment to taxpayers was nearly half a billion pounds. By 2023, the newly unified probation system was still struggling, with the chief inspector admitting he could not guarantee public safety.

The police service

Between 2010 and 2018, funding for police forces was significantly reduced, and police numbers were cut by an estimated 20,000, of which 13,000 were constables and 4,000 were sergeants.[75] As a consequence, officers effectively stopped investigating burglaries, meaning that only 4% ended in prosecution.

Boris Johnson promised to reverse the police cuts in 2019, and claimed to have hired 9,000 additional officers by 2021, but despite an influx of recruits, police numbers in England and Wales – including backroom staff such as analysts – remained 10,000 lower than they were in 2010.[76] There were also six hundred fewer police stations than in 2010.

The water industry

We will clean up our rivers and waterways.[77]

— CONSERVATIVE PARTY MANIFESTO 2015

The privatisation of the water industry had never been a popular policy. Back in July 1989, a poll revealed that 79% of people were opposed to the proposal to privatise the water industry.[78] Throughout the life of the Conservative government dissatisfaction with the water industry had been growing. After 25 years of privatisation water prices had increased by 40% above the rate of inflation.

Despite acquiring the water companies debt-free, the private owners accumulated debt of more than £50bn, which was effectively used to finance dividends to the owners. The annual cost of paying dividends and interest on the debt was estimated to be £2.3bn a year more expensive than it would be under public ownership.

The criticism of the water industry and its poor performance was taken up by an unlikely champion in Feargal Sharkey, the former lead vocalist of the Undertones. In 2018, he gave a keynote address at the Rivers Trust autumn conference and in 2020, he appeared on the popular BBC programme *Mortimer & Whitehouse: Gone Fishing* to discuss the threats from water companies pumping raw sewage into rivers. After this appearance, he became the unofficial leader of a campaign to improve the water industry.

Sharkey claimed that privatisation was a "scam" with water companies gaming the system at the expense of the country's water security and environment. He highlighted research by the University of Greenwich showing that investors had taken £85.2bn in dividends from ten water and sewage firms in England and Wales since the industry was privatised and had increased water bills by 60% in real terms but had underinvested in the country's water infrastructure.

According to Sharkey the water companies had "taken our money which we have given them in good faith to invest in infrastructure and in water supply, and none of that has happened. It has simply gone to benefit their shareholders and drive their corporate greed and profiteering."[79]

Water UK, which represented the water companies, challenged the figures and claimed that investment was twice the level it had been before privatisation. Ofwat agreed that there had been significant investment but also said it shared the concerns of campaigners about the performance of the water companies, which was "simply not good enough".[80]

In 2024, the pumping of raw sewage into the country's rivers and seas reached the worst levels on record.[81] NHS records revealed that the number of people admitted to hospital for waterborne diseases – like dysentery and Weil's disease – had increased by 60% since 2010.[82] In 2024, rowers taking part in the annual Oxford v Cambridge boat race were warned not to enter the River Thames because of high levels of E. coli.[83] There were increasingly high-profile examples of communities losing their water supply and of areas where water wasn't safe and had to be boiled.

In May 2024, the regulator Ofwat argued that water bills needed to rise by a third over the next five years in order to fund improvements in infrastructure. The explanations did little to placate the public. *The Independent* reported "growing public anger over the degraded state of rivers, lakes and coastal waters, rising bills, and the dividends and bonuses paid out by water companies".[84] To the public, it seemed the water industry was not working anymore.

Education

> *Improving our school system is the most important thing we can do.*[85]
>
> — CONSERVATIVE PARTY MANIFESTO 2010

In 2024, the Conservatives claimed that improving school standards was one of their big success stories, driven by Michael Gove's curriculum reforms and the introduction of independently run academy chains. The Conservative Party's ambition when they took office was to make the school system in England one of the best in the world and there are indications that the changes they made had positive results. The 2023 Progress in International Reading Literacy Study (PIRLS), which tests the reading capability of 9 to 10-year-olds, found that England came fourth out of 43 countries compared to eleventh in 2011.

The government claimed to have protected the school education sector from the worst of the austerity cuts, although spending per pupil in England was still reduced by 9% in real terms in the ten years after 2010. Under Johnson's premiership this trend was reversed and pupil spending recovered to similar levels as in 2010.

The same was not true of school construction budgets, which were reduced by 46% in real terms between 2009 and 2022. Despite some increases in investment by 2024, school capital budgets were still over 40% lower than they had been in 2010 in real terms. These cuts led to a huge backlog of school maintenance estimated at over £11bn.[86]

In 2023, the maintenance and rebuilding problems became apparent when, just days before the start of the academic year in September, more than 100 schools were forced to close because of dangerous reinforced autoclaved aerated concrete.

The leader of the Trades Union Congress was furious and, in his speech to the TUC in September 2023, said, "They've had 13 years to sort out crumbling concrete in our schools. But five days before the new term they tell schools they can't open."[87] More than two hundred school buildings were identified as having been built with collapse-prone concrete. It was a fiasco and the direct result of the Conservatives cutting the budget for rebuilding schools even when it was known that large numbers of them had unsafe roofs that could collapse.

A 2023 National Audit Office (NAO) report on school conditions estimated that more than a third of the entire school estate in England, about 24,000 school buildings, were "beyond [their] original design life".[88] The Department for Education claimed that while £5.3bn was needed each year to maintain schools in England, the Treasury had only allocated about £3bn. The growing maintenance backlog attracted increasing attention in the media. A BBC article headed 'Crumbling schools plagued by leaks and cold'[89] was but one example. To the parents of many children their school buildings were no longer fit for purpose.

Higher education

> *We will provide fair access to universities.*[90]
>
> — CONSERVATIVE PARTY MANIFESTO 2010

One of the big educational policy changes the 2010 Conservative administration made was to cut government funding for universities and to allow them to make up the shortfall by tripling domestic student tuition fees to £9,000 per annum. This policy had a very direct impact on the two million-plus students who enrolled on a university course each year. By 2024, the UK contributed the least to a student's higher education of any OECD country, and as a consequence, the country had the most indebted graduates in the world, with the average university student graduating with almost £50,000 of student loan debt.[91]

The £9,000 tuition fee that universities could charge for domestic students was capped by the government, and apart from a modest increase to £9,250 in 2017, the fees were not increased between 2012 and 2024. To keep pace with inflation, fees needed to rise to £12,000 a year by 2024, and it was estimated that universities were making a loss of £2,500 a year on each domestic student. The freezing of domestic tuition fees, along with reductions in teaching grants and high inflation, created a challenging financial environment for universities. Many increasingly sought to recruit more international students for whom there was no cap on fees.

By 2023, the number of overseas students studying at UK universities had risen for the ninth straight year in a row, taking the total number to 679,970 or 24% of the total student population.[92] However, after stricter restrictions on student visas in relation to family members were introduced at the start of 2024, international student enrolments fell, creating an additional problem for universities that were struggling financially. In 2024, Essex University said it had a £13.8m shortfall, which was due to a 38% drop in foreign student applications.[93]

In 2023, over a quarter of publicly funded higher education providers were in deficit and it was forecast the number would rise to 40%.[94] By 2024, 50 universities had announced redundancies and course closures.[95] In 2024, there were increasing numbers of articles warning that the funding model for higher education was broken.[96]

Defence

> *A Conservative government will defend our national security.*[97]
>
> — CONSERVATIVE PARTY MANIFESTO 2010

The Conservative Party had traditionally been a staunch defender of the country's military and police services. However, the Ministry for Defence was not spared from the austerity spending cuts.

Troop numbers were cut by over 40,000 after 2010, causing many military experts to question whether the UK could defend itself in the event of a war. The number of armed forces personnel had fallen to 142,000 in 2023, down from 207,000 in 2000.

The number of frontline fighter jets was also reduced by 40% to 119. Ben Wallace, defence secretary from 2019 until 2023, argued that the armed forces were "hollowed out and underfunded".[98]

While the Conservatives pointed to investment in two new aircraft carriers at a cost of £6.2bn, military experts argued their utility was limited by cuts in other areas, which meant they could not both be properly defended at the same time.

Nothing works anymore – the austerity chickens come home to roost

The damaging effects of the austerity years had been building like a huge wall of water against a creaking dam. The impact of the COVID-19 pandemic was to blow the dam wide open and reveal the vulnerabilities in public services.

After the pandemic, public satisfaction with services such as education, healthcare, and the police service collapsed. According to a More in Common survey in 2023, 58% of people believed that nothing worked anymore.[99] This figure rose to 76% in Red Wall areas.[100] In a separate study three-quarters of people felt that public services had got worse since 2021, and two-thirds of voters described public services as 'underfunded'.[101]

Conservative politicians and government ministers were increasingly questioned about the state of Britain. On *Channel 4 News*, Krishnan Guru-Murthy told the then chancellor Jeremy Hunt, "There is a real feeling at the moment of Britain being broken. You can't get an appointment at the doctor, your letters don't arrive, you can't get a train, you're looking at fuel bills you can't afford, and the government feels like it is running out of ideas."[102]

By late 2023, Conservative commentators were increasingly acknowledging the fact that nothing worked anymore. On X, formerly known as Twitter, this was ironically referred to as the 'great noticing'. This post by the right-wing journalist Isabel Oakeshott, in September 2023, was one example: "Roads, railways, schools, GP services, hospitals, airports, housing, borders, prisons and anything involving call centres – all these things are broken in Broken Britain."[103] A week after Oakeshott's post, the historian Dominic Sandbrook wrote in *The Times* that "Britain is in deep decline, and everybody knows it."[104]

By June 2024, fully 84% of people felt public services were in a bad state.[105] The percentage of people thinking specific services were run down and not working was as follows:

- NHS: 90%
- Hospitals: 89%
- GPs: 85%

- Social care: 84%
- Trains: 75%
- Prisons: 74%
- Police: 71%
- Schools: 67%
- Courts and the justice system: 66%

The narrative 'nothing works anymore' was repeated consistently because it resonated with the public and echoed their experiences. The phrase was used unprompted in focus group after focus group,[106] where people spoke of ambulances not arriving, NHS waiting lists, police not turning up, unaffordable and poor-quality housing, delayed train services, raw sewage being pumped into rivers, the difficulty of getting GP appointments, and decaying physical infrastructure from potholes to crumbling schools.

When asked by More in Common in 2024 to describe the UK in a single word, the top choices of people were 'broken', 'mess', 'struggling', 'divided', 'expensive', 'poor' and 'chaotic'.[107] The majority of people simply felt that nothing worked anymore, and there was deep dissatisfaction that the country was not effectively governed.[108]

Three-quarters of people believed that the country was in a worse state than it was in 2010, including 59% of those who voted Conservative in 2019.[109] It was a view shared by the historians Anthony Seldon and Tom Egerton. In their 2024 book *The Conservative Effect* they argued, "It is hard to find a comparable period in the history of a Conservative, or other, government which achieved so little, or which left the country at its conclusion in a more troubling state."[110]

It was also a view publicly shared by Conservatives, which gave the narrative additional credibility. Danny Kruger, a leading Conservative backbench MP and founder of the New Conservatives, said the party faced "obliteration" at the next election for leaving the country in a worse state than they had found it when they came to power in 2010.[111] Conservative MP Neil O'Brien said the party had presided over the crumbling of public services and not delivered on the public's core concerns.[112] Peter Lilley, a former cabinet minister under Margaret Thatcher, also admitted that under the Conservatives, "Britain is broken – nothing works."[113]

The public narrative part 1 – 'Nothing works anymore'

On the eve of the 2024 general election, a More in Common survey found the percentage of people who believed that 'nothing in Britain works anymore' had increased from 58% to 62%.[114]

Focus groups found that the 'nothing works anymore' narrative resonated so strongly with the public that it was adopted and used by opposition parties as an attack line in the general election campaign. For example:

- When unveiling their 'battle bus' for the election, Angela Rayner said under the Tories, "Nothing works anymore."
- Instagram and Facebook videos published by Rachel Reeves were headed 'Nothing works anymore.'[115]
- In his party political broadcast, Nigel Farage said, "Britain is broken ... Nothing works anymore ... the health service, travelling anywhere, trying to get your kids or grandkids a house. Rents have gone through the roof. Nothing actually works."[116]
- In an ITV televised debate, Daisy Cooper of the

Liberal Democrats said, "Everything is broken and nothing works anymore under the Tories."[117]

- When the Green Party launched their manifesto, they pledged to "mend broken Britain".[118]
- Paul Nowak, the general secretary of the TUC, said, "Nothing works anymore and no one in government cares."
- Keir Starmer pledged to fix broken Britain in his party conference speech, saying what was broken could be fixed.[119]
- Alex Cole-Hamilton, leader of the Scottish Liberal Democrats, argued in the *Edinburgh Evening News* that only the Liberal Democrats could fix broken Britain.

The idea that 'nothing worked anymore' had become a dominant and powerful public narrative that resonated with the public. People had no difficulty in referencing instances that validated the core story or in sharing such examples with their friends and family. It became a common-sense narrative that was seen as self-evident. The question it raised was – why?

9

THE CONSERVATIVES ARE INCOMPETENT

Governments can't afford to mess with competence. Once they are seen as incapable of running the country, the game is up.[1]

— JONATHAN FREEDLAND

It was clear to people in early 2024 that 'nothing worked anymore', but it begged the question of 'Why?'

The most logical starting point for scrutiny was the Conservative government, which had held power for over a decade and had been responsible for austerity. When the public scrutinised the government, it looked chaotic. Rishi Sunak was the Conservative Party's fifth leader and the fifth prime minister since 2016. There were constant reports of party infighting between different factions over Brexit and a continuous turnover of ministers.

There had also been a series of very public scandals from a Tory MP watching pornography on his phone in the House of

Commons to the Paterson and Pincher affairs, to PPE contracts right through to Partygate. Then, in 2022, there was Liz Truss's disastrous mini-budget, which led to her resignation after just 45 days. The obvious answer as to why things no longer worked anymore was that the government was incompetent.

One of the Conservative Party's most important brand strengths historically was its reputation for competence, particularly in economic matters. Geoffrey Wheatcroft, writing in the *Financial Times* in November 2007, claimed it was the Conservative Party's reputation for competence rather than amiability that explained why they had been in office for 84 out of the 123 years before 1997. He later emphasised that nobody ever voted for the Tories because they were 'nice'. Their success, he argued, was founded on a reputation for competence.[2]

In December 2019, when Johnson won his 80-seat majority in parliament, twice as many people trusted the Conservatives over Labour on the economy (39% to 18%).[3]

Polling throughout 2020 continued to put the Conservatives ahead of Labour when it came to managing the economy. Despite the challenges the government faced during the COVID-19 pandemic, the public continued to believe the Conservatives were more competent than Labour. After successfully managing the vaccine rollout programme in early 2021, more than twice as many voters believed that a Conservative government would be better at managing the economy than a Labour government (42% to 18%).[4]

Just three years later, the figures were reversed. Remarkably, Labour led the Conservatives by a record 25 points as the best party to handle the country's economic problems.[5] Robert Shrimsley summed up the public mood in June 2024 when he wrote in the *Financial Times* that "after 14 years, voters have concluded the country is led by serial incompetents and in a worse state than it was a decade ago".[6] The Conservative Party's reputation for economic competence had been shredded, and the public narrative had become 'nothing works anymore *because the Conservatives are incompetent*'.

To understand how this narrative developed and how the Conservative Party became a byword for incompetence, it is necessary to examine two key areas. The first is the party's leadership, and the second is the party's management of the economy.

Leadership

> *Five prime ministers in less than a decade is destabilising and, frankly, humiliating for British democracy.*[7]
>
> — DANIEL FINKELSTEIN

Public perceptions of competence are influenced by their respect for and confidence in political leaders. After Cameron, the Conservative Party chose four leaders who were each in their own way unable to exercise the agency of the post of prime minister and provide a strategic long-term vision. Cameron and his successors were consumed by a series of profound shocks that left them reacting to events rather than crafting a narrative for the future. The party fractured over Brexit, and successive prime ministers struggled to manage the rebels within their own party.

The 2019–2024 government was led in turn by Boris Johnson, Liz Truss, and Rishi Sunak. Johnson's public reputation was damaged below the waterline by Partygate. Just prior to his resignation in 2022, a poll found that the word the public most associated with Johnson was 'liar', followed by 'incompetent' and 'untrustworthy'.[8] By the time Johnson resigned 58% of the public thought the Conservative Party was incompetent, compared to 16% that thought it was competent.[9]

As documented in Part 1, Johnson's behaviour had a corrosive effect on public trust resulting in a dramatic fall in the public's confidence in government. In his jointly edited 2024 book *The Conservative Effect*, Anthony Seldon argues that Johnson's period in charge was "the worst premiership in modern times".[10]

When the Conservative Party removed Johnson, they replaced him with two leaders who were even less politically competent. His successor, Liz Truss, was ultimately elected by just 81,000 Conservative Party members who were far from representative of the public as a whole. More than half of the members were over 55, with four out of ten over 65, and they were more right-wing than the population, with only 15% believing the government should redistribute income from the richer members of society to the less well-off. Political analyst Lewis Baston argued they were insulated from the market economy with their triple-locked state pensions, defined-benefit private pensions, and mortgage-free houses.[11]

Arguably, the party members chose Liz Truss for ideological reasons, such as her tax-cutting zeal, rather than her competence, when for the public what mattered most was competence, not ideology. Truss destroyed the Conservative Party's reputation for competence. Under her leadership the proportion of the public who thought the Conservative Party was incompetent jumped from 49% to 68%.

Truss was replaced by Sunak, who sought to present himself as a competent technocrat but failed to connect with the public, which held him responsible for the economic and policy failures under his tenure as prime minister, and as chancellor. By May 2024, 55% of people believed Sunak was incompetent, and he failed to turn around the public's views about the competence of the Tory Party. By June 2024, 65% of the public still felt that the party was incompetent, compared to just 13% who thought it was competent.[12]

Ian Leslie, an acclaimed writer of books on human behaviour, said of Theresa May, Boris Johnson, and Liz Truss: "Three of the most incompetent prime ministers ever, in a row. What are the odds?"[13]

To have five different leaders in just six years from 2016 to 2022 was on its own extraordinary, destabilising, and a sign of incompetence, but there was even more turmoil further down with constantly changing cabinet and junior ministers.

In the eight years after George Osborne resigned as chancellor of the exchequer in July 2016, there were six different chancellors. In 2022, four different people held the post of chancellor (Rishi Sunak, Nadhim Zahawi, Kwasi Kwarteng, and Jeremy Hunt). There were also eight different foreign secretaries, who were, on average, in post for less than two years.

In education, the turnover was even higher. There were an unprecedented ten secretaries of state in 14 years. In September 2022, Liz Truss appointed Kit Malthouse as education secretary. He became the fifth person to hold the job in under a year and took over from James Cleverly, who had been in the job only two months.

The turnover was even greater when it came to housing. A *Sunday Times* editorial called the level of churn ludicrous, commenting that "Lee Rowley is both the tenth and thirteenth person to have held the role of housing minister since 2016."[14] There were also 13 culture secretaries during the 14 years of the Conservative government, and seven business secretaries in the seven years after the Brexit vote, some lasting just a few weeks in the job.

It was simply impossible to have clear leadership and direction on policy when the ministers were changing so frequently. Anthony Seldon argues the constant turnover of ministers was a disaster: "There was too much churn, too much prime ministerial and ministerial churn to have consistent policymaking."[15]

The constant turnover and changes in direction also created confusion about what the Conservative Party stood for. The government's policy stances bounced from free market economics to strong state intervention, from small state to big state, and from controlling our borders to policies allowing mass immigration. Major policy promises such as Johnson's levelling up were not followed through or even given much attention by subsequent prime ministers.

Robert Shrimsley argued that Brexit was ultimately to blame for the poor choices of leaders. He claimed the party's Brexit revolutionary guards "reshaped the Tories, undermining their base, elevating ideology over pragmatism, distracting them from the issues that matter most to voters, purging their most talented leaders, fetishising one cohort of voter over others and, above all, causing it to elect leaders utterly unfit to run the country".[16]

Economic incompetence

James Carville, a political strategist for Bill Clinton, famously encapsulated voter priorities with the phrase, "It's the economy, stupid." Professor Stephen Fisher concurs, noting that governments rarely survive economic crises. He points out that since 1922, UK governments have been ousted ten times following such crises. Therefore, it is essential for governments to be perceived as competent when it comes to economic management and to demonstrate the ability to navigate the country through challenging times.

Professor Jane Green, political scientist at the University of Oxford, has observed that while an economic crisis can be severe, its political impact hinges on whether the electorate perceives a particular party as responsible. She has suggested that a cost-of-living crisis has the potential to act as a 'competence shock', reshaping public perceptions of the incumbent party's trustworthiness and capability. She also notes that voters hold governments accountable even when difficult economic conditions are sparked by global events, such as the COVID-19 pandemic or major wars.[17]

The failure of a government to manage an economic crisis can damage a party's brand for a very long time. On 16 September 1992, the Conservative government was forced to withdraw from the European Exchange Rate Mechanism despite temporarily raising interest rates to 15% in an attempt to support the pound as the value of the currency plummeted. It became known as Black Wednesday, and following the crisis, the Conservative Party fell behind in the polls. They were never ahead again, and the party lost heavily to Labour in 1997. Norman Tebbit contended that the fallout from Black Wednesday was a major factor in the defeat, as it severely undermined the Conservative Party's reputation for competence. Geoffrey Wheatcroft argued the brand damage from the crisis lasted for nearly 15 years.[18]

The Conservative Party's reputation for economic competence from 2010 to 2024 was badly damaged by:

- the failure to secure investment and growth
- the cost-of-living crisis
- the Liz Truss mini-budget

We briefly examine each of these below.

A failure to secure investment and growth

When Cameron came to power in 2010, investment in the UK was the lowest in the G7 group of countries. The overall investment rate had fallen from around 23% of GDP in the late 1980s to around 17% from 2000 onwards.[19] After the 1980s the level of research and development expenditure relative to GDP had fallen to below 2%. This was relatively low compared with other G7 countries, such as Japan, which was 3.5%, and Germany and the United States, which were both approximately 2.8%.

Public investment in the UK had dropped significantly from an average of 4.5% of GDP between 1949 and 1978 to just 1.5% between 1979 and 2019. In large part this was due to the privatisation programme initiated by Thatcher in the 1980s, and which continued into the 1990s, and the subsequent failure of regulators in key sectors such as energy and water to ensure high levels of investment.

Most economists agree that to generate economic growth, a country needs to increase its level of investment. However, from 2010 to 2016, the Conservative Party chancellor, George Osborne, didn't just cut public spending, he also drastically reduced public budgets for investment, making the country increasingly reliant on private sector investment. Osborne argued that reducing the government deficit would give confidence to the markets to invest in the UK. However, many commentators disagreed and observed that whilst private sector investment had been growing, investors had been reluctant to invest in the UK at comparative levels to other G7 countries for a number of reasons. These included:

- Planning and building regulations, which made projects more expensive
- A lack of domestic construction capacity, which also raised prices
- The difficulty of raising funds in the UK for long-term investments

- Uncertainty in the UK's industrial policy and tax regime
- The availability of low-wage labour in the UK, particularly from Eastern Europe[20]

It was also argued that private investment was discouraged by the government's austerity programme itself, which led to expectations of weak domestic demand and low growth.[21] Critics pointed out that higher levels of public and private investment tend to go together, with the government playing a key role in facilitating investment through its own investments in infrastructure, education, and science.[22]

The decision of the Conservatives to cut public investment after 2010 was particularly criticised by economists because it was a time of low interest rates and cheap borrowing. From 2010 to May 2022, the Bank of England base rate remained below 1%, the lowest in three hundred years. A *Sunday Times* editorial argued that Cameron and Osborne "neglected to take advantage of super-low borrowing costs to build key infrastructure".[23] The permanent secretary to the Treasury at the time, Lord Macpherson, agreed, noting that, "With hindsight we probably should have taken advantage [of low interest rates] and borrowed more when times were more stable ... and invested more."[24]

According to the World Bank, Britain's gross capital formation between 2010 and 2015 placed the country 150th out of 174 countries.

Investment in the UK didn't recover after the 2015 election. Instead, it got worse. Private investment stalled after the 2016 vote to leave the European Union. The Conservatives had remarkably instructed Whitehall not to make any contingency plans in the event of a vote to leave the EU. Hence, after the vote, there were no plans, no sense of direction, and a great deal of uncertainty about the UK's new economic arrangements. It was unclear to investors what type of Brexit the government would pursue – would it stay in the single market or the customs union or leave both?

After the Brexit vote, David Cameron resigned in front of Downing Street and walked back into No 10 whistling a happy tune,[25] but he left the country with no clarity and no prime minister at one of the most critical junctures in its history. The pound's value against the dollar immediately fell to levels not seen since 1985, while the stock market fell 8% and UK government bond yields hit a new record low.[26] The lack of clarity from the Conservative government about its economic plans led investors to put their plans on hold.

The Foreign Affairs Select Committee called the decision not to prepare for a vote to leave the EU an act of gross negligence, which deepened the uncertainty surrounding the impact of Brexit.[27] It was left to the new prime minister, Theresa May, a fervent supporter of Remain, who had cried when the referendum was lost,[28] to set the direction. At the Conservative Party conference in October 2016, she announced that a 'global Britain' would negotiate a trade deal with the EU, set its own rules on immigration and would not be subject to the jurisdiction of the European Court of Justice.

May's speech effectively meant the government would pursue a hard Brexit. Tim Bale claimed this decision blindsided the EU and others because they had assumed that "leaving on that basis was economically so damaging that no sane Prime Minister would advocate it".[29] The shock was also felt in the UK as neither cabinet ministers nor senior civil servants had been consulted. Philip Hammond, May's chancellor, who remarkably had also not been consulted on the decision, later said he had been absolutely horrified.

Economists estimated that the final Brexit deal, which was ultimately agreed by Boris Johnson, would have a negative impact on the economy equivalent to approximately 5% of

GDP.[30] Estimates also suggested that investment in the UK would be around 10% lower than it might otherwise have been without Brexit.[31] It is hard to separate out the precise impact of various factors, such as Brexit and the COVID-19 pandemic, on investment. However, Britain's gross capital formation did not significantly improve, and in 2021, the country was ranked 145th out of 174 countries.

Investors were discouraged by the Conservative government constantly changing its mind on high-profile investment projects such as HS2, a high-speed train line that aimed to connect London, Birmingham, Manchester, and Leeds. The government had approved the project in 2012, with the key aims of increasing connectivity and rail capacity. In 2021, the government cancelled the Leeds leg of the route and in 2023, Rishi Sunak announced in Manchester that his government was also cancelling the Birmingham to Manchester leg. HS2 was reduced to an expensive £50bn high-speed link between London and Birmingham that did little to increase connectivity or capacity.

The Conservative government's decision to cut public investment during the nine years from 2010 to 2019, its decision to have a hard Brexit, and its changing policy decisions all served to heighten investor uncertainty and resulted in a period of chronic underinvestment at a time when it was desperately needed.

The underinvestment amplified the UK's productivity problem. Between 1996 and 2007, UK productivity had risen steadily and GDP per capita doubled during this period.[32] However, after the global financial crash in 2007, it fell sharply and didn't recover in the following 17 years. In 2022, UK GDP per capita was just $46,125, still below the $50,398 it had been 15 years earlier in 2007. The OBR estimated that the post-Brexit trading arrangements had reduced UK productivity by 4% relative to remaining in the EU.

The combination of underinvestment and lack of productivity growth meant that real wages stagnated after 2010. The UK experienced the longest period of no real wage growth since the end of the Napoleonic Wars. By 2024 the average worker earned just £20 more per week than 14 years earlier, after adjusting for inflation.[33] The IFS argued that the 14 years of Conservative government had been "a period of abysmal growth in productivity, and with it, living standards".[34]

Cost-of-living crisis

The reopening of the global economy after the pandemic caused inflation in the UK to rise to 5.1% in November 2021. Professor Stephen Fisher argues that sharply rising inflation and the economic turmoil had a direct impact on levels of Conservative support, which fell from 44% in June 2021 to 36% in November 2021.[35] This significant fall was prior to the Partygate revelations in December 2021 and hence could be attributed in large part to the rise in inflation.

By May 2022, inflation had reached a 40-year high of 9.1%. The costs of food, energy, and rent increased dramatically and far faster than incomes. The cost of living became the public's number one concern.[36]

The National Institute of Economic and Social Research estimated that for one and a half million British households, the costs of food and energy exceeded their disposable income after housing costs. Citizen's Advice reported that food and fuel poverty had more than tripled in just 12 months.[37]

Support for the government's handling of the economy plummeted as the cost-of-living crisis intensified and the country barrelled towards a recession. The percentage of people who felt the Conservatives would be the best party to manage the economy fell from 39% in May 2021 to 23% in May 2022. As confidence drained away from the Conservatives, the public's faith in the Labour Party's economic competence increased, and the party climbed level with the Conservatives.

In June 2022, when Boris Johnson was forced to resign, inflation hit double figures. A YouGov survey reported that one in four people was having to cut back on essentials and that three-quarters of Britons – and two-thirds of Conservative voters – said the government was not doing enough to help people struggling with the cost of living.[38]

The mini-budget catastrophe

When Liz Truss became the new Conservative Party leader and prime minister in September 2022, the country was already in an economic crisis. COVID-19, the Ukraine war, and a global inflation surge had wreaked havoc on the economy. Inflation was at its highest rate in 40 years and government debt had more than doubled to almost 100% of GDP. In her wisdom Liz Truss decided this was moment to embrace radically new economic policies.

As set out in Part 1, Truss's chancellor Kwasi Kwarteng presented a growth plan to parliament on 23 September 2022, which became known as the mini-budget. It proposed a series of tax cuts which would be funded by hundreds of billions of pounds of additional government borrowing.

What followed was a period of chaos. The risk premia on government bonds rose sharply as investors bet against the government's ability to repay its debt. This, in turn, drove down the price of bonds, causing a crisis for pension funds and forcing the Bank of England to intervene. Within weeks nearly all of the measures in the mini-budget were reversed. It was humiliating for the new Prime Minister and shattered the Conservative Party's reputation for economic competence.

It was always the case that interest rates and mortgage rates were going to rise, but any hope the Conservatives had of avoiding the blame was torpedoed by Liz Truss and the mini-budget.

In a Swindon focus group, participants were told that the Conservative Party was claiming that the crisis in mortgage rates had been caused by international factors; did they agree? The immediate response from one respondent was "utter tosh".[39] Another participant said Truss had made decisions like "an 11-year-old". Asked to use one word to describe Truss multiple participants said "shambles".

The feedback from focus groups appeared to support the former Tory chancellor Philip Hammond's claim that Truss had completely trashed the Conservative Party's election-winning reputation for economic competence. Daniel Finkelstein, the Conservative peer, journalist, and political adviser, agreed, saying, "The Liz Truss premiership destroyed a crucial part of the Conservative case, which is that the Conservative Party is prudent with public money and can look after the economy." He added, "It was a calamitous event and not only was it a calamitous event in the life of this government, it has at least the capacity to be of long-term disservice."[40] The mini-budget's damage to the Conservative Party's reputation for competence had the potential to be as significant as Black Wednesday, if not more so.

Taking the blame for higher mortgage rates would inflict ongoing and significant damage on the Conservative brand, as in every single month in the run-up to the 2024 election, tens of thousands of mortgage holders were coming off low-cost fixed-rate mortgage deals. They were experiencing the pain of large increases in their mortgage during a cost-of-living crisis and placing the blame firmly on Liz Truss and the Conservatives. The Liberal Democrats called it the 'Truss tax', arguing the rise in mortgages was the equivalent of a five-pence increase in income tax.[41] There was real anger amongst those who had been striving to get onto the housing ladder but whose dreams had been shattered by higher mortgage rates.

The mini-budget debacle powered a simple public narrative, which became the accepted explanation for the complex series of events that culminated in the economic crisis in late 2022 – namely that Liz Truss had crashed the economy. This narrative was reinforced by opposition politicians and the media. In December 2022, the *Financial Times* published an article on mortgage rates headed 'Liz Truss's "moron premium" still looms over the UK economy.'[42]

Liz Truss became the poster child for Conservative incompetence. When JL Partners (JLP) conducted a survey asking people to give their view of the former prime minister in a single word, the most common answer was 'incompetent', followed by 'useless'.[43]

After the mini-budget, the public's confidence in the Conservative Party's ability to manage the economy collapsed. The proportion of people who said they had confidence in the party's economic competence fell to just 15%.[44] By contrast, 32% said they had confidence in the Labour Party. It was a remarkable reversal in just 18 months.

The public narrative part 2 – 'Nothing works anymore because the Conservative Party is incompetent'

The party's reputation for competence had been well and truly trashed by June 2024. It wasn't just a consequence of the mini-budget. The party's leadership was perceived as chaotic, weak, and incompetent, while the Conservatives' record on the economy was one of failure. The UK economy still had the lowest investment among G7 countries, growth remained anaemic, wages had stagnated, government debt had increased to around 100% of GDP, debt repayments increased by £60bn a year,[45] living standards had fallen during the 2019–2024 parliament for the first time since the 1950s, and taxes as a share of GDP had risen to the highest levels since 1948.[46]

A neutral observer might argue that any government would have struggled given the scale of the crises that the Conservative government faced, such as the COVID-19 pandemic and a surge in global inflation. However, few people were willing to give the Conservatives the benefit of the doubt. The chaos of Brexit, five prime ministers, the perceived dishonesty of the party's politicians, collapsing public services, and the Truss mini-budget had irrevocably damaged the public's view of the party's competence.

The public approval ratings for the government's competence and ability to handle key policy areas were all deeply negative by the start of 2024. In March 2024, they were as follows:[47]

- Immigration -39%
- NHS -33%
- Housing -31%
- Crime -23%
- Economy -21%

The only positive net approval rating was for the government's handling of COVID-19 at +2%.

A party's reputation for competence is particularly critical when issues are salient to voters. In 2024, the public's key concerns were the very issues on which the Tories were perceived as incompetent.

The public believed the five most important issues facing the country were:

- NHS/hospitals/healthcare
- The economy
- Immigration
- Inflation/cost of living
- Housing[48]

These were all issues on which the Conservatives were perceived to have fundamentally failed. Political commentator Stephen Bush argued in the *Financial Times* that by 2024 the Conservative Party's biggest single problem was that it had lost its reputation for competence.[49]

On 5 June 2024, Ipsos Mori published a survey which found that a staggering 83% of people were dissatisfied with the way the government was running the country.[50] A Lord Ashcroft poll days later found that only 6% of people, including only 8% of 2019 Tory voters, said they were satisfied with the current Conservative government.[51] John Burn-Murdoch, writing in the *Financial Times,* argued that "a slow, rolling competence shock" had alienated voters across the spectrum.[52]

The incompetence of the Conservative government was reinforced endlessly by examples highlighted by the press, pundits, pollsters, and politicians. *The Standard* highlighted HS2, which it said was, "Woefully behind schedule, wildly over-budget, subject to the vicissitudes of poor leadership and indecision ... HS2 has achieved the spectacular feat of being the high-tech railway to link London with the north that will no longer be going to the north."[53]

When the former Conservative MP for Dover, Natalie Elphicke, crossed the floor to join Labour in May 2024, she confirmed the views of many when she said, "The Conservatives have become a byword for incompetence and division." Her speech may have been crafted by the Labour team, but the message hit home. Elphicke wasn't the only Conservative to criticise her former party. John Halsall, an ex-Tory council leader, said he was appalled at the incompetence of the Tory government, which had "broken Britain".[54]

Jim Pickard, the *Financial Times* deputy political editor, summed up the public's perceptions of government incompetence when he said, "The Tories have had 14 years of rope with which to hang themselves and they've done a pretty good job of it."[55]

Those who had voted Conservative in the 2019 election were particularly frustrated by the government's incompetence and aggrieved by its failures on immigration and the NHS. When asked why they were planning to defect in 2024, their top reasons were:

- The Conservative Party's failure to deliver: 53%
- The failure to control immigration: 44%
- The Conservative Party are incompetent: 38%
- The problems in the NHS: 37%[56]

The public's frustrations with the Conservative government's incompetence led Professor John Curtice to believe that the 2024 general election was going to be a 'competence' election rather than an ideological election, where voters were going to pass judgement on the competence of the government.[57] Professor Jane Green also argued that the Conservative Party's problems in the election were going to stem from perceptions of trust and incompetence rather than ideological differences. The Conservative Tees Valley mayor, Ben Houchen, agreed, saying that the party was going to be punished because of a lack of competence rather than an ideological failing.

In reality, it can be difficult to separate out ideology from competence. Was the crisis in local government caused by incompetence or by an ideological determination to pursue austerity and make large reductions in public spending? Whatever the truth of these complexities, by 2024, the public had come to the conclusion that *nothing worked anymore because the Conservative Party was incompetent.*

10

THE CONSERVATIVES SHOULD BE PUNISHED

In other countries people would have been dragged out of parliament and lynched in the street because of how corrupt they've been.[1]

— FOCUS GROUP PARTICIPANT

Marshall Ganz, the strategist behind Obama's 2008 grassroots campaign, has extensively researched how narratives can motivate and influence others. He argues that effective public narratives are more than interpretations of the past. They are also 'a story of now' and communicate an urgent need for change. In Ganz's view, the story of now acts as a bridge between *why* people should act and *how* they should act.[2] It sets out the action that needs to be taken to achieve a desirable future.

In 2016, the Leave campaign successfully persuaded people that leaving the European Union was the action required to take back control. In 2024, there was an underlying anger at the

Conservatives for the perceived damage they had done to the country, and the action required by the public narrative was not simply to remove the party from office but to *punish* them.

The anger behind the punishment narrative stemmed from a collective sense of relative deprivation.

Ted Gurr, a former professor of political science, used the concept of relative deprivation to describe the tension that builds up when what a person 'does' have differs from what a person believes they 'ought' to have. This gap, whether perceived or real, can cause feelings of anger, betrayal, and unfairness. These feelings are felt particularly strongly when something that a person or people had before is taken away. Gurr believed that feelings of relative deprivation give rise to anger and aggression.

Relative deprivation can be felt at an individual level, but it is far more powerful when it is felt collectively. In the UK in 2024, there was a collective feeling that things were getting worse, and increasing frustration and anger that they no longer had what they had before. Services they used to rely on were being withdrawn, and facilities were closed. They were also finding that as inflation rose they could no longer afford to buy things which they had previously bought. Younger people felt frustrated that it was more difficult for them to get on the housing ladder than it had been for their parents. Those with above-average earnings particularly felt they 'ought' to be able to buy a home.

People were angry about crumbling public services, such as having to wait longer for hospital operations. They were also angry at the Conservatives' incompetence and their behaviour, including allegations of impropriety, misconduct, corruption, fraud, and lying. From an analysis of focus groups, the public was particularly angry about inflation, Partygate, unfairness, cronyism, poverty, and the Conservatives' lack of respect for people like them.

Anger at inflation and falling household incomes

Inflation is an incumbency killer. When the price people used to pay for something increases, they view it as a form of relative deprivation. The UBS economist Paul Donovan argues that people remember previous price levels and consider higher prices to be unfair.[3] While inflation after the COVID-19 pandemic was a global phenomenon, voters blamed national governments. In Japan, the United States, and the UK, voters expressed their anger at inflation by punishing incumbent governments.

After adjusting for inflation, the Resolution Foundation found that real per capita household disposable incomes in the UK fell between 2019 and 2024, which they claimed was "the first parliament in modern history to see a fall in living standards".[4]

Anger at Partygate

The public's anger at the Conservatives reached boiling point during Partygate, which created a powerful and passionate sense of grievance about the Prime Minister's dishonesty, hypocrisy and the unfairness of 'one rule for them'.

The COVID-19 lockdown was an emotional and distressing time. Hundreds of thousands died and a great many people were not able to sit alongside and comfort their elderly and dying relatives. People were seen trying to communicate with distressed, confused, and vulnerable people through the windows of care homes, where an estimated 270,000 people died during the pandemic.[5] For these people, the revelation that the Prime Minister and his staff had not been following the rules and even held parties caused anger and fury.

The public outrage was most visible in the stories of those who had lost loved ones during the pandemic. The story of

Suzanne McCallum who lost her mother during the pandemic was typical. She told the BBC her mother's funeral had been horrific; she had to go there on her own, stand on her own, and go home to an empty house alone as under the rules no one was allowed to go round to support her. She said she was "absolutely disgusted" by Johnson's behaviour and she had "so much anger", adding: "We followed all the rules. I've lost my mum – she meant the world to me – and they can't even follow the rules that they set out. They're not above anybody else – they are the same and they should have followed their own rules. They shouldn't be allowed to stay. He (Mr Johnson) is a bumbling idiot and just a liar. They have lied to all of us."[6]

Anger at unfairness and cronyism

The use of the 'VIP lane' for COVID-19 contracts and the contracts awarded to those with connections to the Conservative Party created a sense of unfairness and grievance. People particularly resented individuals connected to the Conservative Party making profits from COVID-19 contracts that were fast-tracked without competition. Fifty-one contracts, worth £4bn, went through the 'VIP lane', of which 24 were referred by Conservative politicians or their offices. There were 28 contracts worth £4.1bn that went to those with known connections to the Conservative Party.

There was growing feeling that the Conservatives were just out for themselves. Cases such as the Paterson affair, David Cameron's paid lobbying for Greensill Capital,[7] and the former health secretary Matt Hancock's distribution of public contracts to firms belonging to his friends[8] all reinforced this view.

The public anger about perceptions of corruption and cronyism was visible in focus groups. In one group, a participant expressed this anger, saying in other countries, "people would have been dragged out of parliament and lynched in the street because of how corrupt they've been".[9]

Keir Starmer sought to capitalise on this anger, saying he was sick of people skirting around the issue and the Tories were "wallowing in sleaze". He argued the media should call out the corruption and that he would create an anti-cronyism commission to stop MPs from gorging on money from donors.[10]

Many commentators said Starmer should exhibit more anger and use it the way Tony Blair had done as an opposition leader.[11] One of the most cited examples was Blair's speech in Blackpool in 1994, when he revealed the depth of his anger about the Tory government by saying, "It is time to take these Tories apart for what they have done to our country not because they lack compassion – of course they do, they are Tories – but because they are the most feckless, irresponsible group of incompetents ever to be let loose in government."[12] Starmer took this advice and increasingly referenced his own anger, for example saying, "I am angry because when I see the reputation of our democracy and our country trashed by this Prime Minister, that makes me angry."[13]

Anger about poverty

The Conservative Party's cuts to public services and to benefits had a severe impact on poorer people. The IFS estimated that the effect of Conservative tax and benefit reforms from 2010–11 to 2024–25 had been to reduce the incomes of the top 10% of households and the bottom 40% while increasing incomes in between. The poorest fifth of households were estimated to have lost an average of £1,800, or 10.2% of income, while the richest tenth lost £2,200, or 1.7% of income on average.[14]

Poorer families with children were particularly affected by benefits changes, both because they relied more on benefits, and because reforms such as the 'two-child limit' policy targeted families with children. The IFS estimated that out-of-work families with children lost £5,500 a year on average as a result of benefit reforms while in-work families with children who were below the 40th percentile of household earnings lost £3,100 on average.[15] The *Financial Times* reported that poverty rates for children in large families were almost three times higher than they were for pensioners, with the gap forecast to widen even further.[16]

Under austerity the spending cuts had been brutal, widespread, and often impacted the most vulnerable. In 2024, the number of people in working households below the poverty line was estimated to have risen to over a million. The number of children growing up in poverty was estimated to have increased by over a third. A Joseph Rowntree Foundation report published in January 2024 found that more than one in five people in the UK (14.4m people or 22% of the population) were in poverty.[17]

The government did not increase the Universal Credit allowance in line with inflation, and it fell to its lowest-ever level as a proportion of average earnings. The Financial Fairness report by Donald Hirsch found that the costs of food and heating for many families exceeded 100% of the benefit.[18] The benefit cap (the limit that households can receive in total annual benefits) was also frozen by the government in 2024, meaning that while individual benefits rose, 80,000 families received no increase in their benefits.[19]

In 2024, the Resolution Foundation forecast that child poverty would continue to increase over the next five years, estimating 170,000 more children would be in poverty in 2027–28 than in 2021–22. The New Economics Foundation estimated that if the welfare system the Conservatives inherited in 2010 had been left unchanged, 1.5 million fewer people would be in poverty. In 2022, a study by the University of Glasgow estimated that between 2012 and 2019, there were over 300,000 excess deaths in the most deprived areas of the country attributable to the Conservative government's austerity policies.[20]

When the Conservatives came to power food banks (charitable organisations distributing free food parcels) had been a marginal activity in the UK. However, the number of food banks started to increase very rapidly after 2010. The Trussell Trust, which supports the largest network of food banks in the UK, had around 35 food bank centres in 2010/11, which increased to 650 in 2013/14 and to nearly 1,300 in 2019/20. According to Full Fact government figures suggested around two million people lived in a household which used a food bank in 2021/22.[21] NHS figures revealed a surge in patients admitted with nutrient deficiencies – including scurvy and rickets – with nutrition-related diagnoses increasing by over 39% over the last decade.[22] The average five-year-old in 2024 was also a centimetre shorter than they were in 2010.[23]

The 41st British Social Attitudes report, published in June 2024, found that public concerns about poverty were at an all-time high, with 73% of people concerned about the rising levels of poverty in Britain. In 2024, the former prime minister Gordon Brown observed that the public rightly felt anger at the levels of poverty.[24]

Anger about lack of respect

An overwhelming 96% of voters say that respect for ordinary people is an important quality for a politician – the highest of any attribute tested by More in Common, and something repeated again and again in focus groups.[25]

People felt disrespected by Johnson's blatant lying but they were also upset by the lack of contrition from politicians such as Truss. In her eight-minute press conference after the sacking of Kwarteng, she offered no apology for the chaos she had caused but rather doubled down on her policies.[26] At the end of the conference as Truss rushed for the door, a journalist could be heard asking incredulously, "Aren't you going to say sorry?"

Truss appeared completely indifferent to the problems people had in paying household bills and was often insulting. In an interview with the *Daily Telegraph*, she said the people who claimed she crashed the economy, which was most of the public, "are either very stupid or very malevolent".[27]

The polling firm More in Common found the public felt disrespected by politicians who didn't deliver on their promises and prioritised their own interests against the interests of the country itself.[28] In September 2023, the Conservative Party had a net score of -39% on the question of whether the party respected people like them.[29]

An avalanche of anger

By 2024, the public's grievances were snowballing into an impending avalanche of anger. There was a collective feeling of relative deprivation as public services crumbled or closed, the physical infrastructure deteriorated, and living standards fell. Aristotle defined anger as a desire for revenge which will punish the offender. Removing the Conservative Party from office was no longer enough for voters – they wanted them punished.

George Eaton, the senior editor of the *New Statesman*, argued 2024 was going to be a punishment election.[30] *The Economist* agreed, saying "a punishment beating is on the cards" and quoted Tony Blair in 1997, saying that once the mood had turned against the government, electors became "nothing more than a mob seeking revenge".[31] Political commentators Caroline Wheeler and Harry Yorke argued in the *Sunday Times* that voters wanted "to punish the Tories as much as possible".[32]

Sherelle Jacobs, writing in the *Daily Telegraph*, went further, claiming that furious voters wanted to destroy the party.[33] In *The Spectator* Lionel Shriver claimed that even Conservative voters were furious with the party and so angry they were determined to punish it even if it meant electing a Labour government.[34]

By early 2024, senior Conservatives were openly acknowledging the anger. The former Scottish Conservative leader, Ruth Davidson, said that voters wanted "to see the party punished".[35] Iain Duncan Smith, the former Conservative leader and cabinet minister, claimed there was "a real anger with the government" which I "fully understand". He said the anger reflected the cost of living and levels of migration which were "good reasons why the public is angry, annoyed and fed up".[36] The cabinet minister, Michael Gove, also acknowledged the anger and the public's desire "to eject Conservatives everywhere".[37]

By 2024, the complete public narrative had become:

> *Nothing works anymore because the Conservatives are incompetent and they should be punished.*

It was a narrative that resonated with people and became the accepted story of the 2019–2024 Conservative government.

It was a story of the past, the present, and the future that explained the events of the previous five years, which spoke to people's experiences, and justified their frustration and anger. The shorthand version was simply – 'Nothing works anymore.'

Arguably by 2024 this public narrative had become so powerful and so all-encompassing that the upcoming election, whenever it was called, was going to be unwinnable for Sunak and the Conservative Party.

PART III

A PUNISHMENT ELECTION

11

LABOUR'S MING VASE STRATEGY

While this book is focused primarily on the Conservative Party, it is important to understand how Keir Starmer and his team changed the public's perceptions of the Labour Party and their development of an efficient vote strategy prior to the 2024 general election.

When he made his pitch to Labour Party members to be leader, Starmer appeared in many ways to be Corbyn's heir. He made ten radical pledges,[1] including:

- To increase income tax for the top 5% of earners and reverse the Tories' cuts in corporation tax
- The abolition of Universal Credit
- The abolition of tuition fees
- Nationalisation of public services, including rail, mail, energy, and water, which he said should not be making profits for shareholders
- To ensure full voting rights for EU nationals and to defend free movement as we left the EU
- Repealing the Trade Union Act

- The abolition of the House of Lords and its replacement with an elected chamber or regions and nations
- To end outsourcing in the NHS and local government

However, once elected as Labour's leader in April 2020, Starmer quickly distanced himself from Corbyn and sought to move the party to the centre. An editorial in *The Guardian* in October 2023 commented that "the most striking aspect of Starmer's leadership has been how quickly he distanced the party from its former leader, Jeremy Corbyn".[2]

In October 2020, Starmer suspended Corbyn from the parliamentary party for claiming that antisemitism within Labour had been "dramatically overstated for political reasons" when he responded to the Equality and Human Rights Commission report that the party had unlawfully discriminated against Jewish members.[3]

Starmer understood how to manage organisations and removed the Left from the critical decision-making bodies in the party. As early as November 2020, Starmer and his allies had secured a working majority on the party's National Executive Committee (NEC). The party's membership also changed under Starmer, as tens of thousands of former Corbyn supporters left and were replaced by new members loyal to Starmer.

Starmer's clear objective was to create a more efficient electoral coalition by moving the party to the right to reassure and appeal to more centrist voters in suburban seats. Labour's vote under Corbyn had been deep, narrow, and inefficient. Despite taking 40% of the vote nationally, it only won 262 parliamentary seats in 2017. In 2005, the party's vote had been far more efficient. Blair won just 35% of the vote share but 355 seats. Starmer's strategy was to create a broader and more geographically distributed coalition of voters.

The aim was to win seats from the Conservatives by converting former Conservative and Liberal Democrat voters while holding urban seats despite losing votes to the left. This meant appealing to voters in more suburban and less traditional Labour seats, even if it meant losing some votes on the left in urban Labour areas to the Greens and others. Labour's strengths in these areas meant there were few instances where this would cause it to lose seats. One example was Bristol Central, where concerns over Gaza and Labour's backtracking on their climate spending would put the sitting Labour MP at risk. However, there were far more seats where Labour could gain from a more efficient voting coalition.

As part of this strategy Starmer quickly backed away from his leadership pledges, saying on privatised industries that the future was "in regulating the market, changing the market, rather than simply taking things into public ownership".[4] Starmer also dropped his pledge to end outsourcing in the NHS and local government.

It was clear Starmer made pledges to win the leadership, which he ruthlessly planned to abandon once elected. Ian Leslie argues there was no honest route back to government, and Starmer had to make a left-focused pitch to win the leadership while being fully aware he could not use the same pitch to win an election. Leslie argued Starmer's 2024 election pitch was in "embarrassingly stark contrast" to his previous platform, but he was the only candidate capable of winning both a leadership contest and a general election.[5]

Starmer's actions might have demonstrated the ruthlessness you need to lead a political party, but they also created questions of trust with the public. When he became Labour leader, most of the public (59%) had no view on his trustworthiness, and only 19% distrusted him. The more the public got to see Starmer, the more they distrusted him. When it was revealed that Sue Gray had been offered a job as Labour's chief of staff, the percentage of the public who believed Starmer was untrustworthy jumped from 38% in April 2023 to 45% in May 2023.[6]

Two of the key members of Starmer's team were Pat McFadden and Morgan McSweeney. Pat McFadden had worked alongside Peter Mandelson and Alastair Campbell for Labour in 1997. McFadden had joined the Labour Party at Edinburgh University, citing Neil Kinnock taking on Militant in his 1985 Bournemouth conference speech as an inspiration. He had been sacked from Jeremy Corbyn's frontbench in January 2016. McFadden was seen as someone with extensive campaigning experience who was able to bring discipline to an election campaign.

Morgan McSweeney became the director of campaigns under Starmer and was later to become Starmer's head of political strategy. McSweeney had previously been the director of Labour Together, an organisation which sought to wrest control of Labour away from Corbyn and the Left. Labour Together included people who would become the most senior members of Keir Starmer's Shadow Cabinet, such as Rachel Reeves, Wes Streeting, Shabana Mahmood, and Steve Reed.

It is claimed that McSweeney identified Starmer as a potential leader who could remove Corbyn and move the party to the right, despite Starmer only becoming an MP in 2015. McSweeney became Starmer's leadership campaign manager after Corbyn stood down and used his detailed knowledge of the party's membership to put together the leadership pitch that would win over party members. After Starmer won the contest with 56% of the vote, McSweeney was appointed as chief of staff, making him the most senior adviser in the Labour Party.

Writing in *The Spectator*, Katy Balls argued that the Starmer team's objective was to "nurture a new model army of backbenchers". His team focused on the politics of local Labour branches and the selection of candidates for the top one hundred Labour target seats. The selection was "more tightly controlled than at any previous point in the party's history".[7] Those who held radical left views were purged from candidate lists and replaced with centrist candidates. As an example, North of Tyne's left-wing mayor was blocked from standing for re-election, apparently for appearing on stage with Ken Loach, who had been expelled from the party in 2021. Jon Trickett, MP for Normanton and Hemsworth, claimed in the Tribune that Starmer wasn't respecting the party's pluralist traditions, was being ruthless, and often used spurious reasons to block candidates.[8]

Many of the candidates who were selected had close associations with the Blair government including Douglas Alexander, a former Blair minister, and Emma Reynolds, a Blair special adviser. Party fundraising was also undertaken by former Blairites such as Waheed Alli, Lord Levy, and Lord Sainsbury.

The Ming vase strategy

Labour's strategy in the run-up to the 2024 election was characterised by many as a Ming vase strategy. This was a reference to Roy Jenkins's observation that Tony Blair took so much care not to make mistakes in 1997 that he resembled "a man carrying a priceless Ming vase across a highly polished floor".[9]

Starmer and his colleagues wanted to reassure centrist voters that the country would be safe in their hands and continued to distance themselves from the Corbyn era. In 2022, the shadow chancellor, Rachel Reeves, ditched the Labour Party's policy to nationalise water, saying: "Within our fiscal rules, to be spending billions of pounds on nationalising things, that just doesn't stack up against our fiscal rules."[10] In 2023, Labour MPs called again on Starmer to promise to nationalise water, but he refused, saying, despite evidence to the contrary, that the solution was better regulation.

The Labour strategists believed that if they could win seats in Scotland, they didn't need to significantly increase the party's vote share in other areas. As early as 2021, the leadership had squeezed out Richard Leonard, the party's Corbynite leader in Scotland, and replaced him with Anas Sarwar. Sarwar was the son of a millionaire businessman, Mohammad Sarwar, who had been the UK's first Muslim MP. Encouraged by the implosion of the SNP, Labour shifted significant resources and time to rebuild support in Scotland.

Labour advisers Deborah Mattinson and Claire Ainsley focused on a tight group of voters that they believed Labour needed to persuade to win the election, who they called "hero voters".[11] These were family-orientated, patriotic voters, who they felt were personified by Keir Starmer himself, who had grown up in a semi-detached house with hard-working parents who struggled financially at times. Mattinson and Ainsley believed the party had to focus on their concerns, including affordable housing, reliable public services, and job security.

Starmer and his shadow chancellor Rachel Reeves worked particularly hard to reassure the public that they were not a tax and spend party. As part of this reassurance strategy, Reeves committed the party to the chancellor Jeremy Hunt's main fiscal rule, namely to cut debt as a share of national income in five years, severely restricting the government's ability to borrow. The Labour Party also supported Hunt's cuts in National Insurance from 12p to 8p, despite it requiring significant cuts in public services in the absence of other tax rises. The *Financial Times* commented that Labour appeared very close to the Conservatives regarding tax measures and fiscal rules.[12]

In April 2024, Starmer outlined to the public the six initial steps Labour would take if they won power. These were:

- Sticking to tough spending rules in order to deliver economic stability
- Setting up Great British Energy, a publicly owned clean power energy company
- Cutting NHS waiting lists by providing 40,000 more appointments each week – funded by tackling tax avoidance and non-dom loopholes
- Launching a border security command to stop the gangs arranging small boat crossings
- Providing more neighbourhood police officers to reduce antisocial behaviour and introducing new penalties for offenders
- Recruiting 6,500 teachers, paid for through ending tax breaks for private schools.

The six steps were a marked contrast to the ten pledges that Starmer had made in his campaign to be Labour leader.[13] However, Peter Kellner argued that one of Starmer's main achievements was de-toxifying Labour because that unlocked "the handcuffs that tied millions of reluctant voters to the Conservatives", allowing them the freedom to vote against the Conservatives comfortable in the knowledge that Labour would provide "a pragmatic government led by an experienced public servant".[14]

Vindication – the May 2024 local elections

On 2 May 2024, a series of elections were held, including local elections, the Blackpool South by-election, elections for police and crime commissioners, and also elections for 11 regional and metropolitan mayors. On the day of the election, *The Times* published a poll putting Labour 26 points ahead, and analysts anticipated heavy losses for the Conservatives.

The scale of the Conservatives' defeat was slowly revealed over three days of counting, which culminated in the loss of the West Midlands mayoralty on Saturday evening. By the end of the counting, the Conservatives had lost 474 seats, almost half of the council seats they were defending. Labour gained 186 seats, the Liberal Democrats 104, independents 93, and the Greens 74. In total, the Conservatives lost control of 12 councils.[15]

The Conservatives also lost 10 of the 11 mayoral elections but held on in Tees Valley despite a large swing against Ben Houchen. Tory rebels had decided in advance only to move against Sunak if the party lost both the West Midlands and Tees Valley mayoralties. Ben Houchen's victory appeared to be enough to save Sunak, despite the fact that the swing against Houchen, at 16.5%, was larger than the 3% swing against Andy Street that caused him to lose the West Midlands contest.

The Conservatives retained 19 of the police and crime commissioner posts they had held before the elections but lost 10 as their support fell on average by 10.5 points.[16]

Post-election analysis revealed that the fall in Conservative support was higher in the seats they were defending. In wards where Labour were second to the Conservatives, the Liberal Democrat votes didn't increase, while Labour were up nearly 9%. In wards where the Liberal Democrats were second, their vote was up nearly 6%, while Labour's was up just 2%. This was clear evidence that voters were prepared to tactically support parties that were most likely to defeat the Conservatives. This tactical voting enabled the Liberal Democrats to make gains in areas such as Dorset and Wokingham. The Greens also had their best-ever local election results based on vote share. The level of tactical voting, if repeated in a general election, would cause the Conservatives to lose a large number of previously safe seats.

Worryingly for the Tories, one in five voters said they would be prepared to vote tactically in the general election, with three-quarters saying they would do so to stop a Conservative from winning their seat.[17] To cater for these tactical voters a plethora of websites were set up to identify the party best placed in individual constituencies to beat the Conservatives. These included Tactical Voting, Stop the Tories, and Best for Britain. Naomi Smith, CEO of Best for Britain and founder of the tactical voting platform GetVoting.org, claimed that over ten million people were willing to vote tactically for change in 2024.[18]

There was more worrying news for the Conservatives when the BBC's Nick Eardley highlighted data showing that in council seats where Reform stood candidates, the Conservative vote was down 19 percentage points compared to the result in 2021. The analysis appeared to confirm opinion poll findings that Reform were taking their support overwhelmingly from the Tories, unlike UKIP a decade earlier, which had attracted voters from across the board.

Professor Rob Ford argued that 2 May was, "on any metric, the Conservatives' worst performance in local council elections for a generation".[19] This was a view shared by the *Financial Times* which claimed: "The results for Rishi Sunak's Conservatives in polls in England and Wales on Thursday were about as bad as they could have been ... they are not seen as delivering on key issues for voters in the political centre, including the cost of living and dismal public services."[20]

The Conservatives also lost the Blackpool South by-election to Labour with a huge 26% swing, the third-largest ever recorded at the time. Reform split the Conservative vote as 16.9% of people voted for the party, putting them less than 1%

behind the Conservatives. It was a clear indication of the damage Reform could do to the Conservatives in a general election. Peter Kellner observed that the Conservative share of the vote at 17.5% was "its lowest for at least 100 years in a seat they were defending, replacing Dudley West (18.7% in 1994) as the occupant of this undesirable pedestal".[21]

Kellner argued that the Conservatives had to squeeze Reform's support to avoid a catastrophic landslide defeat at the general election and that if they failed, the Conservative prospects were "truly dreadful".[22]

On Conservative Home, William Atkinson argued that "The voters are sick of us and want us out."[23] He compared the party's situation to that facing Captain Blackadder in the last episode of *Blackadder Goes Forth*, the one where the men finally leave the trench and walk into machine gunfire as the scene dissolves into a field of poppies.[24]

Some Conservative Party members put their hope in the large pool of undecided voters, 60% of whom supported the party in 2019, and in winning back Reform voters. However, the *Financial Times* argued that looking to the party's right was an inefficient way for the Tories to campaign in a general election. The paper argued that winning back 7 percentage points from Reform would only allow the party to hold 186 seats whereas getting back 7 percentage points from Labour would give the Tories 247 seats and potentially deny Starmer a majority.[25]

Professor Rob Ford noted that in areas where the Tories were out of the running the voters had switched in large numbers to the Greens, Reform, and local independents. He wrote in *The Guardian* that this fragmentation "confirms what we see in polling: a restive electorate that is angry at the Conservatives, unenthused by Labour and open to new alternatives".[26] Polls reported that Keir Starmer, while being more popular than Rishi Sunak, was as unpopular as John

Major in 1997. The Labour MP, Jess Phillips, agreed that Labour had "an enthusiasm problem".[27]

Overall support for Labour in the May 2024 council elections was down 1% on the previous year. Labour also lost control of Oldham, and its deputy leader in Manchester lost his seat. The party particularly lost support in areas with large Muslim populations, while in urban areas it lost seats disproportionately to the Greens.

Keir Starmer had gone on the record saying that Labour needed to win Harlow to win a general election, but the party failed to take control of the council. However, the local election results confirmed that Starmer's strategy of moving to the centre and building a more efficient geographical vote was working. The Labour Party gained votes in the bellwether seats that traditionally determine general elections. Labour won councils including Redditch, Nuneaton and Bedworth, and Tamworth. It also gained seats in those it already held such as Milton Keynes, Reading, and Swindon. Labour also won Rushmoor, the home of the British Army, an area that had never had a Labour majority council before.

Prior to the local elections, John Curtice had argued that Labour needed to be 14 points ahead of the Conservatives to gain a parliamentary majority of just one. However, the local elections revealed that the increase in the Labour vote was concentrated in Conservative-held areas. Data from Lewis Baston showed that the swing was 6.3% in Labour-held wards and 11.3% in Conservative-held wards.[28] This meant the Labour vote could be far more efficient at winning Conservative seats, particularly when combined with large-scale tactical voting.

Tim Shipman, chief political commentator of the *Sunday Times*, argued that constructing this more efficient distribution of the party's vote had been Keir Starmer's key objective when he became leader.[29] The strategy was widely seen as moving the party to the right to win over former Conservative and

Liberal Democrat voters in potentially winnable seats while acknowledging it would lose votes on the left. The theory was that Labour's lead was so large in most urban areas that it could afford to lose votes but still win the seats.

Based on the local election results, Labour's Morgan McSweeney argued the party could win a majority with just a six-point lead. It was a view shared by the pollster James Kanagasooriam, who argued Labour's increased vote efficiency, as demonstrated in the May local elections, meant it would need less than a double-figure popular vote lead to win a majority in a general election.[30]

After the election, support for Rishi Sunak's Conservatives fell further. By the start of June 2024, support for the Conservatives was just 21%.[31] The week after the local elections the Conservative MP for Dover, Natalie Elphicke, crossed the floor to join Labour. Elphicke was a member of the European Research Group and on the right of the party. Steve Baker MP tweeted: "I have been searching in vain for a Conservative MP who thinks themself to the right of Natalie Elphicke."[32]

Neil Kinnock was moved to say even broad churches have walls. Other Labour Party members started to ask if there was room for Elphicke in the party, why there was no room for Diane Abbott, who had been suspended for over a year for comments which she had apologised for. For Starmer, it was exactly the comparison he wanted to reassure swing voters. His Labour Party was now one which welcomed right-wing Conservatives but which wouldn't admit left-wing socialists such as Diane Abbott or Jeremy Corbyn.

12

SUNAK CALLS AN EARLY ELECTION

On the morning of Wednesday, 22 May 2024, there was growing speculation that Sunak would call a July election. The latest government borrowing figures had been released, and Robert Peston argued the latest financial forecasts gave Sunak limited room for manoeuvre, meaning there was no scope for a tax giveaway in the autumn. The pressures on public spending and services were also mounting. The asylum budget was overspending by billions of pounds, and the government feared that the failure to get the Rwanda scheme off the ground would mean the numbers of asylum seekers crossing the Channel were likely to increase. To make things worse for the government, the public sector pay review bodies were about to announce a recommended pay increase of around 5% for public sector workers when the government had only budgeted for 2%.

With febrile speculation in Westminster, the SNP's Stephen Flynn asked Sunak directly at Prime Minister's Questions if he intended to call a summer election. Sunak teased MPs with his reply, saying there was "going to be a general election in the second half of this year". July was in the second half of the year. By 4.26 pm there was news that Sunak was going to give a statement outside Downing Street. Three minutes later, a BBC breaking news alert appeared on mobile phones across the country saying, "Sunak set to call a summer election."

As journalists gathered outside 10 Downing Street, the heavens opened and heavy rain drenched the waiting crowd. At 5.13 pm Sunak walked out to the waiting lectern to confirm the election would be held on 4 July 2024. It was difficult to hear Sunak through the rain and above the sounds of 'Things can only get better' being blasted out by the infamous Steve Bray, the anti-Brexit activist, on his sound system at the end of the street. Sunak, without the cover of an umbrella, was getting soaked. His suit became waterlogged and shiny, his shoulders reflecting the lights of the surrounding film crews. He looked broken and bedraggled as he turned and walked back inside. Robert Peston was moved to say he felt sorry for him. It was to be one of the defining images of a badly managed campaign.

The BBC's chief political correspondent said he had two observations on the speech. "Rishi Sunak was absolutely sodden, and it was hard to hear him over the sound of a disrupter blaring music from outside Downing Street."[1] The content of Sunak's speech was completely overshadowed by the context.

In an emergency podcast for 'The Rest is Politics', Rory Stewart called the decision "suicide". The political commentator Steve Richards said it was "the worst prime ministerial launch of an election campaign in modern times. Even PMs doomed to defeat have managed to start the gun with a sense of elegant purpose."[2] Tim Montgomerie, the founder of the Conservative Home website, called it "disastrous", adding MPs "weren't expecting this. They don't think the timing's right."[3] Other commentators pointed out that the only previous July election in the twentieth century was 1945 when the Tories lost 189 seats.

There was a growing sense of incredulity from Conservative MPs that Sunak had bounced them into an election for which they appeared ill-prepared. Rather than consulting the cabinet, Sunak had gone directly to the King and informed his cabinet colleagues only after the decision had been taken. Some suggested this was because, had they had advance notice, the cabinet may have tried to stop him. Conservative central office appeared completely unprepared for an election. They had still not selected over a quarter of their candidates.

Twitter was alight with reports of "furious" Conservative MPs. Rachel Cunliffe, associate political editor at the *New Statesman*, tweeted, "It's hard to overstate just how upset and frustrated Conservative MPs and campaigners are right now." The comments she shared from Conservative MPs included: "It's a terrible idea", "cruel", "heartbreaking", "I don't get it", "really odd", "don't even start", "what a shitshow", "he's given up" and "we deserve to lose".[4] Kitty Donaldson, chief political commentator at *The Independent*, received a message from a Tory MP saying, "This is mad." Another Conservative MP said, "I just don't understand it. The economy is improving. Why not give that more time to bed in?"[5]

Isaac Levido, the Conservative Party's political strategist, had urged the PM to go long and wait until October or November to give more time to show the economy was improving and let the Bank of England cut interest rates. However, Sunak's close advisers including his chief of staff Liam Booth-Smith and his political secretary James Forsyth won the argument for a July election.[6]

The *Financial Times* poll tracker on the day the election was called put support for Labour at 44%, Conservatives at 23%, Reform at 11.6%, Liberal Democrats at 9.5% and the Greens at

6.6%. It was the largest lead any opposition party had held at the calling of an election since 1997. However, the Conservative strategists felt the Labour lead might be overstated by the polls, and the real lead might only be 10 to 12 points. Given that polls typically narrow during a campaign, there was a view that the government could change the narrative once the polls started narrowing and allow the party to start building some momentum. However, it was a risky strategy. In the previous six general elections where the government was behind at the point an election was called, the average swing to the government was just 5.1 points. No governing party had ever clawed back a 20-point polling deficit just six weeks from an election.

Forsyth and Booth-Smith believed by going early Sunak could seize the agenda. They were worried that NHS waiting lists would get worse and illegal migrant boat crossings would increase over the summer. There was also a view they could catch Reform on the hop as they would have limited time to get their resources and candidates together. Finally, they were concerned that if Sunak delayed, the autumn conversations would be dominated by when the election was going to be called, with Sunak being accused of clinging on to power while there was a growing clamour for change. Daniel Finkelstein agreed that the 'time for a change' feeling would only get stronger as the year progressed, saying, "This is as good as it gets however bad it is."[7]

The Conservative strategists also felt it would be a good time to take on the SNP, which had only recently appointed John Swinney as its leader and whose polling was at its worst in a decade. However, it was arguable that Labour would be the major beneficiaries of the SNP's weakness.

When the election was called, the Conservatives were behind Labour on who the public thought would be best to manage the economy[8] and Sunak's personal net favourability rating was -51, his lowest ever as prime minister.[9] Immediately after the election was called Sunak's ratings fell still further. His net satisfaction rating, according to Ipsos, was -53. The previous lowest for a prime minister going into an election had been John Major in 1997, with a rating of -24.[10] The level of dissatisfaction with Sunak was the highest since Ipsos started the survey in 1979.

On the same day that Sunak called the election, the government instructed the authorities to send fewer people to prison as they were effectively full and announced that people should stockpile food for emergencies. It was not a good omen.

One of the Prime Minister's main trump cards is his or her ability to determine when the election is called. The irony of Sunak's decision to call a snap summer election was that Labour were more prepared than the Conservatives. The Labour Party had been constantly watching for signs of an election being called early. A sudden rash of bets shortened the betting odds on a July election which caught the attention of the Labour Party's strategists. Morgan McSweeney felt sure the election was going to be called for 4 July[11] and he put the party on high alert. The day before Sunak called the election Labour Party candidates were preparing their teams and putting into action their social media campaigns.

At 5.46 pm on 22 May 2024, just half an hour after Sunak had appeared in the rain in Downing Street, Starmer appeared indoors in the dry, flanked by two Union Jack flags. He said this was the moment the country has been waiting for, "the opportunity for change". He promised that Labour would "return Britain to the service of working people" and bring a period of stability. He finished with an appeal for people to help Labour "stop the chaos".[12]

What is a good campaign?

Before we review the 2024 election campaign, it is worth reminding ourselves about the attributes of a good campaign. In my book *The Fall of the Red Wall,*[13] I argued that successful election campaigns address six critical elements, namely:

- A vision for the country that resonates with voters.
- Establishing credibility to run the economy and handle big issues like security.
- Promoting a leader that is seen as authentic and a competent prime minister.
- Framing the key questions that will define the election, the core things that voters will be thinking about when they enter the polling booth.
- A strong overarching narrative that addresses the deep concerns of the electorate. Individual policies are no match for the overarching narrative.
- An organisation that can translate support into votes. This includes knowing who your voters are, targeting them and establishing a strong get-out-the-vote operation.

According to Philip Gould, Tony Blair's political pollster and analyst, "The most important thing a party must do in a campaign is listen to what the voters are saying."[14] Gould pioneered the use of focus groups, which have become increasingly important to campaigns to help them understand the core concerns of voters qualitatively.

Focus groups don't simply allow politicians to understand voters, they allow them to identify persuadable voters and, importantly, the language and phraseology to connect with them. The slogan 'get Brexit done' emerged from focus groups run prior to the 2019 Conservative campaign. It is essential for parties to spend time and resources testing, analysing, and honing their messages in focus groups.

Alastair Campbell has argued persuasively that the public decides the key questions in an election. Therefore, Campbell's advice to political parties is "don't waste time trying to change the question, focus instead on getting the right answer that wins support whilst also reflecting your values".[15] This requires listening carefully to polling and focus groups with a view to understanding the electorate and current trends better than the opposition. Through this understanding, campaigns can craft a core overarching narrative and strategy that resonates with voter perceptions. Campbell argues the 1997 Labour slogan 'New Labour, New Britain' encapsulated the party's core strategy to change the country.

Strategists must develop simple, shareable messaging, and a concise narrative, that reflects the party's overall campaign narrative. This needs to connect the past and present with a desirable future. This campaign messaging should use everyday language, such as Margaret Thatcher's message that 'You cannot spend what you haven't earned', which was used to reinforce an overall narrative about controlling public spending.

Election strategists must craft a concise yet broad narrative that accommodates multiple stories and allows voters to insert their own experiences. The power of broad narratives lies in their ability to incorporate diverse stories that reinforce the overall message.

Effective party positioning also requires consistent repetition of campaign messages, as the public pays little attention to political discussions. Despite Starmer and Labour constantly emphasising his normal upbringing by saying that his dad was a toolmaker, by the end of the campaign, only 27% of the public knew this.[16]

Interestingly, academic studies have consistently found that political campaigns have limited persuasion effects, particularly on opposition voters. This suggests that party campaign resources might be more effectively allocated to identifying and mobilising the party's core voters to 'get the vote out'. The increasing adoption of targeted and efficient vote strategies places significant emphasis on identifying potential voters and ensuring they turn out to vote.

13

THE 2024 ELECTION CAMPAIGN

Clear Plan > Bold Action > Secure Future.[1]

— CONSERVATIVE PARTY MANIFESTO 2024

The election was always going to be a formidable challenge for the Conservatives whenever it was held. The party had been in power for 14 years, and no party had ever won five consecutive elections. It had also been in power during some turbulent years, including the COVID-19 pandemic.

At the cabinet meeting on 22 May 2024, Sunak told his colleagues it was time to be bold, saying, "We have got to own the choice and frame the choice."[2]

For challenger parties, a core campaign narrative is invariably the need for change, while for incumbent parties, the core argument is almost always that change is risky, and continuity will lead to a better future. The Conservative strategy was to say the government's plan was working and point to inflation, which had fallen to 2.3%, while arguing Starmer had no plan. Sunak used this framing on the *Today* programme on 23 May 2024, when he said the election was a choice between continuing with his plan, which he argued was working, or the uncertainty and risks of a Labour government. He emphasised the importance of defence and his commitment to raise defence spending to 2.5% of GDP. The first Conservative election advertisement consisted of a blue and red panel. On the blue side, it said, 'Stick with Rishi's clear plan', and on the red side it said, 'Risk it all with no plan'.

The Conservatives had been concerned that Reform would split their vote, and there had been tentative and unsuccessful attempts at brokering a deal. Sunak's team hoped the decision to call a snap election would surprise the Reform Party, who would not be ready for an election. Their plan appeared to work when, on the morning of 23 May 2024, Nigel Farage announced he would not be standing as a candidate, saying, "I will do my bit to help in the campaign, but it is not the right time for me to go any further than that."

In the 2019 election, 72% of people said Brexit was one of the most important issues facing the country. In 2024 it was just 3%.[3] The public's key concerns were the cost of living, the NHS, immigration, and Channel crossings.[4] All areas where the Tories' performance was exceptionally weak.

Lee Cain, the former 10 Downing Street communications director, thought the fundamental public concerns in 2024 meant that the Tories were staring at a heavy defeat. He observed, "All elections are about change or more of the same, and just from the research that we've been doing, you can see that the public is crying out for change in all of the core battlegrounds of an election." Across all major policy areas, from immigration and the NHS to crime, Cain argued the public felt things were worse than in 2019 and certainly worse than in 2010. Cain commented, "The Tory brand is in a terrible place."[5]

It was always going to be difficult for the Conservatives to claim their plan was working and things were improving. People simply didn't believe things were getting better. NHS waiting lists had increased, immigration had soared, and inflation had risen to over 10%. Even though it had fallen back, it only meant prices were increasing less slowly. Prices were still significantly up from a few years earlier. The public believed 'nothing worked anymore' after 14 years of Conservative government.[6]

Lord Gavin Barwell, the Downing Street chief of staff during Theresa May's premiership, argued that the Conservatives found it difficult to craft a "consistent narrative" or vision for the country given the party's constantly changing leadership.

Internally, the party was struggling to raise money, which is considerably harder when you are expected to lose an election heavily. The party's fundraising lagged behind previous election campaigns and, importantly, behind the Labour Party, which meant they would be outspent on digital advertising. This mattered as an Ofcom survey in 2023 found that 10% of people aged 16-plus got their news from TikTok, ahead of BBC Radio 1 and similar to *The Guardian*.[7] Studies estimated that 45% of British internet users were using the app for an average of 28 minutes daily.[8] Traditional outlets were getting an average of 245,000 views per TikTok video but relatively low engagement at 14,000 a video.

Labour spent heavily on social media adverts and far more than other parties. Who Targets Me estimated the party spent over £2.4m during the campaign.[9] Labour strategists were of the view that most TikTok users were already on their side and their aim was to reach swing voters. This was confirmed by Deltapoll surveys, which found if someone was on TikTok, they were already more likely to vote Labour. *The Guardian* reported that the objective of the party's TikTok strategy was to get younger people to download videos and share them in family WhatsApp groups which might reach swing voters.[10] Reform also made inroads with younger people on TikTok, accounting for 7 of the top 13 political accounts.

Sunak's weaknesses as a campaigner were quickly revealed as the campaign got underway. On a trip to Wales, he sought to develop some banter with voters by asking them if they were looking forward to the football, apparently unaware that Wales had not qualified for the European Championships. Sunak also visited the Titanic dockyard on the same day many of his MPs were jumping ship and deciding not to fight a difficult election. A local journalist, James McCarthy, asked Sunak the obvious question: "We are just yards away from where the Titanic was built and designed; are you captaining a sinking ship going into this election?" Sunak simply grimaced and ignored the question.

On Saturday, 25 May 2024, several senior Conservative MPs, including Michael Gove and Andrea Leadsom, resigned, saying they would not be standing in the election. Another Tory MP resigned and encouraged people to vote for the Reform Party. On the same weekend, the Conservatives announced they would introduce a form of national service which would be funded by abolishing the Shared Prosperity Fund, which was a core source of levelling-up investments. It symbolised the party's complete abandonment of the levelling-up promises made by Johnson in the previous election. The national service proposal did not land well with young people even though it was supported by older people. During a walkabout, Rishi Sunak was asked on camera by 16-year-old Henry why he hated young people. The video clip went viral on TikTok.

The following week a leaked internal Conservative poll revealed that more than 100 Tory MPs could lose their seats solely due to people voting Reform.[11] This explained why the party sought to shore up its vote with pensioners. The freezing of tax allowances meant that the basic state pension would soon be higher than the tax-free allowance, dragging millions of pensioners into paying tax. To avoid this, the party promised to give pensioners an additional tax allowance worth £100 a year.

The unresolved and ongoing dispute with junior doctors burst back into life when a five-day walkout was announced and would take place from 27 June to 2 July, just two days before the election.

On 28 May, a JLP poll put the Labour lead at just 12 points, narrowing from 15 a month earlier. JLP used a new methodology based on machine learning to predict how people who said they were undecided would behave. They mapped undecided voters onto political parties by seeing how they responded to certain policies. According to Callum Hunter at JLP, "If a voter says they like Sunak, thinks the Conservatives are better on cutting crime and voted Conservative at the last election, then we predict they will likely vote Conservative again – even if they claim they are unsure about who they are going to vote for this time."[12]

The JLP poll was exactly what Levido and the Conservative strategists had been hoping for. It revealed the polls were narrowing and Labour's lead was falling. They anticipated building momentum around the poll and creating a narrative that the public was getting behind Sunak. This momentum was critical. As New Labour's strategist Philip Gould had argued, "in politics either you have momentum or you are losing momentum, there is no middle way".[13]

The Conservative strategy, however, was immediately

demolished by a cascade of other polls that showed the Labour lead growing. On 29 May, a YouGov poll for *Sky News* put the Labour lead at 27 points (47 to 20) after the first week of the campaign.[14] Survation's poll also revealed that Labour had increased their lead to 23 points (47 to 23) up from 19. On 3 June, the first YouGov MRP poll of the campaign forecast that Labour were on track to beat Tony Blair's 1997 landslide.[15]

The polls had a direct impact on the election narrative and campaign strategies. The polls that put Labour on 47%, which were later found to have drastically overestimated the party's support, undermined the Tory messages about the election narrowing and instead gave momentum to a counter-narrative that there was huge and growing public support for Labour.

According to More in Common, the Tories were holding onto 70% of their 2019 most comfortable voters but only 40% of their 2019 economically insecure voters who were most impacted by the cost-of-living crisis. Sunak said his aim was to build an "ownership society" while at the same time admitting that owning a home in Britain had become more difficult under the Conservatives.[16] The Conservative manifesto said the party would build 1.6m homes in the next parliament and make permanent the stamp duty threshold of £425,000, meaning that about eight in ten buyers would not pay it.

Across the polls as a whole there were no signs of the polls narrowing. Joe Twyman, director of Deltapoll, said that despite the noise surrounding the polls during the first full week of the campaign, the reality is "all pollsters are showing no significant change ... The situation [for the Tories] is as bad as it was at the start of the campaign. If the gap is 27 points, as YouGov has it, it's very, very, very bad for the Tories."[17] Even if JLP was correct that the lead was only 12 points, it meant a three-figure Labour majority.

In an attempt to change the national mood, the

Conservative Party launched a lengthy kitchen-sink manifesto that threw a myriad of different policies at the public including:

- Abolition of National Insurance for the self-employed
- Increase the tax-free personal allowance for pensioners
- Tougher sentences for knife crime, grooming, and assaults against shop workers
- The building of four new prisons that had been previously promised but not built
- Increase the number of police officers by 8,000
- Regularly fly asylum seekers to Rwanda
- Increase defence spending to 2.5% of GDP
- Fund 100,000 new apprenticeships
- Introduce a ban on mobile phones in schools
- Treble offshore wind power as part of their commitment to reach net zero by 2050
- Make £17bn of unspecified public spending cuts to fund their manifesto pledges
- Increase the number of doctors and nurses by 120,000
- Cap social care costs at £86,000
- Introduce a legal cap on migration
- A further 2p cut in National Insurance with a long-term plan to abolish it completely
- 30 hours of free childcare a week for eligible families

The problem with announcing so many different policies, rather than a clear vision with a concise narrative, was that nothing cut through with the public. YouGov found that even where there was strong support for some individual Tory policies, such as national service and increasing tax thresholds for pensioners,[18] these were viewed negatively when proposed by the Conservatives. Many people simply didn't believe the party would deliver on its promises. In their book *The Politics of Competence*, Will Jennings and Jane Green pointed out that a government which loses public trust in its competence will lose public trust across the policy agenda.[19] Luke Tryl argued that the party hadn't just alienated a single group but had lost trust across the board, saying, "It's hard to see an asset they have to bring people back."[20]

It is also arguable that the Tory brand had been so badly damaged by the time of the election that voters were no longer prepared to listen to Sunak or his claims that his plan was working. On 19 June 2024, inflation fell to 2%. Sunak claimed this was clear evidence that his plan was working and urged voters not to risk the future with Labour. However, the public was unmoved. A week later, the percentage of people who felt the Conservatives were best placed to manage the economy fell from 22% to 21%.

The Labour strategy

> *At this election we can change Britain.*[21]
>
> — LABOUR PARTY MANIFESTO 2024

The core overarching Labour narrative was 'time for a change'. It carried clear echoes of the party's election campaign in 1997, after 18 years of Conservative government.

The day after the election was called, Labour launched its first advert, which had Starmer front and centre saying, "It's time for change." The video set out Labour's key messages:

- After 14 years of the Conservatives, nothing seems to work anymore; it's time for change.
- We need to stop the chaos, turn the page, and start to rebuild our country.

Labour's first misstep of the campaign occurred when rumours started to spread that the party would stop Diane Abbott, the first black woman MP, from standing as a Labour candidate. Abbott had been suspended for comments she had made in 2023 and for which she had apologised. The party line was the whip had not been restored to her as there was an ongoing investigation. However, on *Newsnight*, Victoria Derbyshire revealed Labour's investigation had actually been completed five months earlier, and Abbott had been given a 'formal warning' in December 2023.[22]

Under pressure, the party restored the whip to Abbott but would not confirm whether she could stand as a Labour MP. One of Labour's staff then briefed *The Times* that Abbott was going to be banned from standing as a Labour candidate in the seat where she had been an MP for 37 years. The briefing played to Starmer's narrative about a changed Labour Party that had no place for the likes of Abbott and which he believed would be popular with the public. Starmer's view was supported by a YouGov poll which found 37% of Britons thought the Labour Party was right to ban Abbott from standing as a candidate, with just 21% believing it was wrong. However, the decision created a furious reaction from many party members.

The Independent's chief political commentator, John Rentoul, observed that Keir Starmer and his NEC were more ruthless in imposing his favoured candidates on local parties than either Tony Blair or Gordon Brown had been. Hilary Armstrong, Blair's chief whip, had once suggested to Blair that he should deselect Jeremy Corbyn, but Blair, despite having a large majority, felt the party could "tolerate that level of difference".[23] Starmer's NEC found reasons to stop left-wing Corbyn-supporting MPs from standing again and ruthlessly imposed their own loyalists, including some NEC members, as parliamentary candidates in 22 constituencies without consulting local members.

When asked about Abbott, Starmer said that no decision had been taken and it was a matter for the NEC, who had control of the selection process. This was dancing around a technicality. John Rentoul observed that Starmer had clearly already decided what would happen at the NEC meeting. Despite this Starmer continued to claim that no decision had been taken and the party had to go through a process to decide if she could stand. Many on the left feared the party was simply delaying until it became too late for Abbott to run as an independent.

The row distracted from Labour's election campaign, with public figures such as Lenny Henry and David Harewood writing to *The Guardian* saying Abbott should be able to stand. The Diane Abbott affair was raised unprompted in a focus group held in North Swindon on 30 May 2024. The participants said it raised questions about Keir Starmer's trustworthiness and character.[24]

"I worry if I was going to change from one party to another, would I trust somebody that's basically stabbing their own party member in the back?" Others thought it reflected badly on Starmer if this is how "he would treat his own". Starmer and Labour's behaviour were seen as "underhanded", "playing games" and having "messed around" Abbott.

The participants didn't support Abbott but felt she was being dealt with unfairly. Luke Tryl of More in Common, which ran a series of focus groups, said that the principle of unfairness jarred with people. They didn't like that Abbott had done what she was asked by issuing an apology and undergoing training, and then – as they saw it – the goalposts were changed. They believed Abbott was being barred because she was too left wing and didn't think that was a legitimate reason.

As the row dragged on, Angela Rayner went public, saying she thought Abbott should be able to stand if she wanted to. Finally, on 31 May 2024, Starmer was forced to shut down the issue as it had become a major distraction. It was critical to get the focus of the campaign back onto how the Conservative chaos had broken Britain. Starmer told journalists that she would be free to stand as an MP if she wanted to.

The Labour Party manifesto

On Monday 10 May 2024, the polls gave Labour a larger lead than at the same point in the campaign in 1997. Two days later, Keir Starmer launched the Labour Manifesto, which had a photo of him in his rolled-up shirt sleeves on the cover, looking like he meant business and resembling Michael Douglas on the poster for the 1993 film *Falling Down*. Alongside the image of Starmer was the single word 'Change'.

Stephen Bush commented that the word 'Change' on the cover was far more important than the 23,000 words inside. It set out the overarching narrative of the Labour campaign.

The single word 'change' was, in many ways, an extension of the Ming vase strategy. It had the benefit of being vague about what change meant, but to Labour's strategist McSweeney, this was an advantage. Everybody who wanted change could get behind it, even if they wanted different types of change. While it wasn't explicit what change meant, Stephen Bush argued that "It's pretty obvious that most people think it means the NHS waiting list coming down, being able to drink the water from their tap without worrying they are going to get ill, victims of crime not waiting years for their day in court and so on."[25]

Daniel Finkelstein joked that the core Starmer message was 'Britain is broken and we will do nothing about it'. However, he felt it was actually a good electoral strategy as it summed up the mood of the country, as the public believed things were broken and the Tories had to be removed from office, but they didn't want a radical government.

Labour did not set out a big optimistic vision, as Blair had done in 1997. The manifesto referenced the six initial and modest steps that Starmer had previously outlined and left the running on major policy announcements to the Tories. Labour decided to run a defensive campaign, effectively seeking to steal the Tories' clothes on economic management, crime, defence, and patriotism. Morgan McSweeney continually warned Labour not to be complacent and to promise only things they could fund.

A key part of the defensive strategy was to reassure the public on taxes. Labour explicitly ruled out changes to income tax, National Insurance, corporation tax, and VAT, which constituted 71% of all tax income in 2022/23. These promises would severely limit the party's ability to raise tax income when in government, but the initial objective was to reassure voters and win the election. Decisions on how to manage the hole in public finances could come later.

On Tuesday, 29 May 2024, the shadow chancellor Rachel Reeves announced she didn't need any tax rises to fund Labour's programme and said again that there wouldn't be income tax or National Insurance rises. The party was also clear it would not reverse the 4% reduction in National Insurance that had been announced by Jeremy Hunt. Neither party explained how the £20bn cost of the reductions would be met. Hunt's forward budget implied the cost would be met through unidentified public spending cuts.

Starmer wrapped himself in the Union Jack and focused on issues such as defence. On 3 June, the Labour Party launched its defence policies with the party's website displaying a photo of Starmer in a camouflage jacket standing next to a British soldier.[26] At the Fusilier Museum in Bury, the Labour leader was surrounded by military veterans who were standing as Labour candidates in the election, many with medals pinned to their chests. At the launch, Starmer announced he would maintain the country's nuclear deterrent and use it if required.

Many commentators joked about Labour events being draped in the Union Jack. However, Labour's constant use of the flag everywhere appeared to work. A More in Common poll found voters thought the Labour Party under Starmer was more patriotic than the Tories.[27]

As the campaign progressed, Owen Winter, a political data scientist at *The Economist*, conducted an analysis of where Labour were sending activists from their 'How to help' webpage. He found Labour were targeting Tory seats with large majorities, including all Tory seats with majorities of up to 28%, suggesting Labour knew they were well ahead.

Winter also observed that Labour were directing activists "to some of its safest seats in the country, constituencies where Indian, Pakistani and Bangladeshi people make up more than 30% of the population".[28] His analysis suggested that Labour were seriously worried about Muslim voters. A large part of the party's problem with Muslim voters stemmed from Starmer's position on Gaza and, in particular, an interview he gave to LBC in October 2023[29], where he said Israel had the right to withhold power and water from Gaza. The scale of the backlash had forced Starmer to backpedal and claim what he meant was that Israel had the right to self-defence. Internal polling revealed the party was losing the support of British Muslim voters.

The Labour Party had anticipated that the price of its more efficient vote strategy, where it sought to appeal to more centrist voters in suburban seats, would cause it to lose some votes to more progressive parties in urban areas. Internal polling found that the party was losing a lot of support to the Greens in cities, which prompted some concern in Labour circles about the number of young people who might vote Green, safe in the knowledge that the Tories were going to lose the election.

Labour's campaign efforts continued to be targeted at maximising votes in seats where they needed to win over swing voters. Limited effort was put into getting the vote out in safe Labour seats or in seats where the Liberal Democrats were better placed to beat the Conservatives. In *The Guardian,* Rafael Behr argued that Labour were potentially going to win big "on a relatively humble vote-share percentage by knowing exactly where it needs the biggest swings and who will turn out on the day".[30] Andrew Neil commented that "The Labour majority will be as wide as the ocean, but as shallow as a village pond."[31]

Other opposition parties

2024 was arguably Britain's first multi-party election in England with the Greens, Liberal Democrats, Reform, and independents all having viable chances to win seats across the country.

Reform

> *If I were trying to think of the worst thing that could possibly happen for Tory MPs in the next six months, it probably is that Nigel Farage would return.*
>
> — JOHN CURTICE, NOVEMBER 2023

The Conservative Party's relief about Nigel Farage's decision not to stand in the election was short-lived. On Monday 3 June 2024, Farage reversed his previous decision and announced he would stand as an MP in Clacton. He encouraged voters to send him to parliament to be "a bloody nuisance". He also announced that he was to become the leader of Reform.

Sunak's apparent strategy of catching the Reform Party on the hop with an early election followed by policy announcements designed to appeal to Reform voters, such as national service, was in serious trouble. More in Common associate director Jim Blagden spoke to Reform voters after Farage's announcement. He said the voters saw Farage as authentic and consistent which they thought was lacking in mainstream politics.[32] Farage's favourability rating with Reform voters stood at over 70%.

Reform claimed that 2024 was going to be the immigration election, and following Farage's return immigration rose further up the political agenda. The Reform manifesto also promised almost £90bn in tax cuts. These included increasing the minimum threshold for income tax to £20,000, abolishing stamp duty on property purchases and abolishing inheritance tax for all estates under £2m.

In 2019, the Brexit Party's decision not to stand candidates in 317 seats helped the Conservatives significantly in that election. The impact of Reform standing candidates in nearly all English and Welsh seats threatened to split the Conservative vote and allow Labour to win a significant number of seats. Professor Paula Surridge gave the example of Stoke-on-Trent South which had voted overwhelmingly for Brexit in 2016. The Conservatives had won it comfortably in 2019 with an 11,000 majority, but Surridge believed the impact of Reform standing meant it would probably be won by Labour.[33] Surridge was proved correct; Labour won the seat despite only improving their share of the vote from 33.7% to 34.7%, as around 9,000 voters switched from the Conservatives to Reform.

Concerned that Reform could cost the party hundreds of seats, the Conservative MP Marco Longhi appealed unsuccessfully to Nigel Farage to stand down Reform candidates in seats where there were right-wing Conservative MPs.

Farage's major missteps during the campaign were when he claimed Western countries were to blame for Russia's invasion of Ukraine, and stated his belief that the NHS needed to be fundamentally reformed and some form of insurance scheme introduced.

Liberal Democrats

The Liberal Democrats' strategy was to ruthlessly focus their campaign on 80 target seats in order to maximise their chances in the UK's first-past-the-post system. Party activists were encouraged to campaign in these seats and not in those that Labour might win. An analysis by the *Financial Times* found that Labour had also told its members not to campaign in the 80 Liberal Democrat target seats.[34] As a result, there were claims that Labour and the Liberal Democrats had done a secret deal not to put resources into challenging each other in their respective target seats. This was denied, but in many ways it was an inevitable outcome of the strong focus that both parties had on their target seats and encouraging tactical voting to oust Tory MPs.

In all of their target seats, bar three, the Liberal Democrats were competing against incumbent Tory MPs. Their aim was to maximise tactical voting in the so-called Blue Wall seats where they were second to the Conservatives. They specifically targeted two key demographics. The first were the Surrey shufflers, young families who had 'shuffled' out of London to Surrey and Hertfordshire. These shufflers were Labour voters in London but had to vote Liberal Democrat tactically in the home counties to make their vote count against the Conservatives. The second were the lifelong Tories who were disillusioned with the Conservative Party over Brexit and their behaviour.

The Liberal Democrats focused on building strong teams in their target constituencies and, like Labour, focused on these seats rather than on maximising their national vote share. This also applied to the party's digital advertising which was targeted at voters in specific seats. In terms of issues, the party focused on health and social care, but the majority of its messaging was relentlessly focused on tactical voting. After the election, 26% of Liberal Democrat voters said they had voted for the party tactically.

The Liberal Democrat leader, Ed Davey, raised the profile of the party by taking part in a series of stunts designed to garner media attention. These included falling off a paddleboard, riding a water slide on a yellow rubber ring, riding the Colossus roller coaster at Thorpe Park, and bungee jumping in Eastbourne.[35] Mark Pack, president of the Liberal Democrats and political commentator, argued that the party understood the importance of the strong visual images that were created to reach voters not normally interested in politics.[36] By the end of the campaign, Davey had overtaken Starmer and had the highest net favourability ratings of any of the leaders, according to YouGov.

The Green Party

Like the Liberal Democrats, the Greens heavily focused their resources on target seats. They had four target seats. The first was their existing seat in Brighton Pavilion, with the other three being Bristol Central, Waveney Valley, and North Herefordshire. While party members put themselves forward as candidates in a record number of seats to give most people the chance to vote Green, their campaigning was ruthlessly focused on target seats. On election day hundreds of party volunteers poured into the four target seats in a massive 'get the vote out' operation.

The Scottish National Party (SNP)

In the run-up to the general election, the SNP's support had been heavily damaged by an investigation into the party's finances and fundraising. Just before the election John Swinney had been parachuted into the leadership of the SNP and had little time to develop their election strategy. The first line of the party's manifesto on page one was clear on the party's priority. It read: 'Vote SNP for Scotland to become an independent country.' However, the issue of Scottish independence had also become less salient. The most important issues to Scottish voters were the NHS, the cost of living, the economy, and immigration. It was arguably the first election in eight years which wasn't dominated by the question of independence. At the start of May 2024, the Labour Party led the SNP in Scotland by ten points in the polls.[37]

The SNP appeared determined to defend all 48 seats that it

had won at the previous election, and Swinney said it was critical that the party remained the third-largest party.

The key campaign events

The first Starmer v Sunak debate

On 4 June 2024, an estimated nine million people tuned in for the first televised leaders' debate between Sunak and Starmer.

It was a petulant affair with both leaders seeking to make their points. Sunak claimed Labour would raise everyone's tax bill, saying, "Mark my words, Labour will raise taxes, it's in their DNA. Your work, your car, your pension – Labour will tax it." He then added, "Independent Treasury officials have costed Labour's policies and they amount to a £2,000 tax rise for every working family." Starmer responded by saying that taxes were at their highest under the Tories for 70 years but failed to quickly rebuff Sunak's claim about Labour tax rises.

Sunak was put under pressure on NHS waiting lists and unconvincingly argued that the numbers were coming down. Starmer claimed the NHS was in his DNA, pointing out that his wife worked in the NHS and that both his mum and sister had been nurses. Starmer also argued he had changed the Labour Party and put it back in the service of working people, while Sunak continued with his line that his plan was working and Starmer had no plan.

The honesty of both leaders was called into question during and after the debate. Sunak claimed the number of crossings in the English Channel had come down by a third over the last 12 months. However, the next day, it was confirmed that the number of migrants crossing the Channel in 2024 was 10,745, or 41.2% higher than at the same point a year earlier.

During the debate, Keir Starmer claimed he wouldn't use private health if a member of his family was ill in any circumstances, which people simply didn't believe.[38] Ipsos qualitative research found that most people said they would turn to private health if necessary, and indeed many had or knew many people who had. It raised fundamental questions about his trustworthiness. People started to question why Starmer had said in 2019 that Corbyn would make a great prime minister if he didn't believe it. On social media, people also started asking why Starmer had U-turned on his original pledges when he stood to be leader.

During the campaign, the percentage of the public who believed both leaders were untrustworthy increased. The percentage believing Starmer was untrustworthy rose from 43% in April 2024 to 47% by 24 June 2024, while even more people distrusted Sunak, with his numbers rising from 59% to 65%.

During the debate, Starmer had been slow to counter Sunak's claim about Labour's tax rises, but the next day, the Treasury permanent secretary made it clear that civil servants had not been involved "in the production or presentation of the Conservative Party's document". The BBC explicitly said Sunak's £2,000 claim was misleading, as it assumed the costs of Labour's policies would be applied equally to all households and was arrived at by adding up four years of costs which wasn't made clear.[39] The next day Labour representatives took to the airwaves to argue that Sunak had lied.

Sunak's attack on tax rises worked in the sense that it forced Labour to box themselves in on taxes. After promising not to increase the main taxes such as income tax, National Insurance, VAT, and corporation tax, Labour were pressed about possible increases in council tax and whether they would introduce new council tax bands or revalue bands. Jonathan Ashworth, the shadow paymaster general, finally told *Times Radio* that council tax bands would not be changed under Labour, saying, "That's a promise."

The Institute for Fiscal Studies accused both Labour and the Conservatives of a "conspiracy of silence" over stretched public finances. The Conservative Party's cuts in National Insurance left a £20bn shortfall in public finances that had to be filled. Paul Johnson of the IFS argued that, ultimately, this had to come from a combination of public spending cuts, higher taxes, or more borrowing. He argued the manifestos "leave us with no sense as to how the parties will tackle the big problems they'll face in government. On a whole range of tax and spending issues, we really won't know what we are voting for on 4 July."[40] The *Sunday Times* also argued that neither leader engaged meaningfully with the public on taxes as neither party was willing to admit that any incoming government would have to raise taxes, cut public services further, or increase the already high levels of government debt.[41]

Both of the leaders were criticised for studiously avoiding the issue of Brexit, which was almost entirely absent from the campaign. Deep inside the Tory manifesto there were claims the party would seize the benefits of the country's Brexit freedoms by signing further trade deals, cutting red tape, and creating new fishing opportunities.[42] In the Labour Party manifesto, there was just a single mention of Brexit, which was buried in a paragraph almost three-quarters of the way through the document. It said the country would stay outside of the EU, and Labour would seek to make Brexit work in order to seize the opportunities ahead.[43]

D-Day

Thursday, 6 June 2024 was the eightieth anniversary of D-Day and world leaders travelled to Normandy to pay tribute to the thousands who had fought and died during the Allied invasion. It was billed as the last big emotional commemoration where survivors would be present due to their advanced age.

As Joe Biden, Emmanuel Macron, and Olaf Scholz gathered for the international leader's commemoration of D-Day, Sunak headed back to the UK for an interview with ITV and left David Cameron to represent the country. That evening Tim Montgomerie said on *Newsnight* that leaving the D-Day event was "political malpractice of the highest order".[44] The next day's headline in the *Financial Times* described it as "the stupidest of stupid ideas".[45]

There was unrelenting criticism of Sunak's decision which was portrayed as a snub to D-Day veterans. On *Sky News*, Ken Hay, a 98-year-old D-Day veteran, who had been captured as a prisoner of war weeks after 6 June 1944, said that the Prime Minister had let the country down by bailing out. Sunak was forced to apologise and when asked about leaving the event early, he responded: "On reflection, that was a mistake and I apologise. I think it's important, though, given the enormity of the sacrifice made, that we don't politicise this."[46]

It was a naive and forlorn plea in the middle of an election campaign and all of the opposition parties seized on the issue. Liberal Democrat leader Ed Davey and Labour's Jonathan Ashworth both said it had been a dereliction of duty that had brought shame on the country. A lot worse was said in Tory WhatsApp groups whose members said they were so disgusted they were going to turn to Reform. Farage made great play of the fact that he was in Normandy in a personal capacity because it mattered. Starmer also attended the commemoration and secured a photo opportunity with Volodymyr Zelenskyy.

Government extremism adviser Ian Acheson said Sunak's decision "was an act of either colossal stupidity or cynical calculation. Either way, it revealed to me that while I still embrace a conservative philosophy, I am no longer willing to have it outsourced to a bunch of mendacious, incompetent and disreputable clowns. Country before party. Always."[47] The headline in the *Daily Telegraph* posed the question, "How could anyone vote Tory after this?"[48]

Subsequent polls revealed that three in five Conservatives and 68% of Tory 2019 voters thought it was unacceptable that Sunak left the D-Day commemorations early.[49] In a BBC debate on 7 June 2024, Penny Mordaunt, the Conservative leader of the House of Commons, said Sunak's decision had been "completely wrong". During the debate, Nigel Farage also attacked Sunak, saying he "doesn't really care about our history, he doesn't really care, frankly, about our culture". The comment was widely criticised as dog whistle politics, though a More in Common poll after the debate found that 25% of people thought Farage had won the debate, followed by 19% who thought Labour's Angela Rayner won. In third was 'none of the above' with 14%.[50] Later that evening, Luke Tryl, of More in Common, said on *Newsnight*, "In public opinion terms, I genuinely think this is nothing short of catastrophic for Rishi Sunak."

The public's views on Sunak fell to new lows. According to Ipsos, Sunak's net favourability ratings fell to -55 at the end of June 2024.[51] He was trailing Starmer on net favourability by a far bigger margin than Corbyn trailed Johnson at the same stage in the 2019 election. Surveys found that 75% of people were dissatisfied with Sunak's performance as prime minister,[52] and according to YouGov, 70% of the public thought he was untrustworthy, 69% thought he was weak, 63% thought he was incompetent, 61% dislikeable, and 61% indecisive.[53] On 26 June, the front page of the *Evening Standard* had a single headline, '72% say they don't like the Tories', alongside a photo of Sunak.

It became clear that Sunak's decision to leave the D-Day

commemorations early was one of the worst mistakes ever made by a prime minister during an election campaign.

The betting scandal

Just when the Tories thought things couldn't get any worse, they were hit by a betting scandal.

On 13 June, Craig Williams, Sunak's closest parliamentary aide and the Conservative candidate for Montgomeryshire and Glyndwr, admitted to the BBC that he had placed a £100 bet on the election date just three days before it was announced. He apologised, calling it a "huge error of judgement" and said he couldn't comment further as the Gambling Commission was conducting an investigation. It was looking into a flurry of bets on the date of the election made just before Sunak's announcement, bets that had caused the movement in the betting odds and alerted Labour to a summer election.

The *Financial Times* analysed Betfair Exchange data and raised concerns that Sunak's closest aides, those with inside knowledge of Sunak's plans for an early election, may have used this knowledge to place bets on a July election.[54]

The Gambling Commission investigation was extended to include Tony Lee, the Conservative director of campaigning, and his wife Laura Saunders, the Tory candidate for Bristol North West. Both were alleged to have placed bets on the date of the election, and the party announced that Lee was taking a leave of absence. It was also revealed that a police officer assigned to protect the Prime Minister was arrested for making a bet with inside knowledge.

Further revelations came in the *Sunday Times* on 23 June, which reported that the party's chief data officer, Nick Mason, had allegedly placed dozens of bets on the date of the election and had also taken a leave of absence. On 25 June, *Newsnight* reported that up to 15 Conservative candidates and officials were being scrutinised for alleged betting on the timing of the general election.[55]

The scandal was extraordinary. Ruth Davidson, the former leader of the Scottish Conservative Party, said: "I literally have no words. I've been involved in fighting elections for more than 15 years and I literally have no words."[56] The scandal reinforced the public narrative about the lack of integrity in the Conservative Party and the need to punish the Tories. The party was forced to withdraw its support from both candidates who had placed bets on the timing of the election. By the end of June, the Conservative campaign was in complete disarray.

MRP polls and tactical voting

The rise of multilevel regression and post-stratification (MRP) polls in 2024 was to play an important role in the election campaign.

The first YouGov MRP poll of the campaign predicted Labour would win 422 seats and the Conservatives just 140, giving Labour a majority of 194, larger than Blair's majority in 1997.[57] If correct, it would be the worst Tory result in over one hundred years and arguably the worst Conservative result ever.

The YouGov model forecast that Labour would regain almost all of the Red Wall seats won by the Conservatives in 2019. It revealed that the Conservative Party's vote was particularly down in seats that voted to leave the EU in 2016, had more people in working-class jobs, and where voters were older than average and less ethnically diverse. The poll also found that the greatest fall in Conservative support was in seats the party was defending. This was a repeat of the pattern seen in the May local elections.

The YouGov MRP poll, like other MRP polls, also predicted which party had the best chance of unseating Conservative candidates in each constituency and was, therefore, very useful information for voters looking to cast their vote tactically to remove the Tories. As highlighted earlier, there was increasing evidence that people were willing to cast their votes tactically to make their vote count in a first-past-the-post electoral system. An Ipsos survey found that 20% of voters said they were planning to vote tactically and would cast their vote for a party not because they agreed with it ideologically but to defeat the Conservatives. This was far more than in previous election campaigns, where typically between 10% and 12% of voters said they voted tactically.

Keiran Pedley, a pollster at Ipsos, observed that tactical voting was set "to be more widespread than normal, which is why the Conservatives are doing so badly in some seat projections. If you want to predict the scale of the Conservative defeat, you have to understand the impact of tactical voting."[58]

George Eaton argued that the increased likelihood of tactical voting was the result of Starmer's safe, moderate strategy.[59] He pointed out that in 2015, the Tories used voter anxiety about Ed Miliband and the SNP to defeat the Liberal Democrats in the West Country. In 2019, the fear of Corbyn meant that Conservative voters were less likely to defect. Liberal Democrat voters were also less likely to vote tactically for Labour candidates in that year because of their fear of Corbyn. In 2024, these voters were more comfortable voting tactically for Labour under the leadership of the reassuringly moderate Keir Starmer.[60]

The *Financial Times* published the findings of a survey of voters who were planning to switch from the Conservatives in Blue Wall seats. The top reason people gave for switching to Labour or the Liberal Democrats in these areas was 'run down services like the NHS'. The second reason for switching was 'dishonest or dishonourable MPs/Ministers'.[61] A view which had been reinforced by the betting scandal. The third reason they gave was the Conservative Party's mishandling of the economy.

The end game

After the D-Day debacle and the Craig Williams betting revelations, support for the Conservatives plummeted. On 16 June 2024, the *Sunday Times* published a Survation poll that forecast Labour would win 456 seats and Tories just 72. On the BBC, John Curtice said, "Conservative support is now at its lowest ever in British polling history." To add to the Tory gloom, the polls revealed rising support for Reform, with one poll putting them a point ahead of the Tories.

Sunak and his team were braced for a terrible defeat and there was growing concern the party could be wiped out almost completely. Steven Swinford, the political editor of *The Times*, quoted a Tory strategist saying it was no longer a campaign looking to win seats in the Red Wall but had become "a fight for survival".[62]

Isaac Levido believed that the only way to prevent a wipeout was to adopt a new strategy. According to Ben Riley-Smith the strategy was set out in a five-page note and became known as the supermajority strategy.[63] The essence of the strategy was to persuade Conservative voters that they could still influence the outcome of the election and it was essential they voted. It meant warning that the Labour Party was on course for a supermajority which would create long-term risks to the country if there wasn't an effective opposition. The note said it was a "tactical communication to force voters to consider the consequence of their vote".[64]

The new strategy was deployed by Grant Shapps, the defence secretary, on *Times Radio*. He said people should vote Conservative to ensure they had enough MPs to hold the Labour government to account and not to give Keir Starmer a supermajority. The new messaging looked increasingly defeatist. The BBC's Henry Zeffman commented that after listening to Conservative spokespeople, "you could be forgiven for thinking that there is only one possibility – Labour victory".[65]

On 19 June 2024, in a *Sky News* interview, Katy Balls and Stephen Bush both reported that the Tory campaign had become more defensive as the party's internal polling showed them at risk in previously safe seats. Prior to the D-Day catastrophe, Sunak had been visiting seats with an average Conservative majority of 11,894. Afterwards, he started visiting seats where the party had an average majority of 14,317. One in five had majorities of more than 20,000.

The political commentator and former Conservative candidate Iain Dale claimed he had heard of candidates in Tory held seats with majorities of between four and six thousand, who had been ordered to shut down their campaigns and redeploy themselves to help cabinet ministers with majorities in excess of 20,000. If they refused, Dale claimed their computer logins to the party systems were being cancelled and they were being threatened with being removed from the candidates list after the election.[66]

The new messaging went down badly with Conservative campaigners. One furious Tory minister said, "The Labour Supermajority line is completely backfiring. It's totally disillusioning our base. People are saying, "What's the point?" I've had fewer workers out this week than last week."[67]

Iain Dale agreed, saying, "For a succession of cabinet ministers to go on the media and effectively give up the ghost halfway through the campaign is not only unprecedented, but a complete disgrace. Why would any party volunteer go that extra mile and deliver another 100 leaflets just when it is getting dark. Why would they bother?"

There were increasing reports that Tory candidates and

party workers felt let down by a hapless campaign. There was scathing criticism of Sunak – "a total dud in terms of knowing how to fight an election campaign" and Isaac Levido – "no Lynton Crosby. Crosby was an inspirational leader." It was reported that Levido had been going around telling people the party would win fewer than 100 seats.[68]

The narrowing of the polls that Levido had anticipated, and which JLP reported, continued to be contradicted by the other pollsters. According to the majority of polls, Labour's lead over the Conservatives remained close to 20%. The most significant movement they showed was the rise of Reform whose support in the polls increased from 11% to around 16%, and who were forecast to take one in four of 2019 Conservative voters.[69] There was also a small rise in support for the Liberal Democrats. The pollsters' election models all forecast a large Labour majority with the number of Conservative seats falling to between 90 and 150 seats. Many of the Conservative Party's biggest names were at risk of losing their seats, according to the forecasts.

~

As the campaign entered its final stages, the impact of the decisions Labour had made immediately prior to Sunak calling the election was increasingly visible. The party's adverts were all over news sites' web pages, such as *The Sun* and the *Daily Mail*. The betting scandal had not only damaged the Conservative Party's reputation, it had given Labour a significant jump-start when it came to campaign planning. A member of Starmer's team said, "Because of the betting we were much more ready and we were in a position to buy the prime real estate that we assumed the Tories would have ... The betting gave us an unexpected opportunity."[70]

Close to the end of the campaign, two of the UK's richest people, John Caudwell, a former Tory donor, and Jim Radcliffe said they were no longer backing the Conservatives and instead backing Labour. Caudwell said he was particularly critical of the party's mismanagement of the economy and the lowering of ethical standards. Sunak's response was "They're two of Britain's richest men. They can probably afford Labour's tax rises."[71]

The Conservatives also lost the support of the *Sunday Times*, which had backed the party in 2019. In an excoriating editorial on 30 June, the paper argued that since 2016 there had been political chaos which had fatally distracted the Tories from the issues that matter most to voters – healthcare, schools, and the economy. The paper argued it had been embarrassing to have had five prime ministers, seven chancellors, seven foreign secretaries, seven home secretaries, and no fewer than nine education secretaries since 2016. It was also "ludicrous" that Lee Rowley was both the tenth and thirteenth person to have held the role of housing minister since 2016.

The editorial was highly critical of Johnson's Partygate sleaze and incompetence, and the fact that Truss had collapsed the Tories' economic credibility. While the paper acknowledged that Sunak had steadied the ship, it said his election campaign had been woeful with the party lurching through constant self-inflicted mishaps and culminating in a betting scandal. The paper concluded that the Conservatives had forfeited the right to govern.[72]

14

THE 2024 ELECTION RESULTS

At 10 pm on 4 July, the collective Conservative Party held its breath. As the chimes of Big Ben started to ring out across Westminster, the exit poll results flashed across millions of TV screens. The Labour Party was projected to secure a landslide with 410 seats. The Conservatives were forecast to lose over 200 seats and win just 131.

There was a sombre mood in Conservative headquarters and whispers of 'quiet relief' that the party had escaped the humiliation of falling below 100 seats, a fate many pollsters had ominously predicted, but it was a pyrrhic victory.

In the early hours of Friday morning, returning officers across the country stood on stages and delivered a series of devastating blows to the Conservative Party. Their announcements reverberated like a cascade of dominoes as Conservative strongholds were toppled one after another. At 4.45 am Rishi Sunak conceded the election he had called on that fateful, rain-soaked Wednesday afternoon in May. It was a crushing end to 14 years of Conservative rule.

An angry electorate had deliberately punished the

Conservatives. They had engaged in large-scale tactical voting, foreshadowed in the May local elections, that was calculated to inflict the maximum damage on Sunak and his government. There were record-breaking swings away from the Conservative Party. It was a catastrophe for senior Conservative MPs. Cabinet minister after cabinet minister lost their seats, including Grant Shapps, Penny Mordaunt, Gillian Keegan, Steve Baker, Jacob Rees-Mogg, Johnny Mercer, Victoria Prentis, Mark Harper, and Michelle Donelan.

One of the last seats to declare was South West Norfolk, one of the safest Conservative seats in the country where Liz Truss held a 24,000 majority. The returning officer and Truss's rival candidates were kept waiting on stage for ten minutes for the former prime minister. When she finally arrived at 6.45 am, she stood at the far right of the stage looking blankly into the distance as the returning officer announced that she had been defeated by the Labour candidate. She was offered the opportunity to speak to the crowd to thank her supporters but declined and quickly retreated from the stage. Truss became the first former British prime minister to lose their seat in an election for almost 90 years and suffered the largest ever Conservative to Labour swing in a general election (26.2%).

The defeat of Truss capped a terrible night for the Conservatives. The party's vote had almost halved from 2019. The party won 6.8m votes, representing just 23.7% of votes cast, and won only 121 seats. It was the worst-ever result in their 190-year history and the first time they had received less than 30% of the vote. The party ended up losing 251 seats, more than any party had lost at a general election before. Almost half the country's parliamentary seats, 303, switched from one party to another, the greatest number in post-war elections and 65% more than in 1997.

The number of people who voted for the Conservative Party plummeted from 13.97m in 2019 to just 6.83m in 2024. The *Sky*

News deputy political editor Sam Coates commented that the story of the night was "the complete collapse of the Conservative Party".[1]

In the traditional Conservative home counties' heartlands, the party was devastated. For the first time since 1906 Tories didn't win a majority of southern seats.[2] In Berkshire, Bedfordshire, Buckinghamshire, Hertfordshire, and Oxfordshire the party lost 26 seats.

Many of the seats that the Conservatives lost had been held by the party for a very long time:

- Aldershot (1918)
- Ashford (1931)
- Banbury (1918)
- Basingstoke (1924)
- Both Bournemouth seats (1921)
- Bury St Edmunds (1885)
- Chichester (1924)
- Cities of London and Westminster (1931)
- Devon South (1935)
- Dorking (1885)
- Henley (1910)
- Macclesfield (1918)
- Mid Sussex (1885)
- Tunbridge Wells (1931)
- Worthing West (1918)

The Conservatives only held on to 52% of their 2019 voters as their vote fragmented. It flowed in different directions with pollsters estimating that 24–25% went to Reform, 10–12% to Labour and 7% to the Liberal Democrats.[3] While less important, the Remain/Leave split still resonated in the 2024 election, with 44% of those that voted Remain voting Labour compared to only 19% of those that voted Leave. Two-thirds of

Leave voters chose either the Conservatives or Reform. Of the 121 seats the Conservative Party retained, more than half had majorities of 8% or less. In Hartlepool, where the Conservatives had won so dramatically in May 2021, the Conservative candidate came third behind Labour and Reform.

As the results were announced it became clear that Labour had only marginally improved their vote share and would win a majority on just 34% of the vote. Peter Kellner argued the result was "an emphatic rejection of Conservative rule after 14 years in power, but far from an enthusiastic endorsement of Labour".[4] Grant Shapps said the election had been "a collective failure of the Conservative Party" and that "it hadn't been so much that Starmer and Labour won but that we very much lost".[5] Anthony Howard argued back in 2003 that oppositions don't win elections, governments lose them,[6] and 2024 seemed to be a case in point. John Curtice echoed the views of many election analysts when he said, "In many ways, this looks more like an election the Conservatives have lost than one Labour have won."[7]

The real story of the election was the collapse of the Conservative vote. It was "one of the most remarkable collapses for a political party in our history" according to Michael Thrasher, a professor of politics and *Sky News*' election analyst.[8] The Conservatives were probably saved from a total wipeout by a very late increase in their vote share as reluctant Tories returned to the fold and by inefficiencies in tactical voting, primarily in those seats where it wasn't clear which party was in second place.

The Conservative Party failed to get its previous supporters to turn out and vote in the election. More in Common estimated that up to 2.6m of its 2019 voters stayed at home.[9]

Post-election data from the British Election Study puts this figure lower, at an estimated 1.8m people who voted Conservative in 2019 and stayed at home in 2024, which was still more than the 1.1m who switched directly to Labour, though these effectively count double in an election. It appears those not voting took an active decision to abstain, as they felt unable to back another party but wanted to show their disapproval of the Conservatives. For 77% of them, it was the first time they had abstained in an election.

The Conservative Party lost 2.7m of its 2019 voters to Reform, 1.1m to the Liberal Democrats, Greens, and others, while 1.5 million of its previous voters died between the elections.

The Conservative vote fell furthest where the party had been strongest in 2019. Analysis of 53,000 voters surveyed by Focaldata during the campaign found that 2019 Conservative support had fallen most among voters aged over 45, non-graduates, Leave voters, skilled working class, and homeowners. Paula Surridge noted that the Conservative vote among economically left, socially conservative voters had collapsed.[10] The party's vote share among C2 voters was estimated to have fallen from a majority of 52% in 2019 to just 25% in 2024. This was the group of voters who were critical to Thatcher's victories in the 1980s when they switched from Labour to the Conservatives. Reform were the biggest gainer from this group, securing the votes of 25% of C2 voters, though they were still behind Labour, who secured 31% of this group's vote.[11]

Amongst AB voters, the Conservative vote collapsed to 26%, and many of these voters went directly to the Labour Party which won 36% of this group.[12] The Conservative vote share amongst homeowners slumped from 60% in 2019 to 34% in 2024. The Conservative vote was also down 22% among mortgage holders, with Reform gaining ground in this group.

Analysis by Will Jennings found that the more mortgage payers there were in a constituency, the greater the swing away from the Conservatives.

The Conservatives were the preferred party by only one age group, the over 65s. The party secured a mere 5% of the votes of 18 to 24-year-olds and only 10% of the votes of 25 to 34-year-olds. This is particularly worrying for the Conservatives as every year older people die and leave the electorate while new teenagers join it. The conservatising effect of age also appears to be less strong which could be due to people buying homes and having families later than previously. Sociologist Phil Burton-Cartledge also argues that the dominance of the services industry in the UK has helped to shape a younger workforce that is "predisposed to social liberalism, empathy, and tolerance".[13] Whatever the cause, it is apparent that successive generations are less likely to become conservative as they get older. The age at which people were more likely to vote Conservative than Labour, the crossover age, had risen to 71 years old according to Deltapoll data.[14]

The Conservatives again won most votes from those with no formal qualifications, though by a slender lead of 32% to 30% over Labour. Among graduates, the Conservatives trailed a long way behind Labour, who secured 43% of the graduate vote compared to the Conservatives' 19%.

It was notable that the Conservatives did well in seats with large Hindu populations. Leicester East was the only Conservative gain of the night and came in a constituency with a 40% Hindu population. Harrow East, with a 28% Hindu population, delivered the second-largest Conservative majority in the country.

The loss of the Red Wall

The Conservatives lost almost half of their share of Leave voters, with Reform the big gainers in this group. The seats the Conservatives won in Leave-voting areas in 2019 to 'get Brexit done' were almost completely lost. Compared with 2019, support for the Conservatives was down by 12 points in seats where less than 45% had voted Leave but down by 27 points in seats where more than 65% had voted Leave.

In my previous book, *The Fall of the Red Wall*, I identified seats won by the Conservatives in 2019 that had historically been held by the Labour Party and which voted to Leave in the EU referendum. Labour won back all of these Red Wall seats apart from one, Ashfield, where Lee Anderson won for Reform. The average vote share across 40 of the former Red Wall seats[15] was:

- Labour 40.7%
- Conservatives 25%
- Reform 21.3%

Reform won Ashfield and came second in a further ten of these Red Wall seats. On average their vote share exceeded that required by the Tories to retain the seat. As Peter Kellner noted, Labour's landslide owed "a great deal to Reform's success at taking votes from the Conservatives".[16]

While it is difficult to make exact comparisons between 2019 and 2024 because of boundary changes, the Labour vote was up on average in these seats by only 3.5%, from 37.2% in 2019 to 40.7% in 2024. It was the large flow of votes to the Reform Party that split the Conservative vote and allowed Labour to win all but one of the 40 seats. It should also be noted that in 11 of the seats that Labour won in 2024, their vote share was actually lower than when they lost the seats in 2019.

In Burnley, Hyndburn, and Bolton North East, Labour won the seats despite a decline in their vote share of more than five points.

In total Labour won 56 Conservative seats despite winning fewer votes in those seats than it did in the 2019 election.

In surveys after the election, less than a third (31%) of those who voted for Reform said they would have voted Conservative in the absence of a Reform candidate.[17] However, this may reflect the fact that half of 2019 Conservative voters were unhappy with the party and did not vote for them in 2024.

A competence election

To win an election governments need to be seen as competent in the eyes of voters. They must appear capable, reliable, trustworthy, deliver what they say, and respond to issues that matter to voters. These are what political scientists term valence issues, namely aspects of government where everyone agrees on what good looks like. They are also areas where everyone knows what bad looks like, for example, not delivering on promises, not being trustworthy, or not being capable. At its core, the 2024 election was about competence and the public, including many former Conservative voters, concluded the party was not fit to govern the country.

The Conservative Party's electoral defeat can be traced to its failure to deliver on the issues that mattered to voters. Survey after survey confirmed that the public's top three concerns were the cost of living, the NHS, and immigration.[18] By any measure the Conservatives had failed to deliver on these issues. This was acknowledged by Robert Jenrick, the former Conservative minister for immigration, who said, "The fundamental reason we lost is because we failed to deliver what we promised for the British people" and specifically highlighted the failure to deliver on the public's top three concerns, namely a strong economy, a functioning NHS, and a secure border.[19]

The Conservatives could reasonably argue that any government would have struggled to deliver on its priorities given the unprecedented external shocks it had to deal with, such as COVID-19, the Ukraine war, and a global surge in inflation. These were shocks which caused problems for incumbent governments across Western Europe. The public, though, had been in no mood to give the Conservatives the benefit of the doubt. They had been in power for 14 years. Conservative voters were fed up with the party's failure to deliver on promise after promise. The deputy editor of *The Spectator*, Freddy Grey, thought that by 2024, even Conservative voters believed that a more competent Labour Party might be better at controlling immigration and improving the NHS than the Conservative Party.[20]

As far as the majority of people were concerned, the government had made things worse, and many of the wounds were self-inflicted. It was the Conservative Party that had chosen to impose deep cuts in public spending through its austerity programme (including capital spending), that had been responsible for Brexit, that had behaved appallingly over Partygate, that had adopted liberal immigration policies which caused numbers to treble, that had behaved badly with MPs resigning over sex and corruption scandals, that had failed to settle a dispute with doctors which resulted in growing NHS waiting lists, that had chopped and changed policy direction multiple times as a result of party infighting, that had changed prime minister four times, and had voted for Liz Truss's mini-budget which crashed the economy and forced up mortgage rates. To the public, the party's lack of competence, unfitness to govern, and failure to keep its promises were unforgivable.

One focus group participant said, "I was completely torn over what to do, which is unlike me. I just normally don't even think about it. I just go and vote Conservative. But yeah, this time there was a lot of turmoil and in the end, I voted Labour ... I felt it was time for a change and it was a bit of revenge for the betrayal of the Conservatives."[21]

The public's disdain for the party on core valence issues was clearly visible in surveys that asked about the Conservative government's competence, fitness to govern, understanding of the country's problems, and whether it kept its promises. On all of these measures, the Conservative Party's ratings collapsed after 2020.

- The percentage of people who thought the Conservative Party was competent fell from around 40% to just over 10%.
- The percentage of people who thought it was fit to govern fell from over 45% to less than 15%.
- The percentage of people who thought they understood the problems facing Britain fell from around 45% to less than 20%.
- The percentage of people who thought the Conservative Party kept its promises fell from around 25% to less than 10%.[22]

It was, therefore, no surprise when after the election, a Lord Ashcroft poll of Conservative defectors found the top three reasons people gave for not voting Conservative in 2024 were:

- They were out of touch with people like them.
- They hadn't delivered what they promised.
- They were not competent.

When asked by More in Common why the Conservatives lost the election, 64% said they were incompetent.[23]

Ben Houchen argued that the party's failure could be put

down to a lack of competence rather than an ideological failure. He said: "People crave competence from their leaders."[24] John Burn-Murdoch, writing in the *Financial Times*, agreed with Houchen that "the Tories didn't lose this election because they were too right-wing on some issues or too left-wing on others. They lost because voters of all stripes judged them to be incompetent and dishonest."[25]

There was a commonly held view after the election, shared by analysts such as John Curtice, Will Jennings, and others, that people broke with Conservatives over competence rather than ideology. In reality, it is not always easy to separate competence from ideology. It can be argued that the crumbling of public services was an ideological choice that stemmed from austerity rather than simply a competence issue. However, the party was clearly perceived as incompetent. Paula Surridge has argued persuasively that while many voters broke with the Conservatives over their perceived incompetence, where they went was shaped by their values. Thus, those with more authoritarian values switched to Reform.

The public was frustrated that nothing worked anymore and angry at the Conservative Party's incompetence and dishonesty. Paul Bristow, the Conservative MP who lost his seat to Labour in Peterborough, commented: "The public were fed up to the back teeth with us."[26] Bristow said he had knocked on thousands of doors and had heard "time and time again how disappointed and angry people were". It was the public's anger and determination to punish the Conservatives for their incompetence that led directly to an increase in tactical voting, which in turn removed the party from even its safest seats.

Labour's loveless landslide

The Labour Party won 411 seats giving them a landslide majority of 174, close to the exit poll forecast of 170. It was the second-largest Labour majority since Blair's victory in 1997. The party won back almost all of the Red Wall seats they had previously lost. They also gained almost 40 seats from the SNP. In terms of seats, it was a crushing victory. However, the party won just 34% of the votes cast. This was only marginally higher than Corbyn achieved in 2019 and a full six points below the party's performance in 2017. John Curtice commented, "Never before has a party been able to form a majority government on so low a share of the vote",[27] while Gary Gibbon, Channel 4's political editor, termed it a "loveless landslide".

The small increase in Labour's share of the vote in 2024 was entirely the result of a 17-point increase in support for the party in Scotland. There was no increase in the Labour Party's vote share in England from 2019. The fact that Labour didn't increase their vote, when the Conservative government was so unpopular, would indicate the public was far from convinced about Starmer. In Wales, the party's vote actually fell back by four points.

Post-election analysis by More in Common found that if voters had voted with their heart rather than their head and not voted for Labour tactically, the support for Labour would have been four points lower and the Greens three points higher.[28]

The Conservative and SNP voters who switched to the Labour Party were critical because effectively, their votes counted twice – it was one less on the incumbent's vote and one more on Labour's vote.

Many Conservative to Labour switchers consciously made a decision to loan their vote to Labour, in the hope they would deliver on issues such as the NHS and the cost of living. They were not necessarily convinced by Labour but were desperate for things to change. Two participants in a survey run by Labour Together summed up the feelings of many:

> "I was so fed up with the state of everything and I just wanted to change. But it's a gamble. That's the only word I can come up with, because I'm not positive about it ... I think we all felt like there was no choice whether you wanted to believe in the Labour policies or not. We are that desperate for change."

> "I wanted to give Labour a go, I'd like to see if they can do something – I'm on the fence with sticking with them and hopefully they can bring some positive change."[29]

Given the increased costs of mortgages and renting during the 2019–2024 parliament, it was little surprise that 2019 Conservative voters who had a mortgage were significantly more likely to switch to Labour than those who owned their home outright.

Labour finished just 10 points ahead of the Conservatives rather than the 19 to 20 points predicted by many of the polls. The overestimation of Labour's support was the highest ever seen, and the overall margin of error was the worst since the 1992 election. The polls had overestimated the support for both Labour and Reform, and underestimated Conservative and Liberal Democrat support.

The MRP surveys had also overestimated Labour's victory. More in Common and YouGov had overstated Labour's result by 18 and 19 seats respectively. Other MRP polls were far less accurate. Survation's final MRP poll predicted Labour would win 470 seats and the Tories just 68 seats.[30] Pollsters said the scale of the miss would result in a re-examination of their methodologies including sampling, non-response bias, demographic quotas, turnout adjustments, and more.

Labour won 12.88m votes in 2017 and 10.27m votes in 2019. In 2024, the party won just 9.7m votes, although on a lower turnout. The turnout for the election was seven points lower than in 2019, falling to just 59.8%. It was the second lowest turnout since 1885, suggesting there had been no enthusiasm for the election or the party offerings. Lewis Goodall commented, "The public, in many cases, have either felt apathetic or disinclined to choose between what was put before them."[31]

The extensive publication of polls prior to the election indicating a Labour landslide may have also discouraged some voters on the basis that the result was a foregone conclusion. Professor Paula Surridge argued there was likely to be "a significant group who felt that victory was assured and so didn't vote".[32] This view is supported by research evidence that large poll leads can depress turnout, as voters believe that their vote will change little in such situations.[33] However, according to More in Common, just 4% of non-voters stayed at home because they were sure that the party they supported was going to win.[34]

When non-voters were asked why they didn't vote, the top answer selected by 34% was 'I don't trust any politicians.' The second highest answer was 'Voting doesn't change anything.'

In the 63 safest Labour seats, the party's average vote share decreased by 17% from 67% to 50%, and the party lost votes in most of the seats where they had won over 50% of the vote in 2019. The party only really made gains in seats where their previous vote share had been less than 50% in 2019. Labour strategists put this down to the party's ruthless targeting of resources outside its core heartlands, so that its vote became more efficient, allowing it to win where it needed to and avoiding piling up votes in safe Labour seats.

It might also have been that many voters in Labour seats with large majorities felt able to vote for other parties such as the Greens. If the election had been closer or Labour were at risk of losing these seats it is possible the Labour vote might have been higher. Labour Together claims there is some evidence that voters who switched from Labour to the Greens were more likely to decide close to or on the day of the election.[35]

It might also have been that many Labour voters voted tactically for the Liberal Democrats in seats where they were the main challengers to the Conservatives which depressed the Labour vote. However, there were also many seats where there was evidence of Liberal Democrats and other voters supporting Labour where they were the main challengers to the Conservatives, which would have increased the Labour vote share.

Based on data from the post-election British Electoral Study, Dylan Difford estimates that around 500,000 Liberal Democrat voters voted tactically for Labour and a similar number of Labour voters voted tactically for the Liberal Democrats. This suggests a very efficient swap of Labour and Liberal Democrat voters to remove Conservative MPs.[36]

A Lord Ashcroft Poll found that 32% of those who voted Labour said they were voting Labour tactically to try and stop the party they liked least from winning.

Patrick McGuire, a political columnist for *The Times*, claimed the ability to win a landslide majority on such a low vote share was the fruit of a political strategy that had "ruthlessly maximised the efficiency of the Labour vote".[37] This is true, but it was also aided greatly by the broad spread of the Reform vote, which took votes away from the Conservatives across a great many seats, allowing Labour to win without increasing its share of the vote and, in some cases, even winning back seats with a lower vote share than in 2019.

Labour won the most votes in every social class group, as class continued to decline as a predictor of voting behaviour.[38] The big swings to Labour were not in the north and Midlands, and the party did not dominate working-class areas as it used to. In 2024, Labour gained most in affluent areas but lost votes in deprived areas, where their vote share actually fell 6.9%.[39] John Curtice observed that the party wasn't "particularly successful at reconnecting with the left behind voters".[40]

Labour were ahead in every age group except those 65 and over. Labour's highest share was among 25 to 34-year-olds (47%). However, Labour's share fell 21 points among 18 to 24-year-olds, whereas the Greens saw a 16-point rise.[41] Post-election British Electoral Study data revealed a potentially concerning trend for Labour, showing that 800,000 voters who cast their ballots for the party had actually preferred the Greens but voted tactically.[42]

The Labour Party also lost almost a third of its support from Black and Asian communities in the general election, falling from 64% to 46%.[43] The party's stance on Gaza was a factor in areas with large numbers of people who identify as Muslim. The party's vote was down on average by 20.7 points in seats where over 20% of the population identified as Muslim.[44] Analysis of British Election Study data by Dylan Difford found that 51% of 2019 Muslim Labour voters either stayed at home or voted for independent candidates.[45]

Lewis Baston's research found that in the 21 seats where more than 30% of the population was Muslim, Labour's vote share dropped by 29 points from an average of 65% in 2019 to 36% in 2024.[46]

Labour lost four of these seats to independent candidates (Blackburn, Leicester South, Dewsbury & Batley and Birmingham Perry Barr) where voters appeared to object to the party not taking a stronger stance in support of Palestinians and a ceasefire in Gaza. Five more Labour MPs nearly lost their seats from this backlash amongst pro-Palestine Muslim voters. Rushanara Ali's majority fell from 37,500 to 1,700, Shabana Mahmood's from 28,600 to 3,400, Naz Shah's from 27,000 to 707,

Jess Phillips' from 10,700 to 693, and Wes Streeting's from 5,200 to 528.

Luke Tryl argued that these falls in vote share should not simply be attributed to Labour's position on Gaza. In focus groups, he noted there was real frustration over Labour on Gaza, but also a feeling that Labour took Muslim votes for granted and that their communities had been neglected by the party. Participants talked about a lack of opportunities, crime, and the fact no one listened to them. While Gaza was at the forefront of the campaigns of independent candidates, they were also seen as potential champions for their community who'd stand up for them. Thus it was possible that Gaza was a trigger but that many in these communities had started to become disconnected from Labour. Tryl observed that "in an age of electoral volatility traditional loyalties are no longer enough to mean a party can count on the votes of a particular group. Particularly if they feel neglected or taken for granted by that party."[47]

Despite winning a huge landslide in terms of seats, the Labour Party's victory there appeared to be no increase in support for the party. John Curtice claimed there was little enthusiasm for Labour, noting that while Starmer had made his party acceptable, he was "not even as popular as David Cameron was before 2010".[48] To Curtice the election result had been shaped by the failures of the Conservative Party. Rosa Prince, the deputy UK editor at Politico, agreed saying, "There is little doubt that this election was a loss for the Conservatives rather than Labour's gain; there was no surge of enthusiasm for the party."[49] Paula Surridge argued that the desire to see the back of the Tories appeared to outweigh any considerations of policy or even "whether Labour will actually deliver much positive change".[50]

The satisfaction rating for the new Labour government when it was elected, was -21, which was an improvement on the

Sunak government that never rose above -60. However, for Cameron's government it was +10, and for Blair's government it was +37. It took two years for Blair's government to have a negative satisfaction rating.

Keir Starmer was one of the most unpopular opposition leaders to win an election. When he became prime minister he had a popularity rating of plus seven (37% satisfied, 30% dissatisfied). This was low by historical standards for new prime ministers. For example, Cameron's was +30, Blair's +60, and May's +35.[51] It could be argued that Starmer's low ratings reflected the growing public distrust of politicians following the failures of the Conservative government. However, while they should not be overplayed, there were a series of specific concerns raised about his trustworthiness. These included:

- His statements in 2019 that Corbyn would make a great prime minister, which he subsequently admitted he didn't believe.
- Reneging on the promises he had made when campaigning to be the Labour leader.
- Saying in a TV debate that he wouldn't use private health even if one of his family was ill and required treatment.
- His treatment of Diane Abbott and hiding behind technicalities rather than giving his view and saying there was a process to be followed as if the process had nothing to do with him.

In focus groups the public appeared to have low expectations of what he might achieve.[52] This was attributed by Labour List to "the sobering reality that Britain is broken" and the challenges facing the country.[53]

Loveless or not, Keir Starmer turned the biggest Tory majority since 1987 into the biggest Labour majority since 2001.

Tom McTague, the political editor of UnHerd, commented that the scale of the majority meant Starmer had become the "master of Parliament".[54]

A multi-party election

The combined share of the vote for the two main parties has been in long-term decline since the 1950s, and fell to a new post-war low of 57%. In 2024, four separate parties gained over 10% of the vote. Smaller parties also did well, with the Greens and independent candidates both gaining seats and coming second in dozens of constituencies.

The 2024 election was remarkable in the degree to which the Labour Party, the Liberal Democrats, and the Green Party focused their resources on target seats as they sought to maximise the efficiency of their vote rather than their national vote share. Intense tactical voting meant these strategies proved highly successful not just for the Labour Party but also the Liberal Democrats and the Green Party.

Analysis of the 2024 British Election Study data by Dylan Difford revealed that one in eight voters preferred another party to the one they actually voted for.[55] His analysis suggests that 800,000 people who voted Labour preferred the Greens, while 500,000 of those who voted Labour preferred the Liberal Democrats, which almost exactly matched the 500,000 who tactically voted for the Liberal Democrats but preferred the Labour Party.

The Liberal Democrats won 3.5m votes, representing 12.2% of votes cast. The party won 72 of its target seats, making it one of the most successful campaigns in British political history.

While the party failed to take the seat of the former chancellor Jeremy Hunt, it won the seats of three Conservative ex-prime ministers:

- Maidenhead (formerly Theresa May's seat)
- Henley (formerly Boris Johnson's seat)
- Witney (formerly David Cameron's seat)

The success of the Liberal Democrats in winning 72 seats was down to their efficient, concentrated geographical vote and tactical voting. In the election their vote went up in seats where they were challenging the Conservatives but fell slightly in other seats. In seats where the Liberal Democrats were challenging the Conservatives 44% of 2019 Labour voters, who had become more positive towards the Lib Dems, switched their vote to help the party to defeat the incumbent.[56] More than a quarter (26%) of Liberal Democrat voters in 2024 said they had voted tactically.[57]

There is evidence that voters turned to the Liberal Democrats where they had a high-profile local community champion, as 32% said that supporting their local candidate was the top reason for voting for the party.

The Liberal Democrats took seats from the Conservatives in some of the country's wealthiest areas that have the highest proportions of people in managerial and professional occupations.

The Greens recorded their best ever general election performance, winning two million votes and all four of their target seats. The party's focus on winning four seats where they had built a base of support and pouring resources heavily into those seats paid handsomely. Two of the seats they won, Waveney Valley and North Herefordshire, were traditional Conservative seats. In these constituencies it was unlikely that the Green Party had converted voters to their platform of unilateral nuclear disarmament but rather that they had benefited from tactical voting designed to remove the Conservative candidate.

The Green Party's targeted strategy only worked because

they had clearly established themselves as the party best placed to beat the Conservatives in those seats. This allowed them to become the logical home for tactical voters wanting to defeat the incumbent candidates.

The Greens also gained from discontent with Labour among progressive voters. All 40 of their second places came in seats won by Labour. In urban areas the Greens were increasingly competing with Labour for the progressive votes of students, graduates, and young professionals. The Greens picked up 14% of the vote among 18 to 24-year-olds, up 10 points on 2019.[58]

The election strategies of Labour, the Liberal Democrats and the Green Party suggest that these parties have adopted a more sophisticated and successful approach to maximising the efficiency of their vote in the first-past-the-post system. The result is that parliament has a far more liberal set of MPs. For the first time ever voters elected over 500 MPs from left or centre-left parties.

Reform won 4.1m votes, representing 14.3% of votes cast, but only won five seats. This was just one seat for every 820,000 votes it had received. Compare this to the efficiency of the Labour vote, where the party won one seat for every 23,000 votes received. The problem for Reform was that its four million votes were spread evenly and inefficiently across the country. It came second in 98 English and Welsh constituencies. In 13 of these, it was less than 5% behind the winning party, and in 62 seats, it was less than 8% behind the winning party. Reform's approach to the election contrasted markedly with the deliberately targeted approach adopted by the Liberal Democrats and the Green Party. While the party's broad geographic spread of voters hurt the Conservative Party, it was unlikely to win many seats in a first-past-the-post system.

The Reform vote was relatively strong in heavily Leave-voting seats such as the former Red Wall where Boris Johnson's 'get Brexit done' message resonated in 2019. The party won more than a quarter of the vote in the seats that voted most heavily to Leave in the 2016 referendum. According to a More in Common survey the main reason voters gave for voting Reform was immigration.[59]

The other party that suffered by having a broad spread of voters was the SNP. The party's share of the vote in Scotland fell by 15% to 30%, while Labour's rose by 17% to 35.3%. The result meant that the SNP lost 80% of their MPs and were reduced to just nine seats, while Labour won 37 seats. Having a geographically well-spread voter base had been a strength when the opposition was divided, but as Labour support rose, it became a weakness. In every seat the SNP did not win, they came second, but as with Reform, there are no prizes in a first-past-the-post system for second place.

The 2024 election looked like a multi-party election as the Labour and Conservative parties won less than 58% of the national vote, and four different parties in England got more than 10% of the vote for the first time. There was also a wide range of viable alternative parties, including the Greens and independents. Five independent pro-Palestinian MPs won seats at the election. The best known was Jeremy Corbyn, the former Labour leader, who won as an independent in Islington North despite a targeted Labour campaign to remove him. Corbyn referred to the other four independent candidates as his 'comrades'.

A volatile and disproportional election

The increased level of tactical voting and the whiplash changes in the number of seats gained and lost by political parties in recent elections highlight the growing volatility of the British electorate. In England, the seats went up and down like a child's see-saw in 2024 with Labour gaining 211 seats and the

Tories losing 251. According to the post-election data from the British Election Study,[60] over 10m voters voted for a different party in 2024 than they had in 2019.

The number of Liberal Democrat MPs fell to just 8 in 2015 but increased to 72 in 2024. In Scotland, the number of Labour seats fell from 46 seats down to just 1 seat in 2015 and bounced back to 37 seats in 2024. By contrast, the SNP won 56 seats in 2015 but was reduced to just 9 in 2024.

Almost half of the seats in the 2024 election changed hands, with the Conservatives losing 244 seats and Labour gaining 211 seats. This level of change was unsurprising given that 40% of people voted for a different party in 2024 than they had in 2019.[61]

The volatility in seats is due partly to the nature of the UK's first-past-the-post electoral system, as once a party rises above or below a particular threshold level of votes the gain or loss in seats can be dramatic as was seen in Scotland. The winner-takes-all constituency system means that relatively small changes in vote share can be translated by the system into dramatic seat gains or losses. However, part of the growing volatility is due to focused party strategies that target resources at specific seats and the public's willingness to engage in tactical voting.

In 2024, the determination of voters to punish the Conservatives was so strong that voters appeared willing to lend their support to whichever party was best placed to beat Conservative candidates. John Curtice in *The Times* observed that "the scale of anti-Conservative tactical voting was remarkable".[62] In *The Guardian,* Will Jennings also observed that there had been "intense tactical voting".[63] Dr Anton Howes argued that such tactical voting allowed the electorate "to mete out proper punishment" and claimed the 2024 election result showed the first-past-the-post system at its best.[64]

Both the Liberal Democrats and the Labour Party advanced

most where they were the primary opponents to the Conservatives in winnable target seats. Where Labour were the main challenger to the Conservatives, support for the party rose by six points, while support for the Liberal Democrats fell. By contrast, where the main challenger to the Conservatives was the Liberal Democrats, their support rose by nine points compared to just one point nationally. The scale of tactical voting resulted in huge swings against incumbent candidates. Voters were demonstrably switching to the Conservative Party's main challenger to remove their MPs. It was this tactical voting that helped the Liberal Democrats to win 72 seats, their highest since 1923.

The success of targeted, efficient vote strategies and increased tactical voting meant the conversion of votes to seats was highly disproportional. Heinz Brandenburg, a University of Strathclyde political scientist, analysed the election using the Gallagher Index (the standard measure academics use to describe disproportionality) and found the 2024 election scored 24, beating the previous record of 21 in 1931. Thus, statistically, the 2024 election was the most disproportional electoral outcome in British electoral history.

Dylan Difford looked at other measures of disproportionality, such as Loosemore-Hanby and Sainte-Lague indexes, and also found the result to be the least proportional in British election history, commenting, "However you assess it, this election was so extremely disproportional that it is an outlier by western democratic standards, let alone UK ones."[65]

Robert Peston was also quick to emphasise this disproportionality, commenting, "If you believe that the configuration of the Commons should roughly reflect the revealed preferences of voters, this is not a fair result."[66] John Curtice also observed that "Labour's strength in the new House of Commons is a heavily exaggerated reflection of the party's limited popularity in the country."[67]

It can be argued the Labour Party was forced to focus on voter efficiency. In 2017, Corbyn piled up votes in safe Labour seats and won 40% of the national vote but failed to win a majority of seats. Under the first-past-the-post system whether a party wins a seat by a single vote or ten thousand votes doesn't matter in terms of seats won. As Lewis Goodall observed, "Voter efficiency is everything in the British system. If you master that you win."[68]

This was something that the Labour Party, the Liberal Democrats, and the Green Party all recognised. Their focus was on maximising their voter efficiency rather than trying to increase their vote share across all seats. They targeted resources on specific constituencies where they could establish themselves as the main challenger and persuade people to vote tactically to remove a Conservative candidate. The overwhelming success of this approach is likely to shape the future election strategies of challenger parties, including Reform.

PART IV

THE FUTURE

15

THE NEW ELECTORAL LANDSCAPE

We are in an era of unstable voter coalitions.[1]

— JOHN CURTICE & LOVISA MOLLER VALLGARDA

The electoral landscape after 2024 is more fragmented and volatile than it has ever been. Voters are less loyal to political parties and more likely to switch their votes between parties. The old conceptual map of general elections as a pendulum swinging between two main parties no longer works. Stephen Bush has observed that "voters are now more willing to shop around" and vote for other parties.[2]

There is also increasing dissatisfaction with politics. After running dozens of focus groups, Luke Tryl believes the electorate is starkly disillusioned and overwhelmingly distrusts politicians of all parties.[3] Professor Ben Ansell argues the 2024 election highlighted the public's significant disaffection with both of the main political parties and was "a cry for new options".[4]

In the past, both Labour and the Conservatives had a core and loyal electoral base, and elections were decided by a relatively small number of swing voters that moved between the two parties. There was often an assumption that voters were distributed between the two main parties on a bell-curve distribution and that the winning party was the one that could gain the most voters in the centre. This led political strategists such as Peter Mandelson to argue that elections could only be won from the centre.[5] Hence, in previous elections there was a heavy focus on identifying the swing voters that parties needed to win over, such as the Mondeo man or the Worcester woman.

The results of the latest two elections suggest that a significant chunk of voters have become detached from the main parties. Apart from the two Brexit elections of 2017 and 2019, no party has got over 40% of the vote since 2001. Thus, Labour and the Conservatives can no longer take certain seats and their voters for granted, such as those in the Red Wall or the Blue Wall, and simply focus on winning over swing voters.

The broad Labour and Conservative coalitions of the past might have satisfactorily accommodated voters when the main political cleavage was a class-based left-right divide, but this is now far less important in determining how someone votes. Instead, new social, cultural, and economic cleavages are emerging around issues such as immigration and the environment. The old coalitions are increasingly fragile because they contain groups that are diametrically opposed to each other on these new cleavages.

The high level of political distrust in Britain – higher than in every other OECD country other than Czechia – has further increased the fragility of political coalitions. Distrustful and cynical voters are far more willing to switch parties between elections. To use James Kanagasooriam's apt analogy, political coalitions these days are more like sandcastles – impressive but liable to be swept away.[6]

The scale of tactical voting and the aggregate shifts in voting in 2024 were remarkable. For example, the Green Party overturned a 24,000 Conservative majority in North Herefordshire, while an independent candidate overturned a 22,000 Labour majority in Leicester South. The success of smaller parties points to an increasingly fragmented and unpredictable electoral landscape.

Andrew Marr has observed that an angry, anti-politics mood is on the march,[7] which provides new opportunities for smaller parties, including independent, populist and anti-incumbent candidates.

The growth in support for smaller parties lowers the bar for winning parties as the vote is more fragmented. For example, the success of Reform in former Red Wall constituencies lowered the bar for Labour, allowing it to win back seats despite minor increases in its vote share or, indeed, no increase in its vote share at all.

The new political cleavages and the values of voters are increasingly driving vote choices. John Curtice and Lovisa Moller Vallgarda, through the British Social Attitudes Survey, have identified six groups or clusters of voters who tend to consistently share common attitudes and values.[8] They are:

Middle Britons (26%)

The largest group represents the closest approximation to the 'typical' British voter. They often sympathise with left-wing economic narratives but lean towards Euroscepticism and express mild concerns about immigration. Their size makes them a crucial target for all political parties.

Well-off traditionalists (12%)

A highly engaged, predominantly conservative group. Mostly older white men who own their homes and feel financially secure. They strongly align with traditional values and are actively involved in politics.

Apolitical centrists (17%)

The least politically engaged segment. They tend to avoid following news, don't align with any particular party, and generally resist change. Their political apathy is their defining characteristic.

Left-behind patriots (15%)

Economically left wing but socially conservative and nationalist. This group is particularly prevalent in small towns and cities across Northern England and the so-called 'Red Wall' areas. They embody a unique blend of economic progressivism and social conservatism.

Urban progressives (16%)

Typically, university-educated professionals with left-leaning economic views. They view immigration positively and, if they participated in the EU referendum, overwhelmingly voted to Remain. They represent a cosmopolitan, liberal demographic.

Soft-left liberals (14%)

This group tends to be liberal on social issues but more centrist economically. Generally older and more established in their careers than urban progressives, they feel relatively financially comfortable. They balance progressive social views with moderate economic stances.

Other organisations have identified similar cleavages and distinct voting groups, such as More in Common's seven segments[9] and BMG's clans.[10]

It is too early to predict the end of two-party dominance in the UK, not least because Brexit showed how the emergence of a major polarising issue can drive voters back to the two main parties, as it did in 2017. However, in the absence of a major polarising issue, building a stable coalition across these groups will be difficult for Labour and the Conservatives.

Keir Starmer steered a course through this new electoral landscape successfully in 2024, but he was helped by the overwhelming desire of voters to punish the Conservatives and the split of Conservative and Reform voters. Despite its landslide victory in seats, the Labour Party's vote share was still fragile and the fragmentation of its coalition was visible in the seats it lost to independent candidates and the Greens.

The growing volatility of the electorate, their lack of attachment to the main parties, and their greater willingness to vote tactically to punish incumbents has created new opportunities for challenger parties. The Liberal Democrats, the Greens, and independent candidates have all shown how smaller parties can build a base in a constituency through intense local activity and a ruthless targeting of resources. Their aim was to establish themselves as the main challenger and to build a tactical voting alliance to unseat the incumbent MP.

The success of this approach in 2024 suggests we will see it adopted in future elections. Smaller parties are likely to target seats where they can develop a challenger narrative. For example, the Green Party will be focusing on the 40 seats where it finished second to Labour and particularly on the 15 seats where it received over 20% of the vote.

Reform finished second in 98 constituencies in 2024 but arguably had the least targeted campaign. Reform MP and former leader Richard Tice has said his party will seek to learn from the success of the Liberal Democrats' targeted campaign.[11]

Implications for the new Labour government

Labour won a landslide in 2024, but landslides only happen when the ground becomes unstable.

One might imagine that after a landslide, the ground settles, and similar events are less likely to occur in the future. The reality is that such events often increase the likelihood of future landslides. Slopes that don't experience landslips tend to have more vegetation with deeper roots that stabilise the soil. Whereas on slopes that have suffered landslides, the plants have shallower roots and unstable soil. The 2024 Labour landslide was the result of voters becoming detached from political parties, reducing the ideological roots which previously stabilised coalitions and reducing the friction that slowed the movement of voters between parties. Thus, in future, we may see even more dramatic voter shifts.

The Labour coalition was wide and diverse but shallow. An estimated 3.8m of Labour's voters did not vote for the party in 2019,[12] suggesting that around 40% do not have deep roots with the party. Over a million of their voters previously voted Conservative in 2019, while around 900,000 had voted for the Liberal Democrats. Almost three in ten (28%) of those voting for Labour said they had voted primarily to stop another party from winning.

The new government will face challenges in holding

together its electoral alliance. Analysts have pointed to the challenges it faces from Reform on the right, which is second to Labour in 90 Labour constituencies, primarily towns in the Midlands and north, and from the Greens, on the left, who are in second place to Labour in 39 mainly urban seats. However, Labour would appear to be more vulnerable to the 219 second-place Conservative candidates. Not only are there many more of these seats, but the party's average majority over second-place Conservatives is only 14%, compared to 25% for Reform and 34% for the Greens.

Labour's ability to fight off the Conservatives in the seats where they are second will depend not only on Labour's policy successes in government but also on the Conservatives' ability to rebuild their electoral base after the scale of their collapse in 2024.

The increased willingness of people to engage in transactional voting means that even constituencies with large Labour majorities can no longer be considered safe, and the election did not bless the party with large majorities. The party's median majority in 2024 was 6,286, the lowest since 1929. In 25 seats, the Labour majority was less than 1,000 votes and would be lost on a swing of 1% or less. A swing of just 4% would wipe out 75 Labour seats. The Labour government's majority has been compared to a Jenga tower, which has been raised high by taking blocks out of the foundations. The result is a tall tower with a base full of holes that could collapse very quickly.[13]

The potential fragility of the Labour government's electoral base was reflected in its poll ratings. When it was elected, it had a negative favourability rating of -21 according to Ipsos, much lower than that of recent new governments.[14] Two months after the election, YouGov found that only 23% of people approved of the new government, compared to 46% when David Cameron was elected in 2010.[15]

The government's low ratings fell precipitously after it announced a decision to means-test the winter fuel allowance and became embroiled in a scandal that arose over gifts that the Prime Minister had received. The winter fuel allowance decision landed very badly with pensioners, as might be expected, with over 70% opposed to the decision. In focus groups Luke Tryl said he was taken aback at just how negative the initial reactions had been. The decision was also criticised by Martin Lewis, the popular founder of the Money Saving Expert site, who said the targeting through the use of pension credit was too narrow, particularly in the light of the forecast rise in the energy price cap of 10% later in 2024.[16]

By September 2024, YouGov found the new government's approval rating had fallen to -36,[17] while Starmer's personal favourability rating had fallen to -21, the lowest since February 2024.[18]

The day before the Labour Party conference opened in September 2024, Opinium released a new poll for *The Observer*. It reported that Starmer's net approval rating had fallen to its lowest ever in their polls (-26%), down by a remarkable 45 points from his first approval rating as prime minister three months earlier.[19]

In October 2024, YouGov found Starmer's personal favourability rating had fallen further to -36, the lowest since he became Labour leader.[20] Immediately prior to the Budget, in a further sign of electoral volatility, More in Common reported that Starmer had suffered the biggest post-election fall in approval ratings of any Prime Minister in the modern era.[21] His rating had fallen 49 points from +11 in July 2024 to -38 in October 2024.

Following the Budget, there was an uptick in the approval ratings of both Keir Starmer and Rachel Reeves. According to More in Common, Starmer's ratings increased by eight points to -30.[22]

The first Labour Budget

In her first major campaign speech, Rachel Reeves promised that the party's plans for government were fully funded and there would be no additional tax rises beyond those the party set out in its manifesto, "no ifs, no ands, no buts".[23]

During the election campaign, Labour sought to reassure voters again and again that it would not increase taxes or borrowing. For example, when challenged at her press conference on 11 June 2024, Rachel Reeves said, "We don't need higher taxes, what we need is growth." She asserted that Labour's ambitions were "fully funded" and she had no plans "to be a big tax-raising chancellor", while Starmer insisted that, unlike past Labour leaders, he wouldn't "reach for the tax lever".

Both analysts and commentators had been frustrated during the election campaign at the dishonesty of both main parties when it came to the country's financial position. Sam Freedman commented that it was infuriating, as anyone who went through the numbers could see that £40bn of additional taxes was required and that the fiscal rules had to be amended to allow more borrowing, and yet the election was fought "with everyone pretending it wasn't true".[24]

On 30 October 2024, Rachel Reeves unveiled the biggest tax-raising budget since 1993. The Office for Budget Responsibility said it would increase public spending by £70bn annually, with two-thirds on current spending and one-third on capital spending.[25] Half was to be funded through tax increases, which would push the tax take to a record 38% of GDP, while the rest was to be funded by £32bn more borrowing annually. The core tax-raising measure was a £25bn increase in employer National Insurance contributions by raising the rate and lowering the threshold.

The Labour budget was clearly ideological, characterised

by a strong class element with higher taxes on the wealthy, such as increases in inheritance tax, capital gains tax, tax on private schools and more tax on private flights, while increasing the minimum wage and not increasing income tax or employee National Insurance.

Labour had engaged in weeks of linguistic sophistry about protecting 'working people' and sought to maintain a pretence that rising employer National Insurance contributions would not hit employees. However, the OBR downgraded its projections for real household income growth because it expected that a "substantial part" of the employer NICs increase would result in lower real wages. Paul Johnson of the IFS said to suggest the NICs increase wouldn't impact people's incomes was ludicrous.[26] Finally, Reeves was forced to admit that the tax would feed through to workers. The IFS budget analysis showed that staff-intensive businesses employing low-wage employees, such as care homes, would face the biggest hit from the increase in the employer's rate of National Insurance.

In its analysis, the OBR forecast that Britain's economy would grow by more than expected in 2024 and 2025 but by less than previously forecast in the following three years. At the end of five years, the size of the economy would be no larger than prior to the Budget changes. This was particularly worrying for Starmer and Reeves as their claims that their tax-raising Budget was a one-off heavily depended on economic growth. In response Reeves argued that economic growth would be boosted by the government's forthcoming reforms of pensions and planning.

The OBR also forecasted that inflation and interest rates would both be higher because of the decisions in the Budget. This was evidenced by modest increases in gilt rates following the Budget as the scale of the planned spending and borrowing became clear.

The Budget provided an "emergency injection" into the day-to-day running of services by increasing public spending sharply for two years to address the public's concerns about crumbling services and to reverse previous austerity policies. It then proposed three years of spending restraint with very limited increases in day-to-day departmental spending after 2025.

Following the Budget, questions were immediately raised about whether the extra taxes and borrowing were enough to have a demonstrable impact on public services given the aging and growing population. This led to further questions about whether the limited increases in later years were realistic and whether a more generous settlement would be required, along with further tax rises, in the spring of 2025, when departmental spending allocations for future years would be determined.

The BBC's political editor, Chris Mason, commented that after comparing Labour's tax and borrowing promises prior to the election with the decisions in the budget, it would not be uncharitable to conclude the former were "comprehensive baloney".[27]

Instead of making the arguments for additional taxation and borrowing during the election, for fear of damaging the party's chances, Labour attempted to make the arguments after the Budget and sought to persuade people retrospectively they were necessary. The thin veneer Labour used to justify its lack of openness during the campaign was that once in office, they discovered that things were worse than they could ever have imagined. The obvious danger was that despite promising to level with the public, Starmer and Reeves had adopted an approach that might be viewed by the public as evasive and dishonest.

Tom Clark of the Resolution Foundation believed the approach may have further damaged public trust in politicians. He claimed that the Labour Party's best hope was that voters, who were never given the chance during the campaign to be persuaded that decent public services were worth paying for, could be "persuaded by experience instead".[28]

Public expectations: change and deliver

The electorate voted for change, and while the precise nature of the change was not defined by the Labour Party, it was clear that to the public, it meant a more competent government that would deliver improved public services and act in a more ethical manner. Voters were more likely to say they backed Labour at the general election because they saw it as more competent than the Tories, rather than because they preferred its policies.[29]

An Ipsos survey after the election revealed that 58% of the public expected the government to provide more money for public services, and 52% expected the government to improve the NHS by reducing waiting lists and improving access to GPs.[30]

A More in Common survey asked people how they would judge the success of the Labour government after five years. The three top answers were:

- How much they reduce NHS waiting lists (63%)
- How much they lower the cost of living (58%)
- How much they lower immigration (36%)[31]

The election of President Trump in November 2024 reinforced the importance of delivering on these core issues. Deborah Mattinson conducted focus groups in the United States during the election campaign with the 'hero voters' that Harris had to win. Mattinson found that their two main concerns were the cost of living and immigration, which mirrored concerns in the UK. In the United States, there was also a clear anti-incumbency vote, with many electors believing the previous administration had failed on these core issues.

Before the next election Labour will have to be able to demonstrably show that they are competent and have delivered on the changes they promised. Proving competence is one way to unite their diverse coalition as no one is going to be upset at lower NHS waiting lists, fewer train delays, economic growth, or lower inflation. These are not polarising issues, but they are areas where voters expect to see results.

A report on the election from Labour Together implored the party to be cautious and focus on delivery.

> "Labour must never take voters for granted. Indeed, it cannot, because many are simply giving Labour a chance. It must approach every day of governing in the knowledge that it will need to persuade voters again and again and again."
> Labour Together, How Labour Won[32]

Delivery will be difficult given the unrealistic public sector spending plans Labour has inherited. For the first time in many years, the government will have to run a primary surplus, which means it will need to raise more from people via taxation than it will spend on public services. In simple terms, people are going to have to pay more for less. Running a primary surplus will be particularly challenging as the population ages, requiring more spending on pensions and health.

Rebuilding trust

The potentially most difficult inheritance from the previous government is the collapse in the public's trust in politicians. Labour faces not only the huge task of resuscitating Britain's faltering economy and improving the country's crumbling public services but also the daunting challenge of restoring faith in the country's political system. Trust in politicians has been eroded to a point where the public is more sceptical than ever and has widespread doubts about the honesty, integrity, and competence of those in power.

The polls suggest that the public was seeking a new government that "rebuilds their faith in the political process itself, by being open to and respectful of their own attitudes and experiences".[33] This was something Starmer recognised and acknowledged in his conference speech in September 2024. He placed a strong emphasis on respect and promised to build a Britain "where working people are respected".[34]

One of the things that appears to drive Starmer is injustice, which came through in his speeches. When he sought selection as a Labour candidate, he said he was driven by "a burning desire to tackle inequality and injustice".[35] In opposition, his most trenchant criticisms of the Conservatives were about standards in government. The Labour Party's manifesto said that sleaze, scandal, and the failure to deliver on promises had eroded trust in politics, and Starmer promised to uphold "the highest standards of integrity and honesty".[36]

The BBC's Laura Kuenssberg has argued that this may create a problem for the government as by putting high moral standards on the table, they will be judged in a moral way.[37] A critical press will look to test the government's integrity and hold them to their proclaimed 'highest standards'. The public is cynical about politicians of all parties, and if Labour falls short, it will simply not be good enough to say they are better than the last lot. Such an approach will not restore public trust.

The early rows about Starmer and his team accepting free clothing and tickets while cutting the winter fuel allowance for pensioners significantly damaged his personal brand and reputation. If tabloid monikers such as Sir Shameless and Two

Tier Keir take hold, they will not easily be shaken off. Trust is something easily lost and difficult to regain.

In summary, tackling policy issues and making visible improvements in public services will be critically important for the Labour government, but that alone won't cut it in an era of distrust. Starmer has to develop a way of leading that makes people believe, for the first time in a long time, that those in power understand the challenges ordinary people face and are genuinely looking out for them.

16

THE FUTURE OF THE CONSERVATIVE PARTY

It is difficult to overstate the damage done to the Conservative Party brand during their 14 years in government. The scale of the challenge was laid bare in polling by Savanta after the election, which found that seven in ten voters believed the Conservative Party was unelectable, a view shared by 42% of people who voted Tory at the general election.[1]

In 2019, one could argue that it was relatively easy to see what Labour needed to do, even if it was difficult to achieve. Starmer's vision was to reconnect with lost voters by ditching Jeremy Corbyn, accepting Brexit, and moving to the centre. It is far harder to see what the Conservatives need to do after 2024.

The voters that defected from the Conservatives in 2024 split in a number of different directions; an estimated 23% to 25% went to Reform, 10% to 13% to Labour, 7% to the Liberal Democrats, and 3% to the Greens. In total, almost as many people left the party for the more progressive parties on the left as deserted the party for Reform on the right. The party's difficulty will be winning back both previous Remain voters who switched to the Liberal Democrats and former Leave voters who switched heavily to Reform.

In November 2024, Kemi Badenoch was elected as the new leader of the Conservative Party, with 53,000 votes against 41,000 for Robert Jenrick, with around 40,000 not voting. Badenoch received fewer votes than Rishi Sunak when he lost to Liz Truss, though it should be noted that the party's membership had fallen from 172,000 in 2022 to 132,000 in 2024. Back in 2005, the party had 254,000 members. The relatively low member vote for Badenoch, combined with her only winning the support of a third of MPs in the parliamentary stages of the contest, suggested she needed to build her base of support with both members and party MPs.

Polling by More in Common found that voters thought Badenoch could bring something new, different, and refreshing to the Conservative Party. They also thought she was honest and direct and wouldn't sugarcoat issues. Their main concerns were around her lack of experience and perceived lack of warmth.[2]

Following her election, Badenoch faced a number of key challenges:

- The Reform challenge
- The competence challenge
- The narrative challenge
- The demographic challenge

The Reform challenge

One reason the Conservatives have dominated parliament over the last 80 years is that the country's centre-right vote consolidated behind the party while the centre-left vote was divided between parties, primarily Labour and Liberal Democrats. The rise of Reform fatally divided the centre-right in 2024, making it easier for Labour to win seats from the Conservatives.

The threat from Farage and his colleagues is very real. Nearly a third (29%) of the Conservative Party's 2024 voters said they had considered voting for Reform, compared to 17% who said they had considered voting for the Liberal Democrats. This has led a number of Conservatives to argue that the party must win votes back from Reform and stop further voters defecting to them. However, a survey by Savanta suggests that Tory to Reform switchers are probably the hardest voters for the party to win back.[3] Less than a third (31%) of those who voted for Reform say they might otherwise have voted Conservative. The remaining two-thirds say they would have backed other parties.[4]

Many Conservatives believe it is necessary to unite the centre-right vote to win again, which could mean a formal merger or some form of deal with Reform. Tim Montgomerie, for example, has argued that the party should seek an electoral accommodation with Reform, where the parties agree not to compete in certain seats. Others have argued that the party should seek to absorb Reform, but Kemi Badenoch has said Nigel Farage would not be welcome in the party, saying, "We are a broad church but if somebody says they want to burn your church down, we don't let them in."[5]

A YouGov survey after the election revealed that 42% of Conservative Party members would support a merger with Reform, while 51% would oppose such a move.[6] Only 34% of party members felt the party should move to the centre with 51% believing the party should move to the right to attract Reform voters.

Chris Hopkins, the UK political research director at Savanta, said the Conservatives were under-appreciating the stubbornness of Reform voters and the difficulty of convincing them to return to the Conservatives. The other problem is that even if the party could win back every vote that went to Reform in the general election *and* keep all of its 2024 voters, it would still only win 302 seats, which falls short of securing the 326 seats required for a bare majority in parliament.[7]

More moderate Conservatives have argued that rather than seeking to accommodate Reform, the party should move to the centre where elections are normally won. Andy Street, the former Tory mayor of the West Midlands, argues the party must rediscover the values of "moderation, integrity, compassion and service".[8]

It is possible that Reform may implode in some way which will lessen their threat to the Conservatives. The party has already changed its name and branding three times in four elections. While Farage is a charismatic presence in TV studios, it is less clear he is able to build an election-winning machine. However, after the election, Richard Tice and Nigel Farage both claimed they were serious about creating a more professional party.[9] If Reform does become increasingly professional, does more work building a base on the ground in constituencies, and develops a targeted approach to election campaigns, there is a risk that it could become an even greater threat to the Conservatives.

The competence challenge

After 2016, the Conservative Party lost its reputation for competence and lost the trust of key groups of voters. There is evidence that people primarily broke with the Conservatives over the issue of competence, but where they went depended on their values. So, more authoritarian voters went to Reform, while others went to Labour, the Liberal Democrats, or other parties, and others stayed at home.

A key challenge is how the party rebuilds its reputation for competence while in opposition. Some commentators have argued that voters become frustrated with governments and that if Labour begins to look incompetent, then the Conservatives will appear competent by comparison. Thus, time will solve some of the party's problems. The difficulty with this argument is that the voters may desert Labour, but they may not return to the Conservatives. They may express their dissatisfaction with the government by voting for the Greens, independents, or Reform.

To rebuild trust and a reputation for competence, the party must be seen to be united under an effective leader. The leadership team also needs to exude capability and integrity. There needs to be a perception of discipline, not one of constant infighting between factions. Disagreements should be managed privately rather than publicly. Anthony Seldon has referred to the party as fissiparous or liable to tribalism, and further bouts of infighting will damage its reputation for competence.[10]

The party also has to be seen to put the needs of the public above party politics. This will mean supporting Labour when they implement policies that are beneficial for the country.

The party also needs to be honest about its own failings while in government. A 40-page pamphlet promoted by Kemi Badenoch as part of her leadership campaign, *Conservatism in Crisis*[11] was remarkable in failing to address why the Conservatives lost the election. There was no acknowledgement that the party presided over crumbling public services and was perceived as incompetent. The only reference was to the failure to control immigration; there was not a single mention of competence.

The narrative challenge

One of the Conservative Party's key challenges is to define a new narrative or reclaim a previous narrative. Fundamentally, what does the party stand for?

When parties lose general elections, such as that in 2024, there is invariably a period of introspection when the losing party examines why it lost and what it must do to win in the future. The range of Conservative Party groupings, including the One Nation Conservatives, the Popular Conservatives, the New Conservatives, the National Conservatives, and the Common Sense Group, reflects the debate over the party's future direction.

Traditionally, the party has claimed to be the party of sound economic management, and a supporter of the free market, a smaller state, and lower taxes. Following the Truss debacle, it may take some time for the Conservative Party to recover its reputation as economically competent.

If the party is going to advocate for a smaller state, it needs to be clear what this means and the significant reductions in state activity it would like to see. The frequent cries for reductions in foreign aid, fewer regulations, and cuts in funding to arts organisations are too small to make any real difference to the level of state spending. The big spending areas, such as the NHS, schools, and local government, have already been cut heavily, and there appears little scope for further reductions. Indeed, the public in 2024 wanted to see more investment, not less, in these areas while accepting that there could be some scope for greater efficiency. Even the Conservative 2019 voters who defected to Reform wanted to see more investment in public spending and an improved NHS.

It is not clear the Conservatives have yet understood that the electorate is more supportive of state intervention and public services than they are. At their 2024 autumn conference there was a lot of focus on the party's failures on immigration but far less on the party's multiple failures on public services. While it successfully reduced the tax burden on average earners to its lowest level in 50 years,[12] it was achieved through drastic reductions in public services. Reductions that the electorate punished the party for making.

The party does not appear to have acknowledged that its ideological commitment to a smaller state and lower taxes was rejected by the electorate. If the party is going to continue to argue for lower taxes in the future, how will it reconcile this with voters' demands for improved public services and the growing costs of pensions, social care, and healthcare? And what about the party's own desire to spend more on defence, border security, and prisons?

In her pamphlet, *Conservatism in Crisis,* Kemi Badenoch argued that what all Conservatives want is "growth, social cohesion, better public services and sustainably lower taxes".[13] The potential dichotomy of lower taxes and better public services was not recognised. She argues that taxes can be cut significantly while at the same time improving public services. She believes this could be done by reducing regulation, cutting welfare spending, and making cuts in what she terms the bureaucratic class, primarily administrators such as human resources, equalities, and compliance staff.

All of the groups of voters the Conservatives lost in 2024 were to the left of the party on key economic issues, including Reform voters.[14] These voters want to see more public service investment and are not instinctively small-state advocates. The centre-right think tank Onward argues the Conservatives will, therefore, have to craft a strong story that the party can manage and improve public services, particularly the NHS, which will mean a new triangulation around the issue of tax cuts and public spending.

Badenoch's core narrative in her *Conservatism in Crisis*

pamphlet is that a new progressive left has captured the state and promoted extensive interventionism that was 'destroying growth'. Thus, Badenoch argues that the priority is tackling this new progressive bureaucratic class. She argues that a Conservative government will need to ditch radical environmental and identity politics, limit migration, reduce endless HR, compliance, and sustainability rules, and bring down the cost of the welfare state.

As the political commentator Steve Richards argues, narrative really matters in politics as it creates a core sense of purpose and mission that will hopefully resonate with target voters.[15] However, it begs the question, who are the party's target voters?

Prior to Brexit, the Conservative Party was very much a party of the middle class, but following Brexit it has increasingly drawn its support from working-class people. In 2019, the party was just as successful among working-class voters as middle-class voters. It has been particularly successful in winning support from older, more socially conservative voters, who didn't go to university, and by 2024 these people made up around half of the party's voters.

Onward has identified a group of voters that it believes the party should target, which it calls the 'super-demographics'. These people are older, white, mortgage-free homeowners, Brexit voters, who don't hold a degree, are C2 social class, and live in less dense constituencies.[16] Onward claims that the party won 82% of voters with five or more of these super-demographic characteristics in 2019 but just 40% of these voters in 2024, with many defecting to Reform or the Liberal Democrats.

Onward argues that these super-demographic voters have traditionally voted Conservative, and believes this group of voters have to be won back as they are efficiently spread across constituencies. For example, Onward points out that a 10-point swing to the Tories among homeowners would allow the party to win an extra 127 seats because of their efficient spread across constituencies.

On the basis of its analysis, Onward argues that the party's first priority should be winning back the older defectors who went to Reform and the Liberal Democrats. Onward claims these voters share similar underlying values, for example, holding socially conservative values on issues such as crime and immigration. It argues these are the party's more natural voters, and "the party simply won't have any chance of winning again until it can convince 50 to 64-year-olds to vote Conservative again".[17] However, this strategy fails to address the party's longer term and very significant structural and demographic challenges.

The demographic challenge

The party's voting base in 2024 was older than it had ever been. The only age group the Conservatives won in the election was the over-65-year-olds. On current trends, there is a real danger that the Conservative Party will become the pensioner party.

The country's changing demographics will make it increasingly difficult for the party to win unless they can increase their appeal to younger people. Focaldata has estimated that some 17%, or one in six of those who voted Conservative in 2024, will have died by the time of the next election. That would mean over a million fewer Tory voters lost solely as a result of demography.[18] By contrast, the Labour Party is anticipated to gain the support of 800,000 young people who become legally able to vote before the next election, compared to just 160,000 for the Conservatives. If Labour legislates to grant the vote to 16 and 17-year-olds as they intend, the position is likely to get worse for the Conservatives.

Young people's perceptions of the Tories declined markedly

after Brexit. The percentage of 18 to 34-year-olds saying they strongly disliked the Conservative Party jumped from around 20% prior to the Brexit referendum to over 40% by 2023.[19]

This was the age group that Thatcher successfully appealed to in the 1980s. Her policies, including lower taxes, 'right to buy', and the sale of shares in previously nationalised industries, were designed to appeal to young aspirational voters and encourage social mobility. In 1979, 42% of 18 to 24-year-olds and 43% of 25 to 34-year-olds voted for the Conservative Party.[20] In 2024, the party secured just 5% of the votes of 18 to 24-year-olds and 10% of the votes of 25 to 34-year-olds. The party came fifth amongst this younger age group, behind Labour, the Greens, the Liberal Democrats and Reform.[21]

The Conservative Party has arguably been too focused on maintaining the support of the older generation of homeowners and become detached from the aspirations and values of the next generation. This matters because the party can no longer rely on the traditional conservatising effect of age, which was observable in previous generations as voters became homeowners, got married, and had children.

Phil Burton-Cartledge has argued that people are increasingly socially liberal, not because of the role of universities or the decline of conservative institutions but because of their experience of work.[22] As manufacturing industries declined in the UK they were replaced by service industries, and by the time the Conservatives came to power in 2010, around 80% of people worked in the service industry.

Service industries require staff to focus on empathy, care, communication, and tolerance of diversity across customers. Companies run regular courses on these issues and reward those who demonstrate these values and competencies. Thus, younger people's experiences of work are markedly different from those of their parents and grandparents, who worked in manufacturing industries, and are the least socially liberal generation.

Britain's younger generation overwhelmingly voted for the stability of remaining in Europe and are particularly frustrated at the broken housing market. Like the previous generations, they aspire to own their own homes but find it increasingly difficult as house prices and rents have increased relative to salaries.

The difficulties faced by young people in buying their own home are reflected in the decline in young adults (25 to 34-year-olds) owning their own homes since 1990. This decline has been far more marked in Britain than in other countries. In the US the figure has fallen by six percent, in Germany it's down eight percent, in France just three percent but in Britain it has fallen 22%.[23]

The Conservative Party's problems with younger voters are stark. Sam Freedman has observed that the real challenge for the Conservatives is "finding a way to reconnect with younger and middle-aged people earning, or hoping to earn, decent salaries and own a home".[24]

Freedman and Lewis Baston argue that Battersea highlights the challenge faced by the Conservative Party.[25] It is the UK constituency with the highest proportion of graduates and the highest proportion of those in professional and managerial employment. Thirty percent of the population is 25–34 years old, compared to 13% nationally.[26] These young, relatively wealthy professionals might have been considered ideal Tory voters, but Battersea voted 75% to Remain in the EU referendum and voted for Jeremy Corbyn's Labour Party in 2017. The Conservative Party lost the seat as its vote fell from over 50% to 41.5%. The party's vote fell further to 36% in 2019, and their vote collapsed to just 23% in 2024. In the seven years from 2017 to 2024 the Conservative vote in Battersea more than halved.

For the Conservative Party to win again, it needs to find a

way to appeal to young, aspirational, and socially liberal voters. In Europe, parties of the right have done this by promoting practical policies that will materially improve the economic situation of young people.

The future of the Conservative Party?

The scale of the Conservative Party's defeat would typically mean that the party will be out of government for at least two terms. However, the volatility of the electorate, the unpopularity of the Labour government, and the marginality of seats will give the party hope that it can recover quickly. There were 71 seats where the Conservatives were less than 3,000 votes behind the first-placed party and 124 seats where the party was less than 5,000 votes behind.

The party's priority must be to rebuild its reputation for competence. It is a prerequisite to winning back the 1.8m-plus people who voted Conservative in 2019 but stayed at home in 2024, and the five million plus that defected to other parties. While voters may have defected to Reform or the Liberal Democrats, depending on their values, they broke with the party primarily because of concerns over competence.

The party also has to create or reclaim a clear narrative about its vision for the country that will resonate with voters. This narrative appeal has to move beyond its core older base and engage younger, more socially liberal voters while at the same time seeing off the challenge of Reform on its right. It also has to craft a narrative that reconciles its desire for lower taxes with the electorate's desire to rebuild public services.

Ben Riley-Smith has argued that no one should underestimate the Conservative Party's lust for power, which he believes will drive the changes required for it to become electable again. However, the party faces significant electoral, structural, and demographic challenges. Even the 121 seats the party won in 2024 are less secure and more precarious than might be assumed. In 2019, the average Tory majority was 14,500; in 2024, it was just 3,500.

To win an election in the future, the Conservative Party will have to assemble and maintain a broad coalition of voters. Something that will be increasingly difficult amid the growth of new social, economic, and cultural cleavages. High levels of distrust and an angry, anti-politics mood mean that future elections are likely to be more fragmented and unpredictable. The success of smaller parties also means the Conservatives cannot rely on voters becoming disaffected with Labour and turning back to them as they did in the past. The future is not what it was.

If the Conservative Party does not grasp the gravity of its current challenges, the 2024 election could become a defining moment and herald its permanent demise.

AFTERWORD

Dear Reader,

I hope you found this book enjoyable and thought-provoking.

I would love your feedback and would particularly welcome a review on Amazon. It only takes a few minutes to post a couple of sentences that sum up your thoughts. I would really appreciate you taking the time. Here is the short link - https://amzn.to/48fzWsp or you can search for the book on Amazon.

If you would like updates about the book and news about future books, please sign up for my mailing list at www.steverayson.com.

Thank you.

Steve

ANNEX 1 – RED WALL SEATS

Alyn and Deeside (part formerly Clwyd South)
Ashfield
Barrow and Furness
Bassetlaw
Birmingham Northfield
Bishop Auckland
Blackpool South
Blyth Valley (large area moved to Cramlington)
Bolsover
Bolton North East
Burnley
Bury South
Clwyd East (part formerly Clwyd South)
Copeland (now Whitehaven and Workington)
Darlington
Don Valley (now Doncaster East)
Dudley North (now Dudley)
Great Grimsby (now Great Grimsby and Cleethorpes)
Hartlepool (won in 2021)
Heywood and Middleton

Hyndburn
Leigh (now Leigh and Atherton)
Mansfield
Newcastle-under-Lyme
North East Derbyshire
Ossett and Denby Dale (part formerly Wakefield)
Penistone and Stocksbridge
Redcar
Rother Valley
Scunthorpe
Sedgefield (now Newton Aycliffe)
Stoke-on-Trent Central
Stoke-on-Trent North
Stoke-on-Trent South
Wakefield and Rothwell (part formerly Wakefield)
Walsall North (now Walsall and Bloxwich)
West Bromwich East (now West Bromwich)
West Bromwich West (now Tipton)
Wolverhampton North
Wrexham

NOTES

Introduction

1. https://www.tortoisemedia.com/audio/what-just-happened/
2. https://www.ncpolitics.uk/2020/03/rally-round-the-flag/#more-3527
3. https://www.bloomberg.com/view/articles/2020-03-28/coronavirus-gives-boris-johnson-s-political-immunity?embedded-checkout=true
4. https://yougov.co.uk/international/articles/29429-perception-government-handling-COVID-19
5. https://yougov.co.uk/topics/politics/trackers/which-political-party-would-be-the-best-at-handling-the-economy
6. https://www.theguardian.com/politics/2024/feb/17/keir-starmer-reportedly-wanted-to-quit-after-2021-byelection-defeat
7. https://www.thetimes.com/uk/politics/article/boris-johnson-eyes-decade-in-power-5p8hfd72p
8. https://yougov.co.uk/topics/politics/trackers/voting-intention
9. https://www.economist.com/britain/2019/12/21/britains-tories-are-the-worlds-most-successful-party-heres-why
10. https://www.thetimes.com/uk/politics/article/boris-johnson-eyes-decade-in-power-5p8hfd72p
11. https://www.moreincommon.org.uk/general-election-2024/focus-group-live-bury-north/
12. https://www.ipsos.com/en-uk/ipsos-trust-in-professions-veracity-index-2023
13. https://yougov.co.uk/politics/articles/49851-general-election-2024-84-of-britons-say-public-services-are-in-poor-shape
14. https://x.com/WeAreNewBritain/status/1808463115454931132
15. https://www.ipsos.com/en-uk/sharp-improvement-in-economic-optimism-but-little-benefit-conservatives-who-still-trail-significantly
16. https://www.ipsos.com/en-uk/eight-ten-britons-are-dissatisfied-how-government-running-country
17. https://www.ft.com/content/820de7fe-3ec6-4585-a4ce-c450261b3794
18. https://www.tortoisemedia.com/audio/what-just-happened/
19. https://www.economist.com/britain/2024/05/29/the-british-election-is-becoming-an-episode-of-mob-justice
20. https://podcasts.apple.com/gb/podcast/labours-landslide-victory-can-it-get-any-worse-for/id1709628885?i=1000661210459
21. https://podcasts.apple.com/gb/podcast/which-dumped-tory-will-do-strictly/id1718287198?i=1000661593158
22. https://kellnerp.substack.com/p/exposed-the-truth-about-labours-red

1. Fragile Coalitions and Volatile Voters

1. https://www.thetimes.com/uk/politics/article/labour-winning-coalition-political-sandcastle-ukip-keir-starmer-mlkq8zdbp
2. https://www.bbc.co.uk/news/election-2019-50777071
3. https://www.ncpolitics.uk/2020/03/rally-round-the-flag/#more-3527
4. https://news.sky.com/story/general-election-2019-boris-johnson-has-pulled-off-a-victory-to-match-the-best-of-the-thatcher-years-11885210
5. https://www.ft.com/content/4c7594b9-22f3-4a31-8168-4b2622e2d685
6. https://x.com/BBCPolitics/status/1205488514231623680
7. https://www.ft.com/content/4c7594b9-22f3-4a31-8168-4b2622e2d685
8. https://www.ft.com/content/6062ecf0-70d8-4433-bc3b-b2a66dfd162c
9. https://www.independent.co.uk/voices/keir-starmer-poll-sunak-labour-tories-election-b2563201.html
10. https://www.thetimes.com/article/2bbb7d60-3641-11ea-ad7c-b6ce6c640a19?
11. John Curtice in *The Conservative Effect 2010-2024: 14 Wasted Years?*, ed. Anthony Seldon and Tom Egerton (Cambridge: Cambridge University Press, 2014), p. 482.
12. Jamie Furlong and Will Jennings, *The Changing Electoral Map of England and Wales* (Oxford: Oxford University Press, 2024).
13. https://news.sky.com/story/the-similarities-and-differences-between-starmers-support-now-and-blairs-1997-landslide-13161920
14. Edward Fieldhouse, Jane Green, Geoffrey Evans, Jonathan Mellon, Christopher Prosser, Hermann Schmitt and Cees Van Der Eijk, *Electoral Shocks: The Volatile Voter in a Turbulent World*, 1st edn (Oxford: Oxford Scholarship Online, 2020), p. 31.
15. https://www.ft.com/content/28e94b6a-fd64-445f-a258-7ec5c5a6b1cd
16. https://x.com/michael_hal/status/1545528402618327040
17. Margaret Levi, Laura Stoker, 'Political Trust and Trustworthiness', *Annual Review of Political Science*, Vol 3, 2000, 475–507, https://www.annualreviews.org/content/journals/10.1146/annurev.polisci.3.1.475
18. Eri Bertsou, 'Rethinking political distrust', *European Political Science Review*, Vol 11, Issue 2, May 2019, 213–230, https://www.cambridge.org/core/journals/european-political-science-review/article/rethinking-political-distrust/69AD47ECCF3765EFC4F772BB9DFE2596
19. Professor Sir John Curtice, Ian Montagu and Chujan Sivathasan, 'Damaged Politics? The impact of the 2019-24 Parliament on political trust and confidence', National Centre for Social Research, https://natcen.ac.uk/sites/default/files/2024-06/BSA%2041%20Damaged%20Politics.pdf
20. https://ukandeu.ac.uk/trust-distrust-and-the-2019-general-election/
21. Remko Voogd, Tom van der Meer, Wouter van der Brug, 'Political Trust as a Determinant of Volatile Vote Intentions: Separating Within- From Between-Person Effects', *International Journal of Public Opinion Research*, Vol 31:4, Winter 2019, 669–693, https://academic.oup.com/ijpor/article-abstract/31/4/669/5298561?redirectedFrom=PDF

22. Martin Okolikj, Silke Goubin, Dieter Stiers and Marc Hooghe, 'Trust in political parties and ideological proximity voting in Europe: the role of trust in political parties as a heuristic mechanism', *Journal of Elections, Public Opinion and Parties*, Vol 34, 2024, Issue 1, 116–135, https://www.tandfonline.com/doi/full/10.1080/17457289.2022.2113088
23. Professor Sir John Curtice et al (June 2024), 'Damaged Politics? The impact of the 2019-24 Parliament on political trust and confidence', National Centre for Social Research, https://natcen.ac.uk/sites/default/files/2024-06/BSA%2041%20Damaged%20Politics.pdf
24. Ibid, https://natcen.ac.uk/sites/default/files/2024-06/BSA%2041%20Damaged%20Politics.pdf
25. https://www.ippr.org/articles/trust-issues
26. https://strongmessagehere.substack.com/p/getting-to-know-labours-new-electoral
27. https://www.independent.co.uk/news/uk/politics/what-is-tactical-voting-general-election-where-b2556989.html
28. https://strongmessagehere.substack.com/p/the-blue-wall-a-primer
29. https://www.theguardian.com/politics/2021/jun/19/the-blue-wall-what-next-for-the-tories-after-a-shock-byelection-defeat
30. https://www.markpack.org.uk/167813/lessons-from-that-blue-wall-photo-stunt-with-ed-davey/
31. https://www.theguardian.com/politics/2021/jun/19/the-blue-wall-what-next-for-the-tories-after-a-shock-byelection-defeat
32. https://strongmessagehere.substack.com/p/the-blue-wall

2. A Decade of Political Shocks

1. https://www.theguardian.com/commentisfree/2023/dec/05/brexit-leave-remain-tories-labour-voting-trends
2. https://www.theguardian.com/politics/2010/feb/21/gordon-brown-saved-banks
3. Margaret Levi and Laura Stoker, 'Political Trust and Trustworthiness', *Annual Review of Political Science*, 3 (2000), 475–507.
4. John E. Mueller, 'Presidential Popularity from Truman to Johnson', *American Political Science Review*, 64:1 (1970), 18–34.
5. Marc J. Hetherington and Michael Nelson, 'Anatomy of a Rally Effect: George W. Bush and the War on Terrorism', *Political Science and Politics*, 36:1 (2003), 37–42.
6. https://ukandeu.ac.uk/the-rally-round-the-flag-effect-and-covid-19/
7. https://www.ipsos.com/en-uk/uk-opinion-polls/voting-intention-polls-and-trends
8. https://www.bbc.co.uk/news/uk-politics-21625726
9. https://www.bbc.co.uk/news/uk-politics-21625726
10. https://ukandeu.ac.uk/why-david-cameron-had-to-call-an-eu-referendum/

11. https://www.theguardian.com/politics/2015/jul/12/strange-death-of-liberal-democrats-leadership-vote
12. https://ukandeu.ac.uk/emerging-brexit-identities/
13. https://www.britishelectionstudy.com/wp-content/uploads/2019/10/Explaining-Voter-Volatility.pdf
14. https://www.independent.co.uk/news/uk/politics/eu-referendum-brexit-would-spark-ps30bn-in-spending-cuts-and-tax-rises-warn-george-osborne-and-alistair-darling-a7082271.html
15. Professor Sir John Curtice, Ian Montagu and Chujan Sivathasan, 'Damaged Politics? The impact of the 2019-24 Parliament on political trust and confidence', National Centre for Social Research, https://natcen.ac.uk/sites/default/files/2024-06/BSA%2041%20Damaged%20Politics.pdf
16. https://www.ipsos.com/sites/default/files/migrations/en-uk/files/Assets/Docs/Polls/ipsos-mori-veracity-index-2016-charts.pdf
17. https://www.bbc.co.uk/news/uk-politics-47907350

3. Boris Johnson

1. https://www.gov.uk/government/speeches/boris-johnsons-first-speech-as-prime-minister-24-july-2019
2. https://cchq2019.webflow.io/our-plan/introduction-from-boris-johnson
3. https://assets-global.website-files.com/5da42e2cae7ebd3f8bde353c/5dda924905da587992a064ba_Conservative%202019%20Manifesto.pdf
4. https://www.theguardian.com/business/2020/may/12/uk-furlough-scheme-extended-rishi-sunak-coronavirus
5. https://committees.parliament.uk/publications/40174/documents/195996/default/
6. https://commonslibrary.parliament.uk/research-briefings/cbp-9309/
7. https://www.gov.uk/government/publications/COVID-19-19-19-general-public-opinion-tracker
8. https://ukandeu.ac.uk/COVID-19-19-19-and-the-rally-round-the-flag-effect/
9. https://www.independent.co.uk/news/media/emily-maitlis-dominic-cummings-complaints-bbc-newsnight-a9561991.html
10. https://www.theguardian.com/politics/2020/jun/14/poll-uk-government-losing-public-approval-over-handling-of-virus
11. https://yougov.co.uk/international/articles/29429-perception-government-handling-covid-19
12. https://www.nature.com/articles/s41599-021-00850-6
13. https://www.mirror.co.uk/news/uk-news/voice-people-virus-not-boris-23195097
14. https://www.bbc.co.uk/news/blogs-the-papers-55382075
15. https://yougov.co.uk/topics/politics/trackers/boris-johnson-approval-rating
16. https://www.bbc.co.uk/news/uk-politics-68079726

17. https://yougov.co.uk/international/articles/29429-perception-government-handling-covid-19
18. https://podcasts.apple.com/gb/podcast/should-the-tories-stop-chasing-reform-voters/id1706536336?i=1000664745837
19. https://redfieldandwiltonstrategies.com/latest-gb-voting-intention-19-april-2021/
20. https://www.bbc.co.uk/news/uk-politics-57019456
21. https://www.theguardian.com/politics/2021/may/07/keir-starmer-labour-spent-too-long-talking-ourselves
22. https://www.theguardian.com/politics/2024/feb/17/keir-starmer-reportedly-wanted-to-quit-after-2021-byelection-defeat
23. https://www.bbc.co.uk/news/uk-politics-57019456
24. https://www.thetimes.com/uk/politics/article/boris-johnson-eyes-decade-in-power-5p8hfd72p
25. https://www.thetimes.com/uk/politics/article/tories-increase-lead-over-labour-despite-boris-johnson-flat-row-qc9n36pdw
26. https://yougov.co.uk/topics/politics/trackers/is-boris-johnson-trustworthy
27. https://www.dailymail.co.uk/news/article-9510133/Boris-Johnson-said-bodies-pile-high-order-lockdown-sources-claim.html
28. https://www.bbc.co.uk/news/uk-politics-57253578
29. https://www.bbc.co.uk/news/uk-57625508
30. https://yougov.co.uk/international/articles/29429-perception-government-handling-COVID-19
31. https://yougov.co.uk/topics/politics/trackers/is-boris-johnson-trustworthy
32. https://www.theguardian.com/politics/2021/nov/07/return-of-the-sleazy-party-the-conservatives-and-the-owen-paterson-affair
33. https://www.theguardian.com/politics/2021/nov/07/return-of-the-sleazy-party-the-conservatives-and-the-owen-paterson-affair
34. https://x.com/BBCNews/status/1456035462737444876?t=y_fYKcO6_5CCEeakK9koCQ&s=19
35. https://www.thetimes.com/uk/politics/article/even-boris-johnson-loyalists-are-worrying-for-him-6q0lx07g5
36. https://x.com/PippaCrerar/status/1465824698827264007
37. https://hansard.parliament.uk/commons/2021-12-01/debates/A0E282CF-039D-4F26-8F16-946B8C6E2ABC/Engagements
38. https://www.itv.com/news/2021-12-07/no-10-staff-joke-in-leaked-recording-about-christmas-party-they-later-denied
39. https://x.com/DailyMailUK/status/1468709428190924811
40. https://yougov.co.uk/topics/politics/trackers/is-boris-johnson-trustworthy
41. https://yougov.co.uk/topics/politics/trackers/boris-johnson-approval-rating
42. https://yougov.co.uk/topics/politics/trackers/is-the-conservative-trustworthy-or-untrustworthy
43. https://www.bbc.co.uk/news/uk-england-shropshire-59693102
44. https://conservativehome.com/2021/12/09/a-vote-of-no-confidence-in-johnson-has-suddenly-become-more-likely-than-not/

45. https://www.independent.co.uk/news/uk/politics/boris-johnson-flat-whatsapp-text-messages-b1988031.html
46. https://dominiccummings.substack.com/p/parties-photos-trolleys-variants
47. https://www.bbc.co.uk/news/uk-politics-61083402
48. https://www.youtube.com/watch?v=ZqTLiMY5pLo
49. https://savanta.com/knowledge-centre/view/savanta-comres-pmqs-focus-group-2nd-feb-2022/
50. https://www.summitlawllp.co.uk/hmrc-bounce-back-loan-investigation
51. https://www.theguardian.com/world/2022/jun/06/COVID-19-bounce-back-loans-paid-for-cars-watches-and-even-porn
52. https://www.transparency.org.uk/sites/default/files/pdf/publications/Track%20and%20Trace%20-%20Transparency%20International%20UK.pdf
53. https://www.ons.gov.uk/economy/inflationandpriceindices/datasets/consumerpriceinflation
54. https://www.telegraph.co.uk/money/consumer-affairs/britain-faces-worst-cost-living-crisis-generation/
55. https://www.resolutionfoundation.org/comment/spiralling-energy-prices-will-turn-the-uks-cost-of-living-crisis-into-a-catastrophe/
56. https://www.mirror.co.uk/news/politics/more-voters-would-back-labour-26090456
57. https://carnegieuktrust.org.uk/news-stories/lack-of-trust-in-politics-threatens-democracy-new-report-and-poll/
58. https://www.bbc.co.uk/news/business-60506940
59. https://yougov.co.uk/politics/articles/42159-labour-have-caught-tories-best-government-manage-e
60. https://www.bankofengland.co.uk/monetary-policy/the-interest-rate-bank-rate
61. https://www.itv.com/news/2022-05-03/boris-johnsons-mind-blowing-response-to-case-of-struggling-pensioner-elsie
62. https://www.ipsos.com/en-uk/uk-opinion-polls/voting-intention-polls-and-trends
63. Sebastian Payne, *The Fall of Boris Johnson: The Full Story* (Pan Books, 2022).
64. https://www.theguardian.com/commentisfree/2022/jun/25/tories-tactical-voting-tiverton-honiton-election
65. https://www.telegraph.co.uk/politics/2022/06/06/boris-johnsons-hollow-confidence-vote-victory-tears-tories-apart/
66. https://x.com/SimonMcDonaldUK/status/1544206976820854784
67. https://www.theguardian.com/commentisfree/2022/jul/05/the-guardian-view-on-the-cabinet-resignations-endgame-for-boris-johnson
68. https://www.independent.co.uk/news/uk/politics/boris-johnson-pmqs-pincher-starmer-b2116966.html
69. Sebastian Payne, *The Fall of Boris Johnson* (Pan Books, 2022). P258.
70. https://www.spectator.co.uk/article/how-many-of-boris-johnson-ministers-cabinet-have-resigned/

71. https://yougov.co.uk/topics/politics/trackers/boris-johnson-approval-rating
72. https://www.ipsos.com/sites/default/files/ct/news/documents/2022-07/ipsos-political-monitor-june-2022-charts.pdf
73. https://www.ft.com/content/d30bba0c-2105-42ef-b6e9-beade9a554e5
74. https://www.telegraph.co.uk/politics/2022/10/22/tory-voters-think-wrong-force-boris-johnson/
75. https://www.dailymail.co.uk/news/article-11018717/And-social-medias-debate-winner-Tom-Tugendhat-Tory-MP-makes-audience-laugh-quoting-Dumbledore.html
76. https://www.ipsos.com/en-uk/conservative-party-image-weakens-lowest-score-2011-being-seen-fit-govern
77. https://www.ons.gov.uk/peoplepopulationandcommunity/wellbeing/bulletins/trustingovernmentuk/2022

4. Liz Truss

1. https://www.gov.uk/government/speeches/prime-minister-liz-trusss-statement-6-september-2022
2. https://yougov.co.uk/politics/articles/43222-john-humphrys-sunak-versus-truss-who-has-right-ide
3. Ben Riley-Smith, *The Right to Rule: Thirteen Years, Five Prime Ministers and the Implosion of the Tories* (John Murray, 2023), p. 273.
4. https://www.express.co.uk/news/politics/1638934/tory-leadership-contest-conservatives-labour-poll-voting-boris-johnson-resign
5. https://www.telegraph.co.uk/opinion/2022/09/05/liz-truss-can-now-show-what-capable/
6. https://yougov.co.uk/politics/articles/43630-what-do-people-think-liz-truss
7. https://www.bbc.co.uk/news/uk-politics-68079726
8. https://www.thetimes.com/uk/politics/article/like-truss-or-not-we-all-need-her-to-succeed-6tjh9q0jf
9. https://www.thetimes.com/uk/politics/article/behind-the-scenes-in-no-10-when-truss-was-hit-by-a-whirlwind-6vgcrhlhl
10. https://x.com/nickmacpherson2/status/1567907661584236545
11. https://labourlist.org/2022/09/bassetlaw-focus-group-voters-express-disgust-at-unfairness-of-truss-tax-cuts/
12. https://ifs.org.uk/articles/response-energy-price-guarantee
13. https://www.theguardian.com/uk-news/2022/sep/23/kwarteng-accused-of-reckless-mini-budget-for-the-rich-as-pound-crashes
14. https://x.com/AllieHBNews/status/1573415231208013839?lang=en
15. https://ifs.org.uk/articles/mini-budget-response
16. https://ifs.org.uk/articles/mini-budget-response
17. https://www.bbc.co.uk/news/business-63051702
18. https://www.nytimes.com/2022/09/28/business/economy/bank-of-england-bonds.html

19. https://www.telegraph.co.uk/business/2023/02/23/bank-england-slow-fight-against-inflation-rate-setter-admits
20. https://www.bbc.co.uk/sounds/play/p0d439lv
21. https://unherd.com/2022/10/is-truss-the-worst-pm-in-history/
22. https://www.economist.com/leaders/2022/10/11/liz-truss-has-made-britain-a-riskier-bet-for-bond-investors
23. https://www.youtube.com/watch?v=GZv9CYhppdY
24. https://www.youtube.com/watch?v=GZv9CYhppdY
25. https://www.opinium.com/wp-content/uploads/2022/10/MRP_Tables_2022.pdf
26. https://www.youtube.com/watch?v=hYRcV54YIag&list=PL_6zDbB-zRef_M7eXuSLUlGnt7qk66hJq&index=8
27. https://yougov.co.uk/topics/politics/trackers/which-political-party-would-be-the-best-at-handling-the-economy
28. https://x.com/MrLeeCain/status/1797210365152919749
29. https://x.com/MattChorley/status/1787483755722002590
30. https://redfieldandwiltonstrategies.com/latest-gb-voting-intention-16-october-2022/
31. https://www.bbc.co.uk/news/uk-politics-68079726
32. https://yougov.co.uk/topics/politics/trackers/is-the-conservative-trustworthy-or-untrustworthy
33. https://www.ippr.org/articles/freefall-how-a-year-of-chaos-has-undermined-trust-in-politics
34. https://www.ippr.org/media-office/revealed-trust-in-politicians-in-free-fall-after-year-of-chaos-poll-reveals
35. https://www.ippr.org/articles/freefall-how-a-year-of-chaos-has-undermined-trust-in-politics
36. https://www.ons.gov.uk/peoplepopulationandcommunity/wellbeing/bulletins/trustingovernmentuk/2023

5. Rishi Sunak

1. https://www.gov.uk/government/speeches/prime-minister-rishi-sunaks-statement-25-october-2022
2. Ben Riley-Smith, *Blue Murder: The Rise and Fall of the Conservative Government 2010–2024,* (John Murray, 2024). P313
3. https://www.gov.uk/government/speeches/prime-minister-rishi-sunaks-statement-25-october-2022
4. https://www.instituteforgovernment.org.uk/explainer/rishi-sunak-first-cabinet
5. https://www.thetimes.com/uk/politics/article/rishi-sunak-tory-prime-minister-wdvwz0tpp
6. Ben Riley-Smith, *The Right to Rule* (John Murray, 2023), p. 341.
7. https://www.theguardian.com/uk-news/2022/nov/17/autumn-statement-jeremy-hunt-confirms-uk-already-in-recession-as-he-unveils-tax-rises-and-spending-curbs

8. https://www.bbc.co.uk/news/business-63675313
9. https://podcasts.apple.com/gb/podcast/should-the-tories-stop-chasing-reform-voters/id1706536336?i=1000664745837
10. https://yougov.co.uk/politics/articles/49532-sunak-favourability-ticks-up-after-election-announcement
11. https://yougov.co.uk/topics/politics/trackers/rishi-sunak-prime-minister-approval
12. https://www.bbc.co.uk/news/uk-politics-68079726
13. Tim Bale, *The Conservative Party After Brexit: Turmoil and Transformation* (Polity, 2023), p. 296.
14. https://researchbriefings.files.parliament.uk/documents/CBP-7281/CBP-7281.pdf
15. https://www.ipsos.com/en-uk/rishi-sunaks-personal-poll-ratings-improve-labour-retain-strong-lead-voting-intention
16. https://www.ft.com/content/f01f93e0-9e28-4c17-a059-4ff82803b8ae
17. https://www.telegraph.co.uk/politics/2023/05/05/boris-blame-game-triggers-backlash-over-sunak-election/
18. https://www.mirror.co.uk/news/politics/desperate-tories-plot-boris-johnson-29897703
19. https://www.ipsos.com/en-uk/ipsos-issues-index-september-2023
20. https://www.bbc.co.uk/news/uk-politics-67166028
21. https://yougov.co.uk/topics/politics/trackers/is-the-conservative-trustworthy-or-untrustworthy
22. https://general-election-2010.co.uk/2010-general-election-manifestos/Conservative-Party-Manifesto-2010.pdf
23. https://assets-global.website-files.com/5da42e2cae7ebd3f8bde353c/5dda924905da587992a064ba_Conservative%202019%20Manifesto.pdf
24. Tim Shipman, *All Out War: The Full Story of How Brexit Sank Britain's Political Class* (William Collins, 2016), p. 286.
25. https://www.thesun.co.uk/news/politics/24870101/migration-putting-unsustainable-pressure-on-housing/
26. https://www.reuters.com/world/uk/annual-net-migration-uk-hits-672000-year-june-2023-2023-11-23/
27. https://www.huffingtonpost.co.uk/entry/tony-blair-faces-backlash-over-bizarre-immigration-claim_uk_66d98197e4b0830f6e9378b1
28. https://x.com/EdConwaySky/status/1798005491672678768
29. https://www.ft.com/content/674525e8-ce3e-42aa-b5d1-36260d17179a
30. https://inews.co.uk/news/politics/control-cutting-numbers-brexiteer-mps-rishi-sunak-rising-uk-migration-2366440?srsltid=AfmBOop4NmNFXeNgofRWigvL20twodrfaPrdpvM73CbSYbXTzbLvdSK5
31. https://ukandeu.ac.uk/immigration-what-the-public-think-as-the-election-approaches/
32. https://www.ipsos.com/en-uk/ipsos-issues-index-september-2023
33. Gianfranco Addario, Curtis Jessop, Joseph Crowley, Ekaterina Khriakova, March 2024, 'Public attitudes towards immigration and ethnic minorities', National Centre for Social Research, https://natcen.ac.uk/

publications/public-attitudes-towards-immigration-and-ethnic-minorities
34. https://ukandeu.ac.uk/immigration-what-the-public-think-as-the-election-approaches/
35. https://www.instituteforgovernment.org.uk/comment/rishi-sunaks-five-pledges-one-year
36. https://migrationobservatory.ox.ac.uk/resources/briefings/people-crossing-the-english-channel-in-small-boats/
37. https://yougov.co.uk/topics/economy/trackers/how-the-government-is-handling-the-economy-in-the-uk
38. https://www.bbc.co.uk/news/uk-politics-68079726
39. https://www.bbc.co.uk/news/uk-politics-68488467
40. https://yougov.co.uk/topics/politics/survey-results/daily/2024/02/16/03456/1
41. https://www.spectator.co.uk/article/cutting-national-insurance-wont-save-the-tories/
42. https://www.ft.com/content/54068dcd-925c-48d3-bb7b-3c947ba20cb6
43. https://www.ipsos.com/en-uk/conservative-party-brand-image-hits-new-low
44. https://www.ipsos.com/en-uk/majority-of-britons-hold-an-unfavourable-opinion-of-rishi-sunak

6. A Volatile and Distrustful Electorate

1. https://yougov.co.uk/topics/politics/trackers/is-the-conservative-trustworthy-or-untrustworthy
2. https://www.ft.com/content/d30bba0c-2105-42ef-b6e9-beade9a554e5
3. Professor Sir John Curtice, Ian Montagu and Chujan Sivathasan, 'Damaged Politics? The impact of the 2019-24 Parliament on political trust and confidence', National Centre for Social Research, https://natcen.ac.uk/sites/default/files/2024-06/BSA%2041%20Damaged%20Politics.pdf
4. Ibid, https://natcen.ac.uk/sites/default/files/2024-06/BSA%2041%20Damaged%20Politics.pdf
5. https://www.bbc.co.uk/news/uk-politics-65913692
6. https://www.ipsos.com/en-uk/ipsos-trust-in-professions-veracity-index-2023
7. https://www.ipsos.com/sites/default/files/ct/news/documents/2023-12/ipsos-trust-in-professions-veracity-index-2023-charts.pdf#page=9
8. https://news.sky.com/story/a-crisis-of-trust-in-our-politics-spells-trouble-for-the-government-13122344
9. https://www.youtube.com/watch?v=9qZWkwkLmYo&ab_channel=IpsosUK
10. https://www.britishelectionstudy.com/bes-impact/were-all-disillusioned-age-and-political-disaffection-in-the-2024-uk-general-election/#disqus_thread

11. Professor Sir John Curtice et al, 'Damaged Politics? The impact of the 2019-24 Parliament on political trust and confidence', National Centre for Social Research, https://natcen.ac.uk/sites/default/files/2024-06/BSA%2041%20Damaged%20Politics.pdf

7. Public Narratives

1. https://www.nytimes.com/2012/11/04/magazine/still-waiting-for-the-narrator-in-chief.html
2. Larry Hasher, David Goldstein, and Thomas Toppino, 'Frequency and the Conference of Referential Validity', *Journal of Verbal Learning and Verbal Behavior*, 16:1 (1977), 107–12.

8. Nothing Works Anymore

1. https://assets-global.website-files.com/5da42e2cae7ebd3f8bde353c/5dda924905da587992a064ba_Conservative%202019%20Manifesto.pdf
2. https://en.wikipedia.org/wiki/Broken_Britain
3. https://x.com/BBCPolitics/status/1804823654661841331
4. https://www.standard.co.uk/news/politics/cost-living-gas-electricity-food-prices-inflation-latest-mortgages-poll-ipsos-b1097718.html
5. https://www.thesun.co.uk/news/28663239/nothing-in-britain-works-anymore/
6. https://www.thetimes.com/uk/law/article/broken-britain-is-back-and-victims-let-down-says-commissioner-6cfcj0wq2
7. https://www.ft.com/content/69e5e9f8-82bf-4628-aab3-360d4124747c
8. https://www.telegraph.co.uk/news/2022/08/23/britain-broken-nobody-can-bothered-do-anything/
9. https://inews.co.uk/opinion/why-does-nothing-work-in-britain-today-2766096
10. https://www.spectator.co.uk/article/broken-britain-what-went-wrong/
11. https://x.com/DailyMirror/status/1764424136166613296
12. https://x.com/WeAreNewBritain/status/1808463115454931132
13. https://www.ft.com/content/96072f7c-de44-11e2-b990-00144feab7de
14. https://www.theguardian.com/politics/2010/may/17/liam-byrne-note-successor
15. https://www.youtube.com/watch?v=8HutHqVXgac
16. https://www.newyorker.com/magazine/2024/04/01/what-have-fourteen-years-of-conservative-rule-done-to-britain
17. https://www.bbc.co.uk/programmes/m001r7rj
18. https://general-election-2010.co.uk/2010-general-election-manifestos/Conservative-Party-Manifesto-2010.pdf
19. https://lordslibrary.parliament.uk/local-government-finances-impact-on-communities/#:~:text=Spending%20was%2025%25%20lower%20in,and%20regulatory%20services%20(%E2%80%9310.5%25)
20. https://www.worldometers.info/world-population/uk-population/

21. Sam Freedman, *Failed State: Why Nothing Works and How We Fix It* (Macmillan, 2024).
22. https://www.ft.com/content/76c5fd20-04da-4651-8740-e52d21d04541
23. https://www.theguardian.com/politics/video/2022/aug/05/rishi-sunak-admits-taking-money-from-deprived-areas-in-leaked-footage-video
24. https://www.newyorker.com/magazine/2024/04/01/what-have-fourteen-years-of-conservative-rule-done-to-britain
25. https://austeritycity.liverpoolecho.co.uk/
26. https://www.theguardian.com/politics/2024/apr/28/potholes-planning-issues-england-2-may-local-elections
27. https://www.bbc.co.uk/news/business-67441085
28. https://www.thetimes.com/uk/politics/article/worst-council-england-uk-nottingham-xkpb5jzmz
29. https://general-election-2010.co.uk/2010-general-election-manifestos/Conservative-Party-Manifesto-2010.pdf
30. https://www.spectator.co.uk/article/how-much-does-britain-still-love-the-nhs/
31. *The Conservative Effect 2010-2024: 14 Wasted Years?*, ed. Anthony Seldon and Tom Egerton (Cambridge: Cambridge University Press, 2024), p. 140.
32. https://www.newyorker.com/magazine/2024/04/01/what-have-fourteen-years-of-conservative-rule-done-to-britain
33. https://www.instituteofhealthequity.org/in-the-news/news-coverage/what-have-fourteen-years-of-conservative-rule-done-to-britain#:
34. https://www.instituteofhealthequity.org/resources-reports/marmot-review-10-years-on/the-marmot-review-10-years-on-full-report.pdf
35. https://www.kingsfund.org.uk/insight-and-analysis/blogs/counting-cost-nhs-strikes
36. https://x.com/Savanta_UK/status/1817885966389887163
37. https://www.ft.com/content/a4f07a08-b7e9-4330-9915-c2640edf7866
38. https://www.health.org.uk/news-and-comment/charts-and-infographics/REAL-social-care-funding-gap
39. *The Conservative Effect 2010-2024*, ed. Anthony Seldon and Tom Egerton (Cambridge: Cambridge University Press, 2024), p. 144.
40. https://www.wiltshire999s.co.uk/17-ambulances-queue-great-western/
41. https://www.pressandjournal.co.uk/fp/news/aberdeen-aberdeenshire/6285975/ambulances-queued-aberdeen-royal-infirmary/
42. https://x.com/EdwardJDavey/status/1547159099204411393
43. https://www.kingsfund.org.uk/insight-and-analysis/long-reads/solving-issue-gp-access-2019
44. https://www.thetimes.com/uk/healthcare/article/uk-gp-wait-times-nhs-doctors-appointment-2023-525xlm3q5
45. https://www.ft.com/content/7eb75107-c195-40d1-9f78-893d1c7c28b0
46. https://x.com/sachary_/status/1809134301142749553
47. https://assets.kingsfund.org.uk/f/256914/x/0ab966500b/rise_decline_nhs_england_2000-20_2023.pdf
48. https://www.health.org.uk/sites/default/files/upload/publications/2022/Risk%20factors_Web_Final_Feb.pdf

49. https://www.healthwatch.co.uk/blog/2021-12-12/recovery-nhs-dental-care-too-slow-help-thousands-left-pain
50. https://www.nuffieldtrust.org.uk/research/bold-action-or-slow-decay-the-state-of-nhs-dentistry-and-future-policy-actions
51. https://www.healthwatch.co.uk/news/2024-07-08/our-position-nhs-dentistry
52. https://www.nuffieldtrust.org.uk/sites/default/files/2024-01/Nuffield%20Trust%20-%20NHS%20dentistry%20policy%20briefing_WEB_Jan.pdf
53. https://www.thetimes.com/uk/healthcare/article/times-health-commission-nhs-needs-urgent-resuscitation-7wjhbp8s5
54. https://general-election-2010.co.uk/2010-general-election-manifestos/Conservative-Party-Manifesto-2010.pdf
55. https://ifs.org.uk/sites/default/files/output_url_files/BN178.pdf
56. https://www.gov.uk/government/statistics/housing-supply-indicators-of-new-supply-england-january-to-march-2023/housing-supply-indicators-of-new-supply-england-january-to-march-2023
57. https://www.bloomberg.com/graphics/2024-uk-housing-crisis/?embedded-checkout=true
58. https://www.thesun.co.uk/news/politics/24870101/migration-putting-unsustainable-pressure-on-housing/
59. https://news.sky.com/story/uk-spends-more-on-housing-than-almost-any-other-developed-country-and-gets-the-least-value-from-it-too-13099925
60. https://www.statista.com/statistics/386301/uk-average-mortgage-interest-rates/
61. https://www.ft.com/content/bc19bbf4-2939-489e-a113-e21d5baf356d
62. https://www.uswitch.com/mortgages/first-time-buyer-statistics
63. https://www.bbc.co.uk/news/articles/c7209lk8x2wo
64. https://www.bbc.co.uk/news/articles/c7209lk8x2wo
65. https://www.resolutionfoundation.org/publications/through-the-roof/
66. https://www.resolutionfoundation.org/publications/through-the-roof/
67. https://england.shelter.org.uk/media/press_release/at_least_309000_people_homeless_in_england_today
68. https://general-election-2010.co.uk/2010-general-election-manifestos/Conservative-Party-Manifesto-2010.pdf
69. Source: Ministry of Justice, ONS, Home Office, UK Government
70. https://www.bbc.co.uk/news/articles/cg3jnwy8ll2o
71. https://www.instituteforgovernment.org.uk/publication/performance-tracker-2023/prisons
72. https://www.theguardian.com/society/2023/oct/15/two-thirds-prisons-officially-overcrowded-england-wales
73. https://www.newyorker.com/magazine/2024/04/01/what-have-fourteen-years-of-conservative-rule-done-to-britain
74. Sam Freedman, *Failed State* (Macmillan, 2024).
75. https://www.gov.uk/government/statistics/police-workforce-england-and-wales-31-march-2016
76. https://on.ft.com/3VKhMKU

77. https://ucrel.lancs.ac.uk/wmatrix/ukmanifestos2015/localpdf/Conservatives.pdf
78. https://www.ciwem.org/the-environment/how-should-water-and-environmental-management-firms-tap,-retain-and-promote-female-talent
79. https://www.dailymail.co.uk/news/article-13438001/Privatisation-scam-Feargal-Sharkey-hits-water-companies-gaming-shareholders-tens-billions-fail-invest-amid-growing-fury-Brixham-poisoning-scandal-rising-bills.html
80. https://www.ofwat.gov.uk/customer-trust-and-satisfaction-in-water-companies-falling-in-latest-ofwat-and-ccw-research/
81. https://news.sky.com/story/spills-of-raw-sewage-into-englands-rivers-and-seas-are-worst-on-record-13102680
82. https://www.telegraph.co.uk/news/2024/03/29/polluted-water-surge-hospital-admissions-sewage-health/
83. https://www.bbc.co.uk/news/uk-england-london-68674088
84. https://www.independent.co.uk/business/new-regulations-as-labour-tries-to-answer-public-anger-over-water-companies-b2581227.html
85. https://general-election-2010.co.uk/2010-general-election-manifestos/Conservative-Party-Manifesto-2010.pdf
86. https://www.theguardian.com/politics/2024/jan/23/head-of-obr-says-lack-of-budget-details-led-to-work-of-fiction-forecasts-last-year
87. https://www.independent.co.uk/business/tuc-to-accuse-government-of-having-broken-britain-b2408905.html
88. https://www.nao.org.uk/wp-content/uploads/2023/06/condition-of-school-buildings.pdf
89. https://www.bbc.co.uk/news/uk-68021766
90. https://general-election-2010.co.uk/2010-general-election-manifestos/Conservative-Party-Manifesto-2010.pdf
91. https://www.tortoisemedia.com/2024/03/25/broke-and-shrinking-the-downward-spiral-in-british-universities/
92. https://commonslibrary.parliament.uk/research-briefings/cbp-7976/
93. https://www.theguardian.com/commentisfree/2024/mar/29/britain-universities-freefall-saving-them-funding-international-students
94. https://www.officeforstudents.org.uk/media/ly1buqlj/financial-sustainability-report2024.pdf
95. https://commonslibrary.parliament.uk/higher-education-funding-trends-and-challenges/
96. https://benjaminedgar.substack.com/p/uk-universities-are-on-the-brink
97. https://general-election-2010.co.uk/2010-general-election-manifestos/Conservative-Party-Manifesto-2010.pdf
98. https://www.bbc.co.uk/news/uk-politics-64744783
99. https://ukandeu.ac.uk/reports/the-state-of-public-opinion-2023/
100. https://www.mirror.co.uk/news/politics/nothing-britain-works-anymore-say-30063503
101. https://www.ft.com/content/7eb75107-c195-40d1-9f78-893d1c7c28b0
102. https://x.com/Channel4News/status/1602278581366919168

103. https://x.com/IsabelOakeshott/status/1700164559154086078
104. https://www.thetimes.com/uk/politics/article/britains-broken-weve-been-here-before-3qzz9vw8t
105. https://yougov.co.uk/politics/articles/49851-general-election-2024-84-of-britons-say-public-services-are-in-poor-shape
106. https://www.telegraph.co.uk/politics/2024/06/06/general-election-2024-focus-group-wolverhampton/
107. https://www.moreincommon.org.uk/our-work/polling-tables/
108. https://www.ucl.ac.uk/policy-lab/sites/policy_lab/files/the_respect_agenda_ucl_policy_lab-more_in_common_september_2023_1_compressed.pdf
109. https://yougov.co.uk/politics/articles/49596-in-most-ways-most-britons-think-the-uk-is-worse-now-than-it-was-in-2010
110. *The Conservative Effect 2010-2024*, ed. Anthony Seldon and Tom Egerton (Cambridge: Cambridge University Press, 2024).
111. https://www.theguardian.com/politics/2024/jan/07/conservatives-face-obliteration-as-uk-in-worse-state-than-2010-tory-mp-says
112. https://www.neilobrien.co.uk/p/the-everything-bagel-theory-of-the
113. https://www.thetimes.com/uk/politics/article/kemi-badenoch-engineer-fix-britain-dcnw7frrv
114. https://x.com/WeAreNewBritain/status/1808463115454931132
115. https://www.facebook.com/labourparty/videos/nothing-works-anymorerachel-reeves-explains-what-labour-will-do-differently-/857351872889068/
116. https://www.facebook.com/nigelfarageofficial/videos/reform-uk-party-election-broadcast-2024/404048385970803/
117. https://www.itv.com/news/2024-06-07/sunak-was-completely-wrong-to-leave-d-day-ceremony-early-admits-mordaunt
118. https://www.channel4.com/news/greens-launch-manifesto-promising-to-mend-broken-britain
119. https://www.reuters.com/world/uk/pitch-voters-starmer-says-labour-best-placed-fix-broken-britain-2023-10-10/

9. The Conservatives Are Incompetent

1. https://www.theguardian.com/commentisfree/2012/mar/30/george-galloway-labour-tories-detox
2. https://www.theguardian.com/commentisfree/2023/aug/25/natural-party-government-five-pms-conservatives-at-sea
3. https://yougov.co.uk/topics/politics/trackers/which-political-party-would-be-the-best-at-handling-the-economy
4. https://yougov.co.uk/topics/economy/trackers/which-government-would-be-better-at-managing-the-economy
5. https://x.com/DeltapollUK/status/1805286868155555992
6. https://www.ft.com/content/820de7fe-3ec6-4585-a4ce-c450261b3794
7. https://www.thetimes.com/uk/politics/article/can-it-get-worse-for-the-tories-oh-yes-it-can-xvvox2x0n

8. https://x.com/jamesjohnson252/status/1515936769841242122
9. https://yougov.co.uk/topics/politics/trackers/is-the-conservative-party-competent-or-incompetent
10. *The Conservative Effect 2010-2024: 14 Wasted Years?*, ed. Anthony Seldon and Tom Egerton (Cambridge: Cambridge University Press, 2024), p. 253.
11. https://samf.substack.com/p/the-battersea-problem
12. https://yougov.co.uk/topics/politics/trackers/is-the-conservative-party-competent-or-incompetent
13. https://x.com/mrianleslie/status/1575453828773707780
14. https://www.thetimes.com/article/3a79d414-2ae8-4584-aba6-ad39efaa26ea
15. https://www.ft.com/content/6e670e62-57a0-404b-a0a1-66cc5b98ee57
16. https://www.ft.com/content/820de7fe-3ec6-4585-a4ce-c450261b3794
17. https://politicscentre.nuffield.ox.ac.uk/news-and-events/news/political-effects-of-past-and-current-economic-crises/
18. https://www.ft.com/content/979dc308-99e1-11dc-ad70-0000779fd2ac
19. https://www.economicsobservatory.com/boosting-productivity-why-doesnt-the-uk-invest-enough
20. https://www.economicsobservatory.com/boosting-productivity-why-doesnt-the-uk-invest-enough
21. https://economy2030.resolutionfoundation.org/wp-content/uploads/2023/12/Ending-stagnation-final-report.pdf
22. https://www.bath.ac.uk/publications/alternatives-to-austerity/attachments/alternatives-to-austerity.pdf
23. https://www.thetimes.com/article/3a79d414-2ae8-4584-aba6-ad39efaa26ea
24. www.bbc.co.uk/programmes/m001r7rj
25. https://www.youtube.com/watch?v=-Gz6mZYxS0A
26. https://www.bbc.co.uk/news/business-36611512
27. https://www.theguardian.com/politics/2016/jul/20/david-cameron-accused-gross-negligence-brexit-contingency-plans
28. https://news.sky.com/story/theresa-may-was-in-tears-after-the-brexit-referendum-result-11847682
29. Tim Bale, *The Conservative Party After Brexit: Turmoil and Transformation* (Polity, 2023), p. 20.
30. John Springford, 'The Cost of Brexit to June 2022' (Centre for European Reform, December 2022), https://www.cer.eu/insights/cost-brexit-june-2022
31. https://cepr.org/voxeu/columns/impact-brexit-uk-economy-reviewing-evidence
32. https://www.macrotrends.net/global-metrics/countries/GBR/united-kingdom/gdp-per-capita
33. Source: Office for National Statistics.
34. https://www.bloomberg.com/news/videos/2024-06-20/why-the-uk-economy-stopped-working
35. https://www.bbc.co.uk/news/uk-politics-68079726
36. https://www.ipsos.com/en-uk/ipsos-issues-index-june-2022
37. https://amp.theguardian.com/business/2022/jul/30/food-food-fuel-tripled-citizens-advice-charity-eating-heating

38. https://yougov.co.uk/consumer/articles/43504-cost-living-crisis-one-four-have-had-cut-essential
39. https://www.lbc.co.uk/news/lbc-focus-group-swindon/
40. Daniel Finkelstein, 'How to Learn from Liz Truss', *How to Win an Election* (*The Times*, 16 April 2024), https://www.thetimes.co.uk/podcasts/how-to-win-an-election
41. https://www.libdems.org.uk/press/release/truss-tax-mortgage-rise-since-mini-budget-equivalent-to-5p-income-tax-hike
42. https://www.ft.com/content/7bad4783-e6d1-4776-8fa7-4188bbb9d86f
43. https://www.thenational.scot/news/23020724.research-finds-incompetent-word-associated-liz-truss-public/
44. https://yougov.co.uk/topics/politics/trackers/which-political-party-would-be-the-best-at-handling-the-economy
45. https://www.bloomberg.com/news/videos/2024-06-20/why-the-uk-economy-stopped-working
46. https://www.theguardian.com/politics/article/2024/jul/26/eight-charts-lay-bare-tory-labour-inheritance-economy
47. https://x.com/RedfieldWilton/status/1775463565249401223
48. https://www.ipsos.com/sites/default/files/ct/news/documents/2024-06/Issues%20Index_June_v1_PUBLIC.pdf)
49. https://www.ft.com/content/802d399a-7458-47ee-9c12-f6a22e302dd8
50. https://www.ipsos.com/en-uk/labour-lead-conservatives-20-points-first-ipsos-voting-intention-poll-general-election-campaign
51. https://lordashcroftpolls.com/2024/05/with-five-weeks-to-go-less-than-half-of-voters-have-made-up-their-minds/
52. https://www.ft.com/content/d30bba0c-2105-42ef-b6e9-beade9a554e5
53. https://www.standard.co.uk/comment/hs2-travel-national-decline-b1110091.html
54. https://www.mirror.co.uk/news/politics/ex-tory-council-leader-says-32818488
55. https://x.com/DaleVince/status/1798374762475073889
56. https://www.electoralcalculus.co.uk/blogs/ec_condef_20240606.html
57. https://podcasts.apple.com/gb/podcast/the-conservatives-face-their-mount-everest/id1706062286?i=1000658053586

10. The Conservatives Should Be Punished

1. https://lordashcroftpolls.com/2024/06/what-matters-is-that-theyll-try-my-focus-groups-in-doncaster-morecambe-and-tatton/
2. https://narrativearts.org/article/public-narrative/
3. https://www.ft.com/content/115a49cd-c07c-4581-b946-dcc8fd6c8c2c
4. https://www.resolutionfoundation.org/press-releases/current-parliament-remains-on-track-to-be-the-worst-for-living-standards-growth-since-the-1950s/
5. https://www.ons.gov.uk/peoplepopulationandcommunity/birthsdeathsandmarriages/deaths/articles/deathsinvolvingcovid19inthe

caresectorenglandandwales/deathsregisteredbetweenweekending20march2020andweekending21january2022
6. https://www.bbc.co.uk/news/uk-scotland-61092224
7. https://www.politico.eu/article/david-cameron-made-10m-before-greensill-capitals-collapse-leaked-documents-reveal/
8. https://www.independent.co.uk/voices/matt-hancock-jess-phillips-ppe-contracts-peston-b1968727.html
9. https://lordashcroftpolls.com/2024/06/what-matters-is-that-theyll-try-my-focus-groups-in-doncaster-morecambe-and-tatton/
10. https://www.theguardian.com/commentisfree/2021/nov/03/call-out-tories-corruption-conservative-owen-paterson-keir-starmer
11. https://www.ft.com/video/1ba870d3-fd96-453a-aabc-2a35337a5830
12. http://www.britishpoliticalspeech.org/speech-archive.htm?speech=200
13. https://www.facebook.com/BBCPolitics/videos/keir-starmer-pms-actions-corrupt/407936130778404/
14. https://ifs.org.uk/publications/distributional-impact-tax-and-benefit-reforms-2010
15. https://ifs.org.uk/publications/distributional-impact-tax-and-benefit-reforms-2010
16. https://www.ft.com/content/bc19bbf4-2939-489e-a113-e21d5baf356d
17. https://www.jrf.org.uk/uk-poverty-2024-the-essential-guide-to-understanding-poverty-in-the-uk
18. https://www.financialfairness.org.uk/docs?editionId=c9f66338-7c19-4ee8-8634-b0f800c19dc6
19. https://www.netmums.com/cost-of-living/80000-families-at-risk-of-having-benefits-reduced-despite-upcoming-increase
20. https://www.gla.ac.uk/news/archiveofnews/2022/october/headline_885099_en.html
21. https://fullfact.org/economy/labour-tuc-food-bank-figures/
22. https://www.theguardian.com/uk-news/2023/dec/21/surge-in-number-of-people-in-hospital-with-nutrient-deficiencies-nhs-figures-show
23. https://www.theguardian.com/business/2023/jun/21/children-raised-under-uk-austerity-shorter-than-european-peers-study
24. https://www.theguardian.com/commentisfree/2024/feb/08/child-poverty-britain-anger-gordon-brown
25. https://www.moreincommon.org.uk/media/e3in12zd/change-pending.pdf
26. https://www.youtube.com/watch?v=GZv9CYhppdY
27. https://www.telegraph.co.uk/politics/2024/04/15/liz-truss-interview-ten-years-to-save-the-west/
28. https://www.moreincommon.org.uk/media/e3in12zd/change-pending.pdf
29. https://www.ucl.ac.uk/policy-lab/sites/policy_lab/files/the_respect_agenda_ucl_policy_lab-more_in_common_september_2023_1_compressed.pdf
30. https://x.com/georgeeaton/status/1803894376042516917
31. https://www.economist.com/britain/2024/05/29/the-british-election-is-becoming-an-episode-of-mob-justice
32. https://www.thetimes.com/article/4819dbf5-ec7e-4ed1-8ce6-d6f07b0dd256

33. https://www.telegraph.co.uk/news/2024/05/06/britains-next-political-earthquake-could-destroy-the-tories/
34. https://www.spectator.co.uk/article/tory-voters-want-to-punish-their-party-and-themselves/
35. https://www.thetimes.com/uk/scotland/article/ruth-davidson-how-to-rebuild-the-tories-by-someone-whos-done-it-5tg0s7hzk
36. https://uk.news.yahoo.com/voters-angry-annoyed-fed-conservatives-125116064.html
37. https://www.facebook.com/thetimesradio/videos/michael-gove-breaks-down-exactly-why-the-conservatives-lost-the-election/788710413425300/

11. Labour's Ming Vase Strategy

1. https://www.clpd.org.uk/wp-content/uploads/2020/10/Keir-Starmers-10-Pledges.pdf
2. https://www.theguardian.com/commentisfree/2023/oct/07/the-observer-view-keir-starmer-reignited-labour-can-he-do-the-same-for-britain
3. https://www.theguardian.com/politics/2020/oct/29/jeremy-corbyn-rejects-findings-of-report-on-antisemitism-in-labour
4. https://www.bbc.co.uk/news/uk-politics-63028118
5. https://www.ian-leslie.com/p/the-age-of-centrist-heroes-is-over
6. https://yougov.co.uk/topics/politics/trackers/is-keir-starmer-trustworthy
7. https://www.spectator.co.uk/article/the-starmtroopers-how-labours-centrists-took-back-control/
8. https://tribunemag.co.uk/2023/06/trickett-driscoll-case-shows-its-time-for-democrats-to-take-a-stand
9. https://politicalquarterly.org.uk/blog/thirteen-wasted-years-a-strategy-for-starmer/
10. https://labourlist.org/2022/07/nationalisation-just-doesnt-stack-up-against-our-fiscal-rules-reeves-says/
11. https://www.theguardian.com/us-news/article/2024/sep/07/how-lessons-of-uk-election-could-help-kamala-harris-defeat-donald-trump
12. https://www.ft.com/content/69064e7b-dd13-4106-8663-ce735159e451
13. https://www.clpd.org.uk/wp-content/uploads/2020/10/Keir-Starmers-10-Pledges.pdf
14. https://x.com/DAaronovitch/status/1809248259010941295
15. https://www.bbc.co.uk/news/election/2024/england/results
16. https://www.spectator.co.uk/article/things-look-bleak-for-the-tories/
17. https://yougov.co.uk/politics/articles/49886-one-in-five-voters-say-they-are-voting-tactically-at-the-2024-general-election
18. https://www.independent.co.uk/news/uk/politics/what-is-tactical-voting-general-election-where-b2556989.html
19. https://www.theguardian.com/uk-news/article/2024/may/04/local-elections-drubbing-shows-time-is-nearly-up-for-the-conservatives
20. https://www.ft.com/content/c0a7bbd4-f66d-4f19-bf7c-ba2ca458fe4d

21. https://www.prospectmagazine.co.uk/politics/65977/local-elections-2024-rishi-sunak-has-done-nothing-to-revive-his-partys-fortunes
22. https://www.prospectmagazine.co.uk/politics/65977/local-elections-2024-rishi-sunak-has-done-nothing-to-revive-his-partys-fortunes
23. https://conservativehome.com/2024/05/05/goodbyeee/
24. https://www.youtube.com/watch?v=vH3-Gt7mgyM
25. https://www.ft.com/content/54068dcd-925c-48d3-bb7b-3c947ba20cb6
26. https://www.theguardian.com/uk-news/article/2024/may/04/local-elections-drubbing-shows-time-is-nearly-up-for-the-conservatives
27. https://podcasts.apple.com/gb/podcast/elections-debrief-sunak-survives-starmer-solid/id1613562765?i=1000654535854
28. https://twitter.com/lewis_baston/status/1787432559623713251
29. https://www.thetimes.com/uk/politics/article/no-celebrating-keir-starmers-next-steps-to-no-10-b0z6dxkg3
30. https://www.focaldata.com/blog/bi-focal-16-what-will-labours-lead-be-in-the-general-election
31. https://news.sky.com/story/general-election-poll-tracker-will-labour-or-the-conservatives-win-12903488
32. https://twitter.com/SteveBakerFRSA/status/1788174231492002289

12. Sunak Calls an Early Election

1. https://www.bbc.co.uk/news/live/uk-politics-69042935/page/3
2. https://x.com/steverichards14/status/1793319245108945312
3. https://x.com/montie/status/1793316120948043834
4. https://x.com/RMCunliffe/status/1793326467515879926
5. https://www.bbc.co.uk/news/live/uk-politics-69042935/page/2
6. https://www.thesun.co.uk/news/politics/28074650/why-rishi-sunak-called-general-election/
7. https://www.thetimes.com/podcasts/how-to-win-an-election
8. https://yougov.co.uk/topics/politics/trackers/which-political-party-would-be-the-best-at-handling-the-economy
9. https://yougov.co.uk/politics/articles/49500-political-tracker-roundup-may-2024
10. https://www.ipsos.com/en-uk/rishi-sunaks-satisfaction-falls-equal-worst-ever-ipsos-rating-conservative-or-labour-leader
11. https://x.com/JohnRentoul/status/1806716663955341694
12. https://www.bbc.co.uk/news/articles/cz557p4y7750
13. Steve Rayson, The Fall of the Red Wall (2020). P132
14. Philip Gould, *The Unfinished Revolution: How New Labour Changed British Politics Forever* (Abacus, 2011), p. 292.
15. https://www.economist.com/by-invitation/2022/04/29/alastair-campbells-principles-for-politics-today
16. https://www.moreincommon.org.uk/media/e3in12zd/change-pending.pdf

13. The 2024 Election Campaign

1. https://www.conservatives.com/manifesto
2. https://www.thetimes.co.uk/article/inside-the-cabinet-debate-where-election-decision-was-made-xz2vct0tt
3. https://www.ipsos.com/sites/default/files/ct/news/documents/2024-04/ipsos-uk-issues-index-april-2024-charts.pdf#page=18
4. https://www.moreincommon.org.uk/our-work/tracking-public-opinion/
5. https://inews.co.uk/news/politics/rishi-sunak-leading-tories-election-wipeout-worse-1997-landslide-defeat-polls-3084710
6. https://x.com/WeAreNewBritain/status/1808463115454931132
7. https://pressgazette.co.uk/media-audience-and-business-data/most-popular-news-sources-uk-tiktok-ofcom-news-consumption-survey/
8. https://www.emarketer.com/content/uk-tiktok-marketing-2023
9. https://see-media.co.uk/lessons-from-the-tiktok-election/
10. https://www.theguardian.com/technology/article/2024/jun/08/almost-everyone-supports-labour-why-2024-isnt-the-tiktok-election
11. https://x.com/alexwickham/status/1795349195442069817
12. https://www.spectator.co.uk/article/could-the-election-be-closer-than-you-think/
13. Philip Gould, *The Unfinished Revolution: How New Labour Changed British Politics Forever* (Abacus, 2011).
14. https://www.huffingtonpost.co.uk/entry/labour-poll-lead-soars-to-27-points-as-tory-voters-turn-their-backs-on-rishi-sunak_uk_6656d83ae4b0644fd94ebfb5
15. https://yougov.co.uk/politics/articles/49606-first-yougov-mrp-of-2024-general-election-shows-labour-on-track-to-beat-1997-landslide
16. https://www.bbc.co.uk/news/articles/crgglmwwlggo
17. https://inews.co.uk/news/politics/rishi-sunak-leading-tories-election-wipeout-worse-1997-landslide-defeat-polls-3084710?srsltid=AfmBOoogD5uDjnIQgjosZvHy_Xa9O6H7YI9DlLQODnSsCJIl8GNOcnuP
18. https://x.com/YouGov/status/1801932755535544563
19. W. Jennings and J. Green, *The Politics of Competence: Parties, Public Opinion and Voter Preferences in the United Kingdom* (Cambridge University Press, 2017).
20. https://x.com/LukeTryl/status/1802344554311360990
21. https://labour.org.uk/change/
22. https://x.com/vicderbyshire/status/1795344065434620299
23. https://www.independent.co.uk/voices/keir-starmer-left-wing-purge-labour-b2553725.html
24. https://x.com/BurnsConleth/status/1796432286596153721
25. https://www.ft.com/content/e1f94c52-044d-4cfb-8ee1-1e9c4482920e
26. https://labour.org.uk/updates/stories/labours-defence-policy-how-we-will-provide-strong-national-defence-for-britain/

27. https://www.telegraph.co.uk/politics/2024/06/15/voters-find-starmers-labour-more-patriotic-than-tories/
28. https://x.com/OwenWntr/status/1796497104824885457
29. https://www.lbc.co.uk/news/sir-keir-starmer-hamas-terrorism-israel-defend-itself/
30. https://www.theguardian.com/commentisfree/article/2024/may/08/keir-starmer-bland-politics-labour
31. https://x.com/TimesRadio/status/1808990306575995228
32. https://x.com/jim_blagden/status/1797899626386964863
33. https://x.com/p_surridge/status/1801599608407134657
34. https://www.ft.com/content/f60a0cfb-d2e2-4faa-83b2-977839056c95
35. https://www.theguardian.com/politics/gallery/2024/jul/02/ed-for-heights-lib-dem-leader-davey-campaign-stunts-in-pictures
36. https://www.libdems.org.uk/news/article/how-did-the-general-election-result-happen
37. https://yougov.co.uk/politics/articles/49880-general-election-2024-labour-leads-snp-in-scotland-by-six-points
38. https://www.youtube.com/watch?v=9qZWkwkLmYo&ab_channel=IpsosUK
39. https://x.com/BBCSounds/status/1798607214925815945
40. https://x.com/PJTheEconomist/status/1805142627378995463
41. https://www.thetimes.com/article/3a79d414-2ae8-4584-aba6-ad39efaa26ea
42. https://public.conservatives.com/static/documents/GE2024/Conservative-Manifesto-GE2024.pdfIt
43. https://labour.org.uk/wp-content/uploads/2024/06/Change-Labour-Party-Manifesto-2024-large-print.pdf
44. https://x.com/BBCNewsnight/status/1798844486254223487
45. https://www.ft.com/content/0596349e-2b33-4a84-a16b-002fdeb4bf12
46. https://www.lbc.co.uk/news/rishi-sunak-apologises-d-day-starmer-labour-not-to-politicise-his-decision/
47. https://x.com/christopherhope/status/1799088247320035595
48. https://www.telegraph.co.uk/politics/2024/06/07/rishi-sunak-dday-row-how-could-anyone-vote-tory/
49. https://x.com/Savanta_UK/status/1799139356159926668
50. https://x.com/LukeTryl/status/1799203206553080254
51. https://www.ipsos.com/en-uk/labour-maintains-lead-conservatives-falling-back-equal-their-lowest-ever-vote-share
52. https://www.ipsos.com/en-uk/rishi-sunaks-satisfaction-falls-equal-worst-ever-ipsos-rating-conservative-or-labour-leader
53. https://x.com/YouGov/status/1807333287288819744
54. https://www.ft.com/content/1cc50124-e19c-481d-bd91-fdecb3d64528
55. https://www.channel4.com/news/factcheck/factcheck-the-election-betting-scandal-explained
56. https://podcasts.apple.com/gb/podcast/what-are-the-odds-a-betting-scandal-sinks-the-tories/id1613562765?i=1000659705275
57. https://yougov.co.uk/politics/articles/49606-first-yougov-mrp-of-2024-general-election-shows-labour-on-track-to-beat-1997-landslide

58. https://www.theguardian.com/politics/article/2024/jun/27/labour-lib-dem-tactical-voting-plans-impact-tory-seats
59. https://www.newstatesman.com/politics/2024/06/why-tories-fear-tactics-are-failing
60. https://www.focaldata.com/blog/bi-focal-16-what-will-labours-lead-be-in-the-general-election
61. https://www.ft.com/content/6d88c42a-8714-416f-9d7f-b52645f5c42f
62. https://x.com/Steven_Swinford/status/1803183714698141762
63. Ben Riley-Smith, *Blue Murder: The Rise and Fall of the Conservative Government, 2010–2024* (John Murray Press, 2024), p. 362.
64. Ben Riley-Smith, *Blue Murder: The Rise and Fall of the Conservative Government, 2010–2024* (John Murray Press, 2024), p. 363.
65. https://www.bbc.co.uk/news/articles/cv221jple3jo
66. https://www.iaindale.com/articles/is-starmergeddon-coming-for-the-tories
67. https://x.com/DPJHodges/status/1803372839040409833
68. https://www.iaindale.com/articles/lions-led-by-donkeys-how-the-tory-leadership-has-let-down-the-poor-bloody-infantry
69. https://x.com/BBCPolitics/status/1807390074700472700
70. https://x.com/Peston/status/1807500964737458329
71. https://www.dailymail.co.uk/news/article-13546035/Labour-tax-rises-Rishi-Sunak-Tory-donor-John-Caudwell-Brexit-Man-UtdJim-Ratcliffe-Starmer.html
72. https://www.thetimes.com/article/3a79d414-2ae8-4584-aba6-ad39efaa26ea

14. The 2024 Election Results

1. https://podcasts.apple.com/gb/podcast/labours-landslide-victory-can-it-get-any-worse-for/id1709628885?i=1000661210459
2. https://x.com/Dylan_Difford/status/1818189284073259337
3. https://yougov.co.uk/politics/articles/49978-how-britain-voted-in-the-2024-general-election
4. https://www.wilsoncenter.org/microsite/7/node/121033
5. https://podcasts.apple.com/gb/podcast/should-the-tories-stop-chasing-reform-voters/id1706536336?i=1000664745837
6. https://www.thetimes.com/article/oppositions-dont-win-elections-governments-lose-them-v753zr7v063
7. https://www.bbc.co.uk/news/articles/c2x0g8nkzmzo
8. https://news.sky.com/story/labour-and-lib-dem-vote-efficiency-is-a-remarkable-feature-of-this-election-13171901
9. https://www.moreincommon.org.uk/media/e3in12zd/change-pending.pdf
10. https://x.com/p_surridge/status/1804785809880482226
11. https://www.ipsos.com/en-uk/how-britain-voted-in-the-2024-election
12. https://www.ipsos.com/en-uk/how-britain-voted-in-the-2024-election
13. https://tribunemag.co.uk/2021/07/the-crumbling-foundations-of-the-conservative-party

14. https://x.com/MatthewPrice01/status/1802947402434740341
15. See Annex A for the full list.
16. https://www.prospectmagazine.co.uk/politics/67878/why-labour-should-be-nervous
17. https://www.moreincommon.org.uk/media/e3in12zd/change-pending.pdf
18. https://lordashcroftpolls.com/2024/07/how-britain-voted-and-why-my-post-vote-poll/
19. https://www.thetimes.com/uk/politics/article/robert-jenrick-we-lost-because-we-got-brexit-done-but-nothing-else-vs3zmdnpr
20. https://podcasts.apple.com/gb/podcast/uk-election-the-view-from-the-right-w-freddy-gray/id1653753850?i=1000660140100
21. https://www.moreincommon.org.uk/media/e3in12zd/change-pending.pdf
22. https://www.ft.com/content/d30bba0c-2105-42ef-b6e9-beade9a554e5
23. https://www.moreincommon.org.uk/media/e3in12zd/change-pending.pdf
24. https://www.thetimes.com/uk/politics/article/competence-will-redeem-the-tories-tacking-right-will-not-9xz93xzpj
25. https://x.com/jburnmurdoch/status/1809103281009926147
26. https://conservativehome.com/2024/08/05/paul-bristow-we-wont-win-again-unless-we-say-sorry-and-understand-why-we-lost/
27. https://www.thetimes.com/uk/politics/article/john-curtice-general-election-labour-victory-results-7cpgvbrcs
28. https://www.moreincommon.org.uk/media/e3in12zd/change-pending.pdf
29. https://www.labourtogether.uk/how-labour-won-2024-report
30. https://www.survation.com/final-survation-mrp-projection-of-the-2024-general-election/
31. https://x.com/lewis_goodall/status/1809124572291113265
32. https://fabians.org.uk/scratching-the-surface/
33. https://www.qmul.ac.uk/media/news/2024/hss/could-labours-massive-poll-lead-affect-as-well-as-reflect-how-it-performs-at-the-election-three-things-the-evidence-tells-us.html
34. https://www.moreincommon.org.uk/media/e3in12zd/change-pending.pdf
35. https://www.labourtogether.uk/how-labour-won-2024-report
36. https://bsky.app/profile/dylandifford.bsky.social/post/3l47jhpfvbw2w
37. https://www.thetimes.com/article/80c8bcb2-9b4e-4c1d-8394-f9d2679f2ee1
38. https://www.ipsos.com/en-uk/how-britain-voted-in-the-2024-election
39. https://x.com/LukeTryl/status/1810619416431808661
40. https://podcasts.apple.com/gb/podcast/the-conservatives-face-their-mount-everest/id1706062286?i=1000658053586
41. https://www.ipsos.com/en-uk/how-britain-voted-in-the-2024-election
42. https://x.com/Dylan_Difford/status/1835223126436638921
43. https://www.independent.co.uk/news/uk/politics/labour-party-black-asian-voters-b2584177.html
44. https://x.com/LukeTryl/status/1809067838348349777
45. https://x.com/Dylan_Difford/status/1847931683212796403
46. https://hyphenonline.com/2024/07/06/the-impact-of-muslim-voters-at-the-2024-election-was-even-bigger-than-you-think-apsana-begum-

shabana-mahmood-birmingham-perry-barr-blackburn-leicester-dewsbury-uk-election/
47. https://x.com/LukeTryl/status/1809885910797807652
48. https://www.thetimes.com/uk/scotland/article/john-curtice-why-the-polls-could-be-wrong-about-the-election-3pv8tnhmw
49. https://www.politico.eu/article/labour-election-victory-weaker-than-you-think-keir-starmer-nigel-farage/
50. https://www.theguardian.com/politics/article/2024/may/31/if-the-pollsters-have-it-right-the-conservatives-need-a-miracle-in-five-weeks
51. https://www.youtube.com/watch?v=QDDXaix9d9I
52. https://podfollow.com/660638948/episode/5b2b34f4fffccc c76b9a8370d4af51c603ef1a30/view
53. https://labourlist.org/2023/05/keir-starmer-new-labour-politics-trust-red-wall-broken-britain/
54. https://unherd.com/2024/07/how-starmer-slaughtered-the-tories/
55. https://x.com/Dylan_Difford/status/1835222859930652822
56. https://www.britishelectionstudy.com/bes-impact/the-liberal-democrats-in-2024-vote-efficiency-and-tactical-voting/
57. https://x.com/chris_annous/status/1835263182924865586
58. https://www.focaldata.com/blog/how-britain-voted-2024
59. https://x.com/LukeTryl/status/1810632291208642590
60. https://www.britishelectionstudy.com/data/
61. https://www.moreincommon.org.uk/media/e3in12zd/change-pending.pdf
62. https://www.thetimes.com/uk/politics/article/john-curtice-general-election-labour-victory-results-7cpgvbrcs
63. https://www.theguardian.com/politics/article/2024/jul/07/labour-safe-seats-marginals-landslide-victory-vote
64. https://x.com/antonhowes/status/1809212147924402601
65. https://makevotesmatter.org.uk/news/2024/7/6/election-2024-our-least-representative-election-ever/
66. https://www.itv.com/news/2024-07-05/why-this-is-the-most-important-election-of-modern-times
67. https://www.thetimes.com/uk/politics/article/john-curtice-general-election-labour-victory-results-7cpgvbrcs
68. https://x.com/lewis_goodall/status/1809124572291113265

15. The New Electoral Landscape

1. https://samf.substack.com/p/mapping-voter-coalitions
2. https://www.ft.com/content/6533de73-1d38-4dc3-b2a1-b8d0c0b6eaac
3. https://x.com/LukeTryl/status/1808956911187837206
4. https://benansell.substack.com/p/morning-after-poll
5. https://www.independent.co.uk/voices/peter-mandelson-labour-left-blair-b1826082.html
6. https://www.thetimes.com/uk/politics/article/labour-winning-coalition-political-sandcastle-ukip-keir-starmer-mlkq8zdbp

7. https://www.newstatesman.com/politics/uk-politics/2024/10/the-row-over-labours-freebies-wont-end-any-time-soon
8. https://natcen.ac.uk/dividing-lines
9. https://www.britainschoice.uk/segments/
10. https://www.bmgresearch.co.uk/wp-content/uploads/2024/06/BMG-VICs_The-Broken-Coalition-The-2024-Election-and-Sunaks-Clan-Crisis_REPORT.pdf
11. https://www.theguardian.com/politics/2024/sep/20/reform-can-learn-from-lib-dems-on-ground-campaigning-says-richard-tice
12. https://x.com/Dylan_Difford/status/1835581888129368144/photo/1
13. See Robert Ford https://www.theguardian.com/politics/article/2024/jul/07/labour-safe-seats-marginals-landslide-victory-vote and https://fabians.org.uk/governing-to-win/
14. https://www.youtube.com/watch?v=QDDXaix9d9I
15. https://yougov.co.uk/politics/articles/50410-political-tracker-roundup-august-2024
16. https://www.moneysavingexpert.com/news/2024/07/eligibility-changes-winter-fuel-payment/
17. https://x.com/YouGov/status/1833879500435677512
18. https://yougov.co.uk/politics/articles/50435-the-honeymoon-is-over-keir-starmers-net-favourability-falls-to-lowest-level-since-february
19. https://x.com/OpiniumResearch/status/1837571997489836154
20. https://yougov.co.uk/politics/articles/50648-keir-starmer-now-as-unpopular-as-nigel-farage
21. https://www.politico.eu/article/uk-keir-starmer-labour-suffers-historic-drop-in-approval-ratings/
22. https://x.com/LukeTryl/status/1853060554593636426
23. https://www.bbc.co.uk/news/articles/ce990eg3rq20
24. https://x.com/Samfr/status/1851607763643752807
25. https://obr.uk/hero/budget-delivers-large-increases-in-spending-tax-and-borrowing/
26. https://x.com/PJTheEconomist/status/1851631776122228970
27. https://www.bbc.co.uk/news/articles/c8rl5pnm47do
28. https://www.prospectmagazine.co.uk/ideas/economics/68420/budget-2024-evasions-out-taxes-up
29. https://www.moreincommon.org.uk/media/e3in12zd/change-pending.pdf
30. https://x.com/keiranpedley/status/1811655276895822134
31. https://www.moreincommon.org.uk/media/e3in12zd/change-pending.pdf
32. https://www.labourtogether.uk/how-labour-won-2024-report
33. https://www.moreincommon.org.uk/media/e3in12zd/change-pending.pdf
34. https://labour.org.uk/updates/press-releases/keir-starmers-speech-at-labour-conference/
35. Tom Baldwin, *Starmer: The Biography* (William Collins, 2024). P256
36. https://labour.org.uk/wp-content/uploads/2024/06/Change-Labour-Party-Manifesto-2024-large-print.pdf
37. https://www.tiktok.com/@bbcsounds/video/7417143173056597280

16. The Future of the Conservative Party

1. https://x.com/HenryRiley1/status/1822189843155234851
2. https://www.moreincommon.org.uk/media/r4hodhtk/conservative-leadership-election-focus-groups-media-briefing-2-sept-2024.pdf
3. https://www.politicshome.com/news/article/reform-voters-hardest-for-tories-to-win-back-new-poll-suggests
4. https://www.moreincommon.org.uk/media/e3in12zd/change-pending.pdf
5. https://www.independent.co.uk/news/uk/politics/kemi-badenoch-prime-minister-tax-break-private-school-b2631266.html
6. https://yougov.co.uk/politics/articles/50401-what-do-tory-members-think-the-future-direction-of-the-conservative-party-should-be
7. https://bsky.app/profile/benansell.bsky.social/post/3l4jnpx6uni2j
8. https://www.thetimes.com/comment/columnists/article/tories-will-find-great-dangers-in-opposition-6zfxhznhp
9. https://www.bbc.co.uk/news/articles/c20j3428vyyo
10. *The Conservative Effect 2010-2024*, ed. Anthony Seldon and Tom Egerton (Cambridge University Press, 2024), p. 140.
11. https://cdn.prod.website-files.com/66e290977b0f17041797e6ae/66fb3a4aa6d5bf17f7481ed1_Conservatism%20in%20Crisis.pdf
12. https://ifs.org.uk/articles/how-tax-burden-high-when-most-us-are-taxed-so-low
13. https://cdn.prod.website-files.com/66e290977b0f17041797e6ae/66fb3a4aa6d5bf17f7481ed1_Conservatism%20in%20Crisis.pdf
14. https://pollingsnippets.substack.com/p/broken-coalitions-2019-voters-in
15. https://podcasts.apple.com/gb/podcast/why-are-the-conservatives-still-talking-to-themselves/id1384867286?i=1000671314577
16. https://www.ukonward.com/wp-content/uploads/2024/09/Onward-Breaking-Blue-General-Election-2024-4.pdf
17. https://www.ukonward.com/wp-content/uploads/2024/09/Onward-Breaking-Blue-General-Election-2024-4.pdf, p. 8.
18. https://www.huffingtonpost.co.uk/entry/sixth-of-tory-voters-likely-to-die-before-next-election-analysis-finds_uk_669e0e89e4b008fc7de10c6c
19. British Election Study Internet Panel, waves 1-25
20. https://www.ipsos.com/en-uk/how-britain-voted-october-1974
21. https://yougov.co.uk/politics/articles/49978-how-britain-voted-in-the-2024-general-election
22. Phil Burton-Cartledge, *The Party's Over: The Rise and Fall of the Conservatives from Thatcher to Sunak* (Verso, 2023), p. 316.
23. https://www.ft.com/content/165f9aee-1180-4be8-903b-b166dc4e4fa1
24. https://samf.substack.com/p/on-the-edge
25. https://samf.substack.com/p/the-battersea-problem
26. https://commonslibrary.parliament.uk/constituency-statistics-population-by-age/

ACKNOWLEDGEMENTS

I want to start by thanking my wife, Christine, for her love and patience while I was researching and writing this book.

I would also like to thank my editor, Louise Lubke Cuss, and my cover designer, Kate Chesterton, for their encouragement and support.

Thanks also go to all those who took the time to read the draft manuscript and provide me with feedback, including Rob Ashton, Virginia Bader, Sarah Bartlett, Charlie Beckett, Rachel Brastock, Peter Casebow, Donald Clark, Chris Cullen, Gordon Drummond, Mike Everett, Simon Greany, Deborah Grubb, Darren Holmes, Peter Fairfax, Ian Farringdon, Colin Franks, Dru Furneaux, John Helmer, Neill McWilliams, Jonathan Oakley, John O'Brien, Teresa Pole-Baker, Reg Race, Behailu Shiferaw, Philippe Shoosmith, David Warren, Stephen Walsh, and Li Whybrow.

Printed in Great Britain
by Amazon

53663705R00175